THE

CHARLES WILKINS

WILD RIDE

A History of the
North West Mounted Police   1873–1904

Stanton Atkins & Dosil Publishers

Vancouver

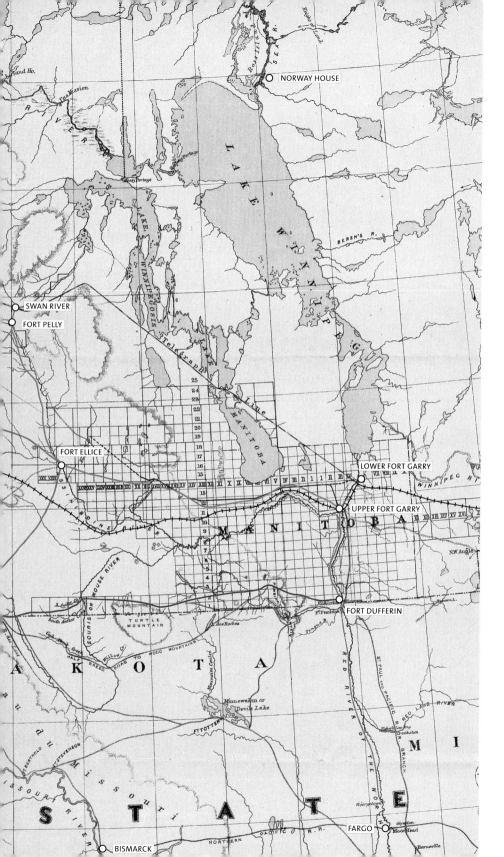

BETWEEN Canadian Confederation in 1867 and the beginning of the twentieth century, the territory represented by the map on these pages was, for better or worse, transformed and transformed utterly. What began as a great tract of open wilderness populated largely by aboriginal people became, in a matter of decades, an alliance of territories, provinces and municipalities that have defined the land ever since. The map is dotted with place names, every one of which was the setting for some vivid drama or series of dramas that, taken together, have become the story of the building of a country: Red River, Fort Dufferin, Fort Whoop-Up, Fort Walsh, Cripple Camp, Maple Creek, Cut Knife Hill, Frog Lake, Batoche.

Along the way, no person or institution contributed more to the transformation of the territory than a few hundred men in red coats, the earliest members of the North West Mounted Police. In their enthusiasm, and often their naivete or ignorance, the early Mounties did what they were told to do, or felt needed doing, in the push to make one world disappear and another come into being. The map, it might be said, is the cartography of their role in history.

MAP LEGEND

— Commissioner G.A. French's outward route to Sweet Grass Hills

— Commissioner G.A. French's return route to Fort Dufferin

— Inspector W.D. Jarvis' route from La Roche Percée to Fort Edmonton

— Assistant Commissioner J.F. Macleod's route from Sweet Grass Hills to Fort Macleod

● 1885 Nort-West Rebellion battle sites

+++ Canadian Pacific Railway

THE BATTLE FOR THE GREAT NORTH-WEST

THE YEAR IS 1870, THE HOUR just past noon on a frigid day in early March. At the heart of the Red River Settlement the heavy oak doors in the south wall of Upper Fort Garry burst open and a gang of weathered irregulars spill out, some dressed in buffalo-skin coats and fur hats, some waving rifles, the lot of them jostling and hollering in French. In their midst, a young man held at gunpoint can be heard screaming at his tormentors, repudiating their authority, belittling their sanity and integrity. *You're all cowards!* he hollers as he stumbles through the crusted snow.

A pair of grim-faced Metis in shirt sleeves, despite the cold, push forward carrying a hastily constructed plank coffin. As they come alongside the prisoner, he realizes for the first time that the death sentence passed on him the previous day is no mere political ploy. His voice cracks, he stumbles, and the clergyman helping him along struggles to keep him upright.

On what would otherwise have been an unremarkable afternoon in this settlement of farmers, traders and hunters, a crowd begins to gather, women and children on its fringes. Some are excited by the show, others appalled at what is happening.

The defiant and traumatized prisoner is Thomas Scott, a twenty-five-year-old surveyor from southern Ontario, an Irish immigrant, who a few months back had arrived in Red River, at the forks of the Red and Assiniboine, along with a cadre of his Protestant compatriots, his purpose was to begin preparing the west for the advance of Canadian Confederation. The great vision of Prime Minister Sir John A. Macdonald to build a country from sea to sea had taken root three years earlier, when Macdonald and the Fathers of Confederation brought Canada's first four provinces into a reluctant alliance. Now, in its determination to move west, Macdonald's government had sent surveyors and administrators to the largely French settlement of Red River. Townships, property lines and straight roads would have to be established. Protestant churches and English schools had to be built.

This is said to be the earliest known photo of Louis Riel, taken in 1858 when he was 14 years old, shortly after he entered la Collège de Montréal.

What Macdonald had not counted on in his determination to annex Red River and its surroundings was the presence of another fiery twenty-five-year-old, a St. Boniface mystic named Louis Riel, whose resistance to Confederation, at least in Red River, was as vehement as Macdonald's determination to see it succeed. The charismatic young organizer was the oldest of eleven children born to a Metis family whose roots in Red River dated to the settlement's founding in 1812. At the tender age of thirteen, he had been sent to Montreal for training as a priest and for education in the arts and sciences. But he gradually lost interest in the priesthood and in 1864, at the age of nineteen, went to work for a year in a Montreal law firm. By this time, he had developed a passion for politics, particularly as it affected minorities such as the Metis. After stints of employment in the United States, in Chicago and St. Paul, he returned to Red River in July 1868.

Full of political fervour, and in the face of advancing Confederation, Riel quickly developed a noteworthy vision of his own. At its core was the founding of a jurisdiction quite unlike what Macdonald had in mind, a place where Metis and Native rights would be held in highest regard, where French would be a respected language, and where Native and French culture would not be just served, but celebrated.

Not that Riel had anything against English-speaking settlers in Red River. At the time there was a growing number of them, recently arrived from Ontario and the northern US. But in the face of English insensitivity toward the Metis, Riel was determined that his people would not be overrun by the expanding anglophone culture – or by Macdonald's commitment to serving that culture.

In Riel's earliest vision, he foresaw a Metis territory stretching west from the Red River Settlement to the Rockies. It would be called Assiniboia.

Meanwhile, deeply disturbed by Ottawa's attempts to subordinate Red River without consulting its inhabitants, Riel and his confreres established what they

THE RED RIVER Settlement was a colonization project set up in 1811 by Thomas Douglas, the Fifth Earl of Selkirk, on land granted to him by the Hudson's Bay Company. At the time, social upheaval in Scotland caused by the introduction of sheep farming and the ensuing Highland and Lowland clearances had left many Scots destitute. Lord Selkirk was determined to give the disinherited farmers a chance at a better life in a new colony he called Assiniboia. To that end, he purchased a controlling interest in the Hudson's Bay Company, which was partially owned by his family, and set up the aforementioned land grant – some 116,000 square miles drained in part by the Red and Assiniboine rivers. During the summer of 1811, Selkirk sent out a small group of Scots to the area, but they were forced to pause for the winter at York Factory. They arrived at the Red and Assiniboine during the summer and autumn of 1812, and wouldn't have survived their first winter had it not been for the help of the North West Company and the Metis. Ultimately, conflicts developed between the colonists and the fur traders, and by 1815 the settlement had been deserted. Meanwhile, the struggle for control of the fur trade intensified between the North West Company and the Hudson's Bay Company.

In the spring of 1816, the Hudson's Bay Company destroyed the North West Company fort at the junction of the Red and Assiniboine rivers. Hudson's Bay Company attacks and North West Company reprisals through the region led to the Battle of Seven Oaks in June 1816, when the Hudson's Bay Company governor and twenty of his men were killed by a group of Metis.

But Selkirk refused to give up. He subsequently recruited new settlers, who arrived in Red River in July 1818 and proceeded to watch hordes of grasshoppers destroy their crops both that summer and again in 1819.

After the merger of the Hudson's Bay Company and the North West Company in 1821, the Red River Settlement became more stable and grew with the arrival of retired fur traders and their families – particularly the Metis.

In 1835, following the death of Lord Selkirk, the settlement was transferred back to the Hudson's Bay Company. However, the resident Metis refused to accept the company's authority and continued to assert their right to deal as free traders in furs, pemmican and buffalo robes. In 1849, a court decision forced the Hudson's Bay Company to allow them that freedom.

While the Red River Settlement itself was often unstable, at times radically unsuccessful, it eventually became the base on which the province of Manitoba was founded.

Throughout the tragic early years of the Red River Settlement, the defenceless colonists were often befriended by Chief Peguis of the regional Saulteaux or Ojibwa. During Selkirk's visit to the colony after the Battle of Seven Oaks, he expressed open gratitude to Peguis who, in return, in 1817, with other regional chiefs, conveyed to Selkirk control of native-held lands within the District of Assiniboia.

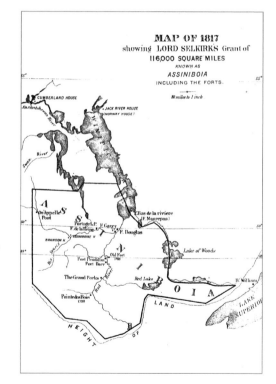

This somewhat otherworldly photograph, taken at St. Boniface in 1869, shows Louis Riel surrounded by the members of his Metis National Committee. Front, on floor, left to right: H.F. O'Lone, P. Proulx. Centre, seated: P. Poitras, J. Bruce, Louis Riel, W.B. O'Donoghue, F. Dauphinais. Back, standing: C. Larocque, P. Delorme, T. Bunn, X. Dagee, A. Lépine, B. Tourond and T. Spense.

called the Metis National Committee and, with it, a provisional government in the settlement. Riel was appointed president of that government, and his makeshift militia forcibly took control of Upper Fort Garry, a one-time Hudson's Bay Company post used less for trade than as an administrative centre for the company.

NOW, INSIDE THAT FORT, a local Catholic priest, Father Lestanc, and a newly arrived emissary from Ottawa, Donald A. Smith, pleaded with Riel to spare Thomas Scott's life. Not only had Scott been sentenced by a court martial of dubious authority, but the charges against him had been somewhat overstated. Smith argued that Scott was being executed not so much for treason as for mere insults to Riel and the Metis, a version of insubordination.

But the fiery president, who since childhood had been known for his stubbornness, was in no mood for pardons. He had already commuted the death sentence of Major Charles Boulton, Scott's ally, who, in the name of Canada, had joined Scott

and thirty-two others several weeks earlier in an attempt to wrest control of the fort from Riel and his troops. The attack had been turned back, and the attackers arrested and imprisoned in the fort.

If Riel and his men had expected contrition from their foes, they did not get it. Scott, in particular, had proven to be a loudmouth and a hothead and for weeks now had been a goad to his guards and to the self-esteem of the provisional government. From his cell he screamed taunts and spit curses at anybody who came within earshot. *The Metis were cowards! They would never have the guts to put him to death! Riel himself was a coward!* Scott's thick Irish brogue had become a near-capital offence in itself.

Riel had originally attempted to mollify the mulish Orangeman to assure him that his rights and those of his co-conspirators would be protected under Metis authority. But gradually he had grown to loathe Scott – and to loathe the government whose decidedly Orange preferences now echoed so aggressively within the fort.

PUBLIC NOTICE TO THE INHAB- ITANTS OF RUPERTS LAND.

The President and Representatives of the French-speaking population of Rupert's Land in Council, "the Invaders of our rights being now expelled") already aware of your sympathy, do extend the hand of friendship to you our friendly Inhabitants, and in do- ing so invite you to send twelve Representa- tives from the following places, viz.

St. John's, St. Margret's 1. Headingly 1, St. James 1, St. Mary's 1, Kildonan 1, St. Paul's 1, St. Andrew's 1, St. Clement's 1, St. Peter's 1, Town of Winnipeg 2 in order to form one body with the above Council con- sisting of twelve members to consider the present political state of this Country, and to adopt such measures as may be deemed best for the future welfare of the same.

A meeting of the above Council will be held in the Court House at Fort Garry on Tuesday the 16th day of November at which the invited Representatives will attend.

By order of the President,
LOUIS RIEL,
Secry.

Winnipeg Nov. 6th 1869.

Louis Riel's belief in the process of fair represen- tational government is inherent in the notice he posted on November 6, 1869, encouraging the municipalities and dis- tricts in the area of the Red and Assiniboine rivers to send represen- tatives to form a council that would consider the future and politics of the area and of the country at large. (The name missing in the notice is St. Peter's.)

T HE HUDSON'S BAY Company (HBC) is the oldest incorporated merchandising enterprise in the English-speaking world and has played a significant role in both Canadian and US history.

The French explorers Médard Chouart des Groseilliers and Pierre-Esprit Radisson were the first to propose the creation of a trading firm that would reach the interior of North America by way of Hudson Bay. In 1665, they sailed to England and secured the support of Prince Rupert, who subsequently persuaded his cousin, King Charles II, as well as several other noblemen and merchants, to finance a fur trading expedition. The venture proved incredibly successful and, in 1670, led to a royal charter granting the "Governor and Company of Adventurers" exclusive trading rights in the territory drained by rivers flowing into Hudson Bay.

The vast region was named Rupert's Land and its most valued commodity was the beaver pelt. Back in England and Europe, the North American pelts were painstakingly transformed into stylish and popular waterproof hats. Unfortunately, the felting process required the use of mercury, and many hatters were poisoned by the toxic vapours, a fact reflected in the expression "mad as a hatter."

In 1821, declining beaver populations and increasing conflict and competition led the HBC to a merger with the North West Company and the acquisition of the latter's trading area, the North-Western Territory. This new version of the HBC became increasingly involved in governing the settlers that had followed the fur traders into the north and west, and in providing government services for both Selkirk's colony in present-day Manitoba and the colony of British Columbia. This practice continued until 1869, when the HBC sold Rupert's Land and the North-Western Territory to the government of Canada. In subsequent years, the company's real estate holdings in Canada were limited to merchandising ventures both in large cities and in dozens of communities across the north.

Using simple human-powered presses such as the HBC version shown above, fur buyers and shippers could compress dozens of beaver pelts, sometimes weighing hundreds of pounds, into tightly packed bales for shipping.

There has long been debate over what happened to the body of Thomas Scott after his extended execution in 1870 at Upper Fort Garry. Later when it was discovered that the buried coffin was empty, it was rumoured that on the night of his death his remains had been taken from the fort in the wee hours and pushed through a hole in the ice. He is seen at right in 1869.

By this time Riel perhaps harboured a measure of self-doubt. After all, he was not by temperament an executioner. He was an intellectual. He was also moody and insecure and unfortunately had become trapped in his need to stand up to the Canadian government, to let Macdonald know that the Metis meant business and were not to be taken lightly.

As a last resort, Smith argued that the one great merit of Riel's campaign so far was that it had been peaceable – and as such showed Ottawa that the Metis were worthy of consideration, both moral and legislative. From Smith's point of view – and perhaps even from Riel's – Macdonald's annexation of Red River and its surroundings was inevitable. The best Riel could hope for was protection for his people and their culture.

"Why risk vengeance?" begged Smith.

"We must make Canada respect us," answered Riel, who terminated the meeting with the comment that he had done a good thing in sparing the life of Boulton, adding – "but I must execute Scott."

Riel's chief lieutenant, Ambroise Lépine, who had been listening from the shadows, now assured Riel that the sentence would be carried out promptly, and left the room. With bloodless calm, Riel turned to Lestanc and suggested he offer a prayer for the condemned man. Smith did not wait to hear it.

Having learned that there would be no clemency, one of Scott's guards ordered the now-trembling prisoner to his knees. Lépine fastened a blindfold across his eyes.

The firing squad stood in line some twenty feet from their mark and loaded and raised their rifles, uneasy in their role. None of them had ever shot a man. Their minds raced. *Was the sentence right in the eyes of God? Or were they themselves committing murder and risking eternal damnation?*

When the order came, they fired – four rifles, four rounds, only two of which found their mark, ripping through the condemned man's shoulder and chest. Scott fell face forward, blood seeping quickly into his clothes and onto the snow. His taunts were replaced by groans of pain.

One of Riel's lieutenants stepped forward and fired a round into the fallen man's head. But the bullet lodged in his jaw without killing him. In the seconds that followed, several members of Riel's militia wrenched Scott off the snow and dumped him into his coffin. Having nailed down the lid, they carried Scott quickly into the fort.

Riel, who had observed the botched execution from a distance, spoke sharply to those who had gathered, ordering them back to their homes.

If Scott's cries had antagonized the fort dwellers in preceding weeks, they must now have created torment. All afternoon and into the evening the Irishman's muted howls could be heard emanating from his coffin. In the middle of the night, he begged to be set free or killed.

Only in the early morning did he fall silent.

RIEL'S DETERMINATION to control Red River for his people – and Macdonald's to control it for Confederation – were both of course part of a broader flow of events.

This survey map of the Red River Plain was drawn by Canada's chief surveyor J.S. Dennis in 1869 but is based on surveys that were done prior to the transfer of Rupert's Land to Canada in that year. The most important line on the map is the Winnipeg or Principal Meridian, which became the basis for all further surveys of the west and can be seen running straight up the middle of the map. The angled writing in the centre of the map, just to the east of the Principal Meridian, describes the spot where Major Webb's survey party was stopped by Louis Riel and the Metis on October 12, 1869. The occurrence was the first overt resistance of the Red River Rebellion. The little "quilt" of squares in the lower right corner represents the 64 sections of land (800 acres each) that made up each of the map's townships as drawn at the time. However, the delay in surveying caused by Riel allowed the adoption of the American system of a 6 mile-square township divided into 36 sections of 640 acres each.

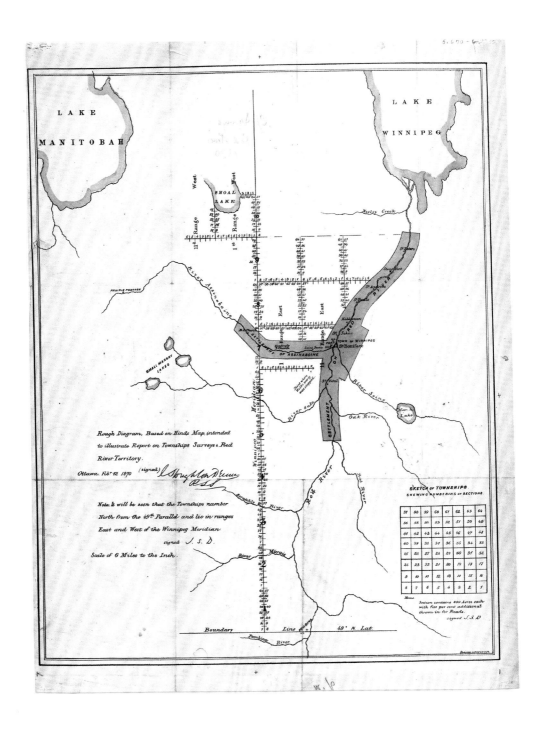

The York boat, modeled after Orkney Islands fishing boats (themselves a descendent of the Viking longboat), was a stable and durable inland craft used by the Hudson's Bay Company to carry furs and trade goods along inland waterways during the eighteenth and nineteenth centuries. It was named after York Factory, the headquarters of the HBC at the mouth of the Hayes and Nelson rivers on Hudson Bay in what is now Manitoba. One of the boats is seen here, under sail, near the HBC settlement of Oxford House.

Macdonald knew that if his vision of Canada was to succeed, his government needed to lay undisputed claim to the great central wilderness and prairie – to Rupert's Land, as it was then called.

For the past century, the Hudson's Bay Company (HBC) had controlled the territory by British charter, mapping waterways and building forts in its inexhaustible quest for furs. Under HBC rule, some eleven thousand Metis and tens of thousands of Indians had enjoyed relative stability and fair trade through the forests of what is now northwestern Ontario and across the prairie and wilderness to the west. Both Metis and Indians had travelled freely in their quest for buffalo, maintaining their traditions and self-respect. To keep them productively involved in the fur trade, the HBC had rigorously denied them access to alcohol and had kept American whisky traders at bay.

But with Ottawa's purchase of Rupert's Land from the HBC on November 19, 1869, Macdonald's government had set the stage for immense change – little of which would ultimately be positive for the land's original inhabitants. No longer would the land and hunting grounds belong to the Indians and Metis (within decades, most Natives would be herded onto reserves and deprived of their religion and language). No longer would the farm lots be laid out in long tracts touching the river according to the old French seigneurial system, which gave each lot access to water. It was suspected that, under Macdonald's grand vision, Catholicism itself would be challenged in Red River. Certainly, the tribal religions would be endangered.

A more immediate concern was that, in the absence of the HBC and its paternalistic attitude toward the Natives, whisky would flow like poison through the tribes, mainly through the nefarious practices of American whisky traders. Even as Canadian surveyors were arriving in Red River, such traders were establishing themselves in illegal "whisky forts" along the US border, or "medicine line" as it was known to the Blackfoot, Cree and Sioux.

The truth about the great north-west was that in the absence of the HBC, with its functional ethics and disciplines, there would be no effective law – and no lawmen. In the US, such a void had led to gunslinging and mayhem, to the mass killing of Natives, and to Native reprisals.

Macdonald was well aware of the American "wild west" and was determined to bring order to Rupert's Land before chaos could erupt there, too. The first step, he believed, would be to make a province of the easternmost part of the territory. It would be called Manitoba, and its centre would be the growing town of Winnipeg.

WHEN NEWS of Scott's execution reached southern Ontario, the reaction was swift and vengeful, particularly among Orangemen who, with the support of members of the Ontario legislature, demanded that a military force be sent to Red River to deal with the insurgents. Unwilling to offend Quebec or jeopardize bringing Manitoba into Confederation by hammering the Metis, Macdonald dodged the issue by declaring that, since Manitoba was not yet

This cover of the *Canadian Illustrated News* for March 4, 1870, suggested to readers in eastern Canada that Thomas Scott's execution was a clear-cut affair in which Scott died quickly, perhaps of a single gunshot, and was placed with a degree of dignity in a coffin and buried in a proper grave outside the walls of Upper Fort Garry. Unfortunately, such was not the case.

officially a part of Canada, the matter was in the hands of the British Crown. Whatever the jurisdictional concerns, a military expedition led by the British colonel Garnet Wolseley was dispatched to Red River in early May. Macdonald vociferously denied that the purpose of the trek was to exact revenge or bring Riel to trial. Rather, it was to secure peace, to establish order on the eve of annexation – and to illustrate to the US that the British intended to be a presence in the north-west, where the US also looked to expand. For committed Orangemen, however, the purpose remained clear – especially to those who formed part of Wolseley's militia.

Meanwhile, at Upper Fort Garry, Riel had been rebuked by his own people for his reckless handling of the Scott affair, and had reassessed his position. Canada, he allowed reluctantly, was in the west to stay, and the best opportunities for Metis and Indian rights lay in political negotiation.

Thus it was that on March 24, 1870, three representatives from Riel's provisional government, including his chief spokesman, Father Noël-Joseph Ritchot, set off for Ottawa to negotiate the creation of the province. Their demands were clear: that French culture, language and education be enshrined in the provincial statutes and that land rights be secured.

A scant six weeks later, the *Manitoba Act* was passed by Parliament, based on the Metis List of Rights drawn up by Riel and his advisers. One section of the act protected Metis lands and guaranteed the Metis the right to their religion and the use of their language in the legislature and the courts. As head of the provisional government, Riel was ordered to maintain peace while awaiting the arrival of Manitoba's first lieutenant-governor, Adams G. Archibald, who would be travelling in the care of Wolseley's troops.

IF MACDONALD was acting at all precipitously in his attempts to expand the country, it was largely because America itself was looking to expand north of the border, where many US politicians wanted to see US control extended as far as the Arctic.

It is both a curiosity and an irony that the Metis List of Rights, considered an all but heretical document by Parliament for its various "provocations," called for several advances that the government dearly wanted in the country, including the application of law and of court-administered justice, and the writing of treaties with the tribes "to ensure peace on the frontier." In fact, there was very little in the List of Rights that did not reflect the spread of democratic rule in Canada. What rankled Ottawa was not so much the demands themselves as the thought of ceding power over Manitoba to Louis Riel and his band of "half-breed" irregulars.

LIST OF RIGHTS.

1. That the people have the right to elect their own Legislature.

2. That the Legislature have the power to pass all laws local to the Territory over the veto of the Executive by a two-thirds vote.

3. That no act of the Dominion Parliament (local to the Territory) be binding on the people until sanctioned by the Legislature of the Territory.

4. That all Sheriffs, Magistrates, Constables, School Commissioners, etc., be elected by the people.

5. A free Homestead and pre-emption Land Law.

6. That a portion of the public lands be appropriated to the benefit of Schools, the building of Bridges, Roads and Public Buildings.

7. That it be guaranteed to connect Winnipeg by Rail with the nearest line of Railroad, within a term of five years ; the land grant to be subject to the Local Legislature.

8. That for the term of four years all Military, Civil, and Municipal expenses be paid out of the Dominion funds.

9. That the Military be composed of the inhabitants now existing in the Territory.

10. That the English and French languages be common in the Legislature and Courts, and that all Public Documents and Acts of the Legislature be published in both languages.

11. That the Judge of the Supreme Court speak the English and French languages.

12. That Treaties be concluded and ratified between the Dominion Government and the several tribes of Indians in the Territory to ensure peace on the frontier.

13. That we have a fair and full representation in the Canadian Parliament.

14. That all privileges, customs and usages existing at the time of the transfer be respected.

All the above articles have been severally discussed and adopted by the French and Eeglish Representatives without a dissenting voice, as the conditions upon which the people of Rupert's Land enter into Confederation.

The French Representatives then proposed in order to secure the above rights, that a Delegation be appointed and sent to Pembina to see Mr. Macdougall and ask him if he could guarantee these rights by virtue of his commission ; and if he could do so, that then the French people would join to a man to escort Mr. Macdougall into his Government seat. But on the contrary, if Mr. Macdougall could not guarantee such rights, that the Delegates request him to remain where he is, or return 'till the rights be guaranteed by Act of the Canada Parliament.

The English Representatives refused to appoint Delegates to go to Pembina to consult with Mr. Macdougall, stating, they had no authority to do so from their constituents, upon which the Council was dissolved.

The meeting at which the above resolutions were adopted was held at Fort Garry, on Wednesday, Dec. 1, 1869. Winnipeg, December 4th, 1869.

Below: Pack trains such as this, in Barkerville, BC, in 1868, were a common sight during the Fraser Valley gold rush, transporting supplies and luxuries at great effort and cost.

The depletion of gold within a few years left thousands of US miners in the British colony and, for some, a sense that BC's future might better be tied to the US than to Canada.

Right: In a near-futile search for gold, a Chinese man washes gravel tailings in the Fraser River in 1875, long after most prospectors had given up and gone home.

Brother Jonathan, a fictional character created in the 1800s to personify the US, rides the "annexation engine" into Canada. As the cartoon at right shows, US annexation was still a subject of public fascination in 1886 when this item appeared in J.W.A. Bengough's *A Caricature History of Canadian Politics*, published by the famed Grip Printing and Publishing Company in Toronto. The cartoon's caption: *Annexation comes in by the rail, while liberty flies off in the smoke* expresses Canada's fear of America's earlier intentions to expand north of the border all the way to the Arctic.

THE WAY BROTHER JONATHAN WILL ASTONISH THE NATIVES.
ANNEXATION COMES IN BY THE RAIL, WHILE LIBERTY FLIES OFF IN THE SMOKE.

By 1870, US federal and state governments were focusing on growth as a way to hasten recovery from the American Civil War. There was already a railway across the US and an expanding steamboat system, which together provided access to most parts of Rupert's Land and the north-west. Moreover, hundreds of US settlers had poured north from Minnesota to Red River, giving Minnesotans back home the notion that the state might just as well annex the territory.

Meanwhile, on the west coast, thousands of US prospectors and miners had migrated into the Fraser River Valley in the wake of gold discoveries there. In some areas along the Fraser, Americans outnumbered the British by three or four to one. However, by the late 1860s, with the gold rush over, the colony of British Columbia had lapsed into economic decline, giving some residents the idea that, with so many Americans already on BC soil, their best interests lay in joining the United States.

Beyond all of this, there was in the US an anti-British bias that had its roots in the Revolutionary War and that made expansionists of those who, more than anything, wanted to see the US flag where the Union Jack was now flying.

SUCH WERE the tensions between Canada and the US that in May 1870, when the Wolseley Expedition was about to leave Ontario, the US government denied the forces passage onto American soil and thus access to the most obvious and developed route to Manitoba.

The expedition included four hundred British troops and eight hundred semi-trained militiamen from Ontario and Quebec. This small army was generally believed to be incapable of surviving the trip through the formidable forests west of Lake Superior. And with good reason. The first stage of the trek, by boat through the Great Lakes, was relatively manageable. But the route west from Prince Arthur's Landing through northwestern Ontario followed the recently opened Dawson Route, which was not so much a road in any conventional sense as a nightmarish

The beadwork and embroidery on these deerhide gloves from the late 1800s are an echo of the intricacy and elegance of Metis art and design from an earlier era. By this time, however, such designs were somewhat influenced by European designs brought by missionaries who taught Metis girls sewing in the mission schools.

THE WORD "Metis" comes from the Latin verb "miscere" (to mix) and was originally applied to children from the marriages of Cree, Ojibwa and Saulteaux women to French and Scottish fur traders in the mid-1600s.

As the Metis increased in number and married among themselves, they developed a distinctive culture and identity, neither European nor Native but a fusion of the two.

With their mixed traditions and command of both European and Native languages, the "mixed-bloods," as they were often called, were logical intermediaries in the commercial relationship between the two civilizations. They were, for example, indispensable to the fur trade, working as guides, interpreters and provisioners, supplying the new forts and trading companies with pemmican, fresh meat and hand-stitched clothing made of buffalo and deer hide. They also provided transport for furs and goods and, in so doing, adapted European technology to the wilderness. For example, their invention and use of Red River carts and York boats made it possible to transport large volumes of goods and supplies to and from even the most distant outposts of the fur trade.

Music and creativity were central to Metis identity – as was their language, Michif, an amalgam mostly of Cree and French, but with some additional borrowing from English as well as from Native languages such as Ojibwa and Assiniboine. The culture's legendary fiddlers brought jigs and reels into their music. Their attire included woven sashes, embroidered gun sheaths, deer hide caps and quilted and beaded pipe bags. To the Cree and Ojibwa, the Metis were known as the "flower-beadwork people" because of their elaborately decorated clothing and belongings.

By the early nineteenth century, Metis villages had been established in and around fur trade posts from the Great Lakes to the Mackenzie Delta. One of the chief endeavours of the prairie Metis was the organization of seasonal commercial buffalo hunts through which they supplied the fur trade with pemmican and hides. So rigorous was their approach to the harvesting of buffalo that for each hunting foray they elected a provisional government to make and enforce the laws of the hunt. The expertise and persistence that made the Metis incomparable hunters also made them durable and relentless soldiers, as the government and North West Mounted Police would discover during the North-West Rebellion.

The Metis also developed a unique political and legal culture with strong democratic traditions. By 1816, they had challenged the Hudson's Bay Company's monopoly in the fur trade and had begun to develop a strong national consciousness and a sense of political entitlement.

Efforts by the Scottish settlers to restrict Metis hunting and trading practices at the Red River Settlement during the early 1800s led eventually to the settlers' defeat by the Metis in 1816 at the Battle of Seven Oaks. It was the same site where the victorious Metis, led by Cuthbert Grant Jr., first unfurled the flag of the Metis Nation.

For the next half century, the Metis were in the majority at Red River, but they were never properly acknowledged or fairly treated by the governing powers in eastern Canada. In 1869, they took up arms in a losing cause against Sir John A. Macdonald and the advances of Confederation. They did so again in 1885, in the area of Batoche, Saskatchewan, where Louis Riel and Gabriel Dumont led the Metis in the North-West Rebellion, a catastrophic attempt to establish legal and cultural respect for their people.

Today, some 300,000 Metis live across Canada and in the northern US In Canada, their struggle for rights and cultural recognition is carried on with growing success by the Metis National Council.

series of portages, rapids and barely pass-
able trails through the mosquito-infested
bush. In all, the thousand-mile trip took
just under four months and would not have
been possible without the help of more
than seven hundred Metis voyageurs and
Indians, knowledgeable woodsmen who
were hired along the way as pack carriers,
guides and paddlers.

Among Wolseley's militiamen was
a resilient young farm boy named Sam
Steele, an Ontario teenager, who many
years later, in his book *Forty Years in Canada: Reminiscences of the Great North-
West*, would describe clawing his way up
thirty miles of rapids at a stretch, hauling
thousand-pound boats up forty-five-
degree slopes through impassable spruce
forests, traversing rain-swollen cataracts
and shouldering supply packs so heavy
that every step was a potential misstep
– perhaps a crushed shoulder or fractured
skull. Steele described a Metis guide who,
anxious to show what he could do on a
portage west of Fort Frances, "hoisted
two barrels of pork and 1000 rounds of

ammunition – a weight of 528 lbs."

Some of the men got sick. Others
broke legs and injured backs. In descend-
ing Le Grand Descharge rapids by boat,
one of Steele's comrades snapped an oar,
sending the boat they were rowing into a
maelstrom of churning waves and back-
wash. "We were helpless," wrote Steele.
"Death stared us in the face as we surged
past the rocks and whirlpools." The blackflies were a pestilence, and parts of the
route were so confusing that Wolseley
himself got lost for two days among the
islands of Lake of the Woods.

The Metis wanted to believe Macdonald's
promise that the troops would bring peace
to Red River. But as the forces approached
Fort Garry, rumours grew that Scott's
death would be avenged. When the soldiers were within sight of the fort, Riel
was persuaded to flee into the countryside
with several of his men. He eventually
made his way to the US, where he would
live for many years.

Meanwhile, Wolseley's ragged and weary
troops arrived in Red River, where their

Michel Quesnelle was a
Metis from Cheyenne,
Wyoming, who became
a NWMP scout and, in
1875, brought the first
horses across the bor-
der from the US to Fort
Walsh.

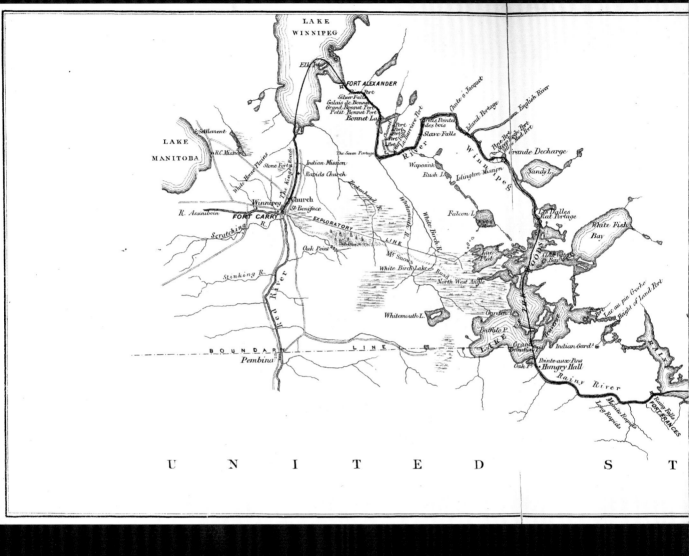

This portrait of a rather slim and ascetic-looking Sir John A. Macdonald reveals little of the first prime minister's hard-driving stubbornness, indomitable ego, capacity for chicanery, or fierce alcoholism. Nor does it reveal his imaginative brilliance or enormous sense of vision and destiny.

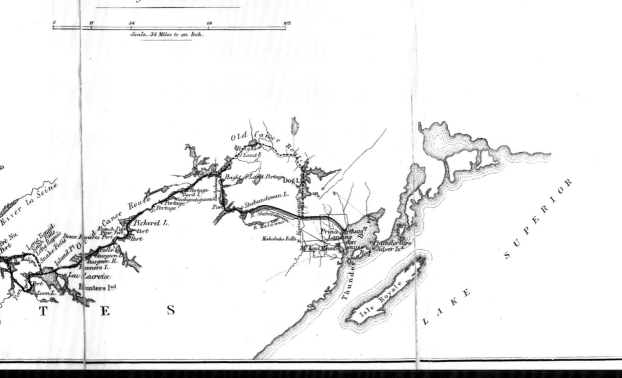

Plan of
Route followed by
RED RIVER EXPEDITIONARY FORCE
FROM
LAKE SUPERIOR TO FORT GARRY,
during the summer of 1870.

Scale.. 34 Miles to an Inch.

This impeccably orderly map showing the route of Colonel Wolseley's Red River Expedition to put down Riel during the summer of 1870 might suggest an equally impeccable and orderly passage through the wilderness of north-western Ontario. But quite the opposite was true. The expedition suffered almost every calamity known to bush travel: swamped canoes, rain-sodden gear and clothing, plagues of blackflies and mosquitoes, misread maps, knee-deep mud, broken bones, shortages of food, and worn out boots. The expedition's first few hundred miles, on the Dawson Route, required the troops to drag heavy boats and guns across forty-seven portages, one of them three miles long, uphill.

PUNCH'S FANCY PORTRAITS.—No. 96.

SIR GARNET WOLSELEY.
SHORT SERVICE AND QUICK RETURNS.

Field Marshall Garnet Joseph Wolseley's career in the British army began in 1852, spanned nearly half a century and included significant postings in Burma, the Crimea, India, China, Africa and, of course, Canada where he led the Red River Expedition in 1870. His brilliantly executed Ashanti campaign in West Africa in 1873–74 made him a household name in Britain. The phrase "Everything's all Sir Garnet," meaning "Everything is in order," is a tribute to Wolseley's widespread reputation for tidiness and efficiency.

spirits were anything but raised. According to Sam Steele, "The main street was a sea of black mud, caused by the recent rains. In it, voyageurs, whites, half-breeds, and Indians fought, wallowed and slept in all stages of drunkenness, induced by the poison dispensed over the bars of the vile saloons of the place."

Left to their prejudices, many of Wolseley's militiamen joined English-speaking residents of the settlement in open hostility toward the Metis. One night in a local hotel, a couple of settlers, jacked up on grain liquor, accosted Elzear Goulet, who was thought to have commanded the firing squad that had executed Thomas Scott. Goulet ran from the hotel and, terrified that his pursuers were going to shoot him, jumped into the Red River and attempted to swim across. But to no avail. His pursuers fired from the riverbank, and Goulet disappeared beneath the surface.

"It was supposed up to this time," wrote Steele, "that the body of poor Scott was buried within the walls of Fort Garry." But when members of the settlement's public works department opened the grave, they found Scott's pine coffin contained only a few rocks. Speculation that the Irishman's corpse, or perhaps his living body, had been weighted with chains and dumped through a hole in the ice did little to reduce tensions between the Canadians and the Metis.

In Riel's absence, Colonel Wolseley and most of his soldiers returned east within a matter of weeks, leaving a peacekeeping force in charge of the settlement. But the tensions of the past few weeks were unresolved. The Metis quickly discovered that their new "rights" were theoretical only, and that they still had no legal claim to the land they had occupied for decades. Their farms were hastily surveyed and in some cases turned over to English-speaking settlers or other newcomers. Disillusioned, many Metis left for the free country of the Saskatchewan Valley or for unregulated land in the United States.

Riel, meantime, was banished from the country by the Canadian courts for a period of five years, which would eventually be extended to ten. It is one of the more intriguing oddities of Canadian history that when federal elections came along, the people of Red River made Riel a Member of Parliament by proclamation. There is proof that at least once he came back into the country in disguise and travelled to Ottawa, where he appeared secretly in the House of Commons and signed his name on the parliamentary roll.

BACK IN OTTAWA, Macdonald, who was increasingly curious about the country to the west of Red River, decided to send out a non-military expedition, the aim of which would be to bring back a report on life and conditions on the prairie and in the remote north-west. To lead the mission, the prime minister turned to one of the great soldier-adventurers of the nineteenth century, an indefatigable Irishman named William Francis Butler, a man who revered Napoleon and who had travelled ahead of the Wolseley Expedition, often in danger, gathering intelligence and sending it back to the colonel.

Below: The Red River Expedition at Kakabeka Falls, by Frances Anne Hopkins. This idyllic rendition of Colonel Wolseley's stop west of Prince Arthur's Landing might suggest a rather leisurely trip west by the government's forces.

Rather, the trip was fraught with what one soldier referred to as "misadventure, hardship and daily peril."

Right: Colonel Wolseley was by all accounts an egoist who loved the trappings, ceremonies and any other ego-gratifying accoutrements of his rank in the British army. Even in the boreal wilderness, he is said to have demanded pomp and ceremony to whatever degree these could be achieved by cold and hungry troops in tattered uniforms. He eventually attained the rank of field marshall in the British forces and carried the baton shown here with its presentation box.

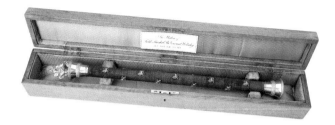

THE SCIENCE OF CHEEK; OR, RIEL'S NEXT MOVE.
RIEL (loq.)—"FIVE THOUSAND DOLLARS! BY GAR, I SHALL ARREST ZE SCOUNDREL MYSELF!"

The ambitious inquiry, which would cover some 2,800 miles, would look into possibilities for agriculture and industry, bridges and roads – and whether a railway could be constructed through the mountains to join the wide-open prairie to the tea-swilling colony by the Pacific.

If a railway through the mountains was not feasible, Macdonald needed to know right away, since the next step in his dream of building a country sea to sea would be a promise to British Columbia to put rails across the prairie and through the mountains to the Pacific. How else but with a rail link could he convince Governor Anthony Musgrave and his fellow British Columbians to join Confederation? The coastal dwellers were three thousand miles from Ottawa, with two mountain ranges and near-endless prairie and wilderness between. Many residents in the British colony, and indeed in the American north-west, thought the colony would be better off annexed to the US, which had recently purchased Alaska from the Russians.

Macdonald was also curious about the condition of the tribes. Were they thriving? Or even healthy? How had they been affected by the long-time presence of the Hudson's Bay Company? And now by its absence? What policing might be needed to keep peace among the Natives and the future settlers?

Butler was as tough as a railway spike and as impervious as a raven to cold and storms. Travelling with a few horses and carts, and at most a guide or two, he slept under the stars, even in blizzards and −40°F weather. He ate pemmican and rabbits, and almost anything else that turned up. Near Duck Lake, in what is now central Saskatchewan, he described setting a fire and dining in the snow with a Cree traveller named Starving Bull:

What dinner might have been under ordinary circumstances, I cannot state; but, unfortunately on the present occasion, its preparation was attended with unusual drawbacks. Starving Bull had succeeded in killing a skunk during his

Using an intricate code of symbols and numbers, the early Natives kept what were called "winter counts," in effect calendars that recorded the major events and passages of a year or succession of years.

The one shown here, was started by Bull Plume of the Pikani, part of the Blackfoot Confederacy, logged Pikani events ranging from 1764 to 1917, a total of 153 years, making it one of the most extensive of the Blackfoot winter counts in existence. The English notations were added later by Canon W.R. Haynes, an Anglican missionary stationed at Brocket, Alberta.

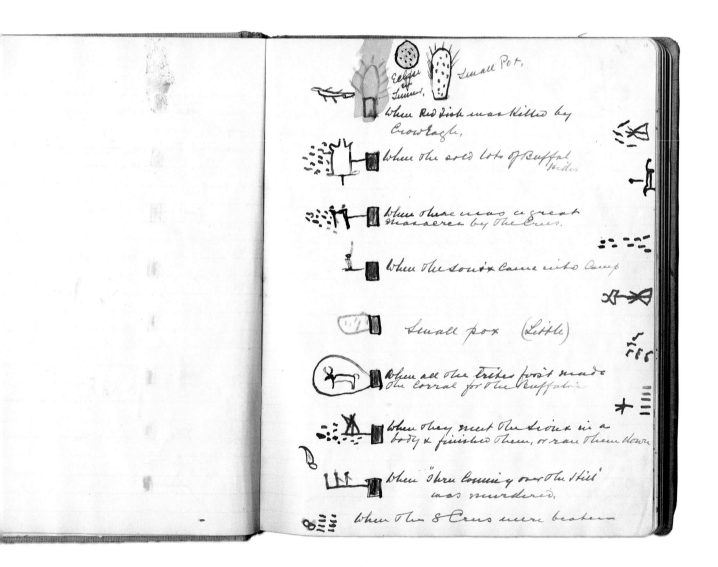

William Francis Butler served as intelligence officer with Wolseley's forces and a short time later accepted Sir John A. Macdonald's commission to travel across the west and report back on everything from the condition of the Natives to the opportunities for industry and agriculture. Most poignantly, he reported on the plight of the tribes stricken by smallpox – "poor, plague-stricken wretches who by streams and lake, by willow copses and upon bare hillsides, often shelterless from the fierce rays of the summer sun… lay down to die."

journey. This performance, while highly creditable to his energy as a hunter, was by no means conducive to his success as a cook. Bitterly did that skunk reverie himself upon us who had borne no part in his destruction. Pemmican is at no time a delicacy; but pemmican flavoured with skunk was more than I could attempt. However, Starving Bull proved himself worthy of his name, and the frying-pan was soon scraped clean under his hungry manipulations.

Butler's book on his travels, *The Great Lone Land*, speaks hauntingly of the distances and isolation of the prairie: "Between this little camp-fire and the giant mountains to which my steps were turned, there stood in that long twelve hundred miles but six houses [tribal encampments], and in these houses a terrible malady had swept nearly half the inhabitants out of life."

The "terrible malady" Butler mentions was smallpox, a scourge that raged across the prairie and plains in 1870, moving from the midwestern United States into the farthest corners of the North-West Territories.

The grossly disfiguring disease, particularly virulent for people never before exposed to the smallpox virus, was first brought north on a Missouri River steamboat. An infected man is said to have left a blanket on board, which was taken by a Gros Ventre tribesman, who caught the disease and spread it to his people, inflicting upon hundreds of them pustulating facial and body sores and, eventually, a painful death. A war party of Bloods that had gone south to steal horses came upon a Gros Ventre camp in which the dead lay bloated and disfigured, and the only living beings were the horses still grazing around the tents. The Bloods, who knew nothing about smallpox, took both the horses and the buffalo robes of the dead, hastening the spread of the disease through the Blackfoot, Cree and Stoney people.

There were neither doctors nor medicines in the west at the time, and smallpox eventually claimed more than half the Blackfoot and Cree, killing over ten thousand Cree. "Of all the fatal methods of destroying the Indians which his white brother has introduced in the West," wrote Butler, "this plague of smallpox is the most deadly."

For thousands of miles across the prairie, the trail was marked with the unburied bodies and bleaching bones of those Butler called "the wild warriors of the West." At Fort Pitt, in what is now northern Saskatchewan, more than a hundred infected Cree, forbidden from entering the fort, perished outside the stockade. The dead lay for days until finally, tentatively, hungry wolves emerged from the forests and fought over the decomposing bodies. Some stricken Natives believed that if they could give the disfiguring sickness back to the non-Natives around Fort Pitt – return it to those from whom it had come – they would cease to suffer from it themselves. And so they hung around the houses outside the fort, put their marred faces against the pump handles and spit on the doorknobs.

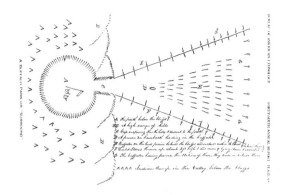

The term "buffalo jump" implies something almost playful about the method that, for millennia, the Natives used for hunting and harvesting buffalo. But the process of driving two-thousand pound animals into corrals and then over fifteen- or twenty-foot cliffs – causing them smashed legs, ribs and spines – was a most serious endeavour indeed.

Considering that he was an appointee of Macdonald's, it is ironic that Butler had nothing good to say about the European colonists of the era, including the Scots, and their effect on the Natives. "It is the same story from the Atlantic to the Pacific," he wrote in his book. "First the white man was the welcome guest, the honoured visitor; then the greedy hunter, the death-dealing vender of fire-water and poison; then the settler and exterminator – everywhere it has been the same story."

WHILE DISEASE was the most immediate challenge facing the Metis and Indian populations, it was certainly not the only one. For centuries, the Blackfoot, Assiniboine and Cree – indeed all the prairie tribes – had depended on the buffalo for everything from food and clothing to weapons, tools and bow strings. The animal's hide could be made into boats, moccasins, and coats. Its horns became powder flasks and jewellery. Its flesh could be roasted or mixed with fat and pounded into the staple of the Metis diet, pemmican. So significant

was the latter to survival on the prairie at the time the Europeans showed up, it wasn't long before the fur traders and settlers – and then the soldiers, too – were either trading for it or making it themselves and carrying it on their patrols.

It is difficult from the vantage point of the early twenty-first century to comprehend the size of the buffalo herds. In their annual migrations in search of fresh grass, these huge-headed animals shook the ground from Texas in the south to the foothills of the Rockies in the north-west. The valleys and flatlands were at times said to be black with them, and it was common for a wagon train to be camped for two days while a herd passed. During the mid-1800s, Colonel Richard Irving Dodge of the US Cavalry reported that in Montana he had ridden for twenty-five miles through an unbroken parade of them – an estimated half-million animals.

The traditional hunt involved dozens, sometimes hundreds, of men and women who spread themselves in long lines across the prairie and gradually

steered the buffalo into a funnel-shaped corral, and finally into a pound where the animals were slaughtered with spears. Sometimes the buffalo were driven over an embankment – a "jump" – where they piled up on one another, roaring and kicking, immobilized by broken legs and backs.

After a successful hunt came elaborate feasting, then the painstaking process of preparing hides and making pemmican. The women did much of this work, and when it was done they stitched robes from the tanned hides, made moccasins, mitts and leggings, then decorated them with beads and porcupine quills.

While buffalo was invariably the foundation of any feast, wild fish, fowl and game also featured in tribal and Metis celebrations and at the tables of the fur traders. On a trip west during the mid-1800s, the artist Paul Kane described a Christmas feast among the Metis and traders at HBC Fort Edmonton:

At the head, before Mr. Harriett, was a large dish of boiled buffalo hump; at the

THE BUFFALO and buffalo hunt were, for centuries, the central focus of life for the Natives of the prairie and plains. But even though this majestic mammal was plentiful prior to the arrival of the Europeans in the west, no part of any slain animal was wasted. The hide was used for robes, teepees, bull boats, blankets and moccasins, while the bones went into hand tools, pipes, arrowheads, hoes and hide scrapers. The sinews were turned into bowstrings, thread and snowshoe webbing, the horns into jewellery and cooking and eating utensils.

The dung was used for fuel, the brains for tanning hides, the fat for candles and soap. The hair became rope and yarn, the stomach a container for carrying water.

More than anything, it was hunger that drove the hunt, and very little of the buffalo's soft tissue was not consumed as food. The nose, tongue, heart, liver and stomach were all considered edible delicacies – as were the eyeballs and brains.

The muscle tissue was butchered into roasts and steaks, while any remaining fat, gristle and organs were fed raw to the dogs.

In addition, much of the meat from any hunt was made into pemmican, essential nourishment for the months to come and a major trading item. The Metis dominated the pemmican trade, supplying first the North West Company and then the Hudson's Bay Company to provision the fur trade. Without this nutritious and compact food, many traders would have gone hungry.

This long-lasting fare was made by cutting the meat into strips, which were dried over a slow fire, or in the hot sun, until they were hard and brittle. They were then placed in a trough and pounded into powder-like bits with a stone or large wooden pestle. The result

was mixed with the rendered fat of the bone marrow in a ratio of approximately 50 percent meat and 50 percent melted fat. In some cases, dried fruits such as saskatoon berries, cranberries, blueberries or chokecherries were pounded into powder and then added to the mixture – particularly if the pemmican was going to be used on ceremonial occasions. The concentrated mixture was then sewn into "green" rawhide packets for storage and eventual shipment in ninety-pound sacks to far-flung outposts.

A cache of pemmican discovered recently was analyzed to determine what was in the dried meat mixture. It was found to be the complete energy bar of its day and was still edible after more than a hundred years.

The word "buffalo" derives from the French word "boeuf," meaning ox or bullock, used by French fur traders to describe these immense prairie mammals. Buffalo can grow to six feet six inches in height and up to ten feet in length, and can weigh up to 2,200 pounds. The animal's lifespan in the wilds is about fifteen years.

Below: This versatile fur trader bought and sold a range of pelts and skins that included those of fox, beaver, buffalo and deer. Some of them were used for clothing and winter warmth on the prairie, while others were shipped to the fashion houses of London and New York. Note the buffalo skulls in the foreground, left and centre.

Right: An experienced buffalo skinner is said to have been able to take the hide from a slaughtered animal in ten or twelve minutes. In the worst days of overslaughter, skinned carcasses were often left rotting on the prairie or plains until they were eventually picked clean by wolves, foxes, ravens, crows, coyotes, shrews… and so on down to maggots and microbes, until there was nothing left but bleached bones in the sun.

foot smoked a boiled buffalo calf. Start not, gentle reader, the calf is very small, and is taken from the cow by the Caesarian operation long before it attains its full growth. This, boiled whole, is one of the most esteemed dishes among the epicures of the interior. My pleasing duty was to help a dish of mouffle, or dried moose nose; the gentleman on my left distributed, with graceful impartiality, the white fish, delicately browned in buffalo marrow. The worthy priest helped the buffalo tongue, while Mr. Rundell cut up the beavers' tails, and the other gentleman spent his time in dissecting a roast wild goose.

The buffalo hide was not the only skin used in the making of winter clothing. Fox and rabbit skins were also used, as were the skins of wolves, which were of course part of the same ecosystem as the buffalo.

However, by the mid-nineteenth century, the ecology of the prairie was changing as rapidly as the political landscape. The presence of fur traders and settlers meant that more buffalo were

being slaughtered for meat and clothing. The use of muskets acquired through the Hudson's Bay Company made the killing of the animals easier and quicker. Breech-loading rifles available from American traders from the late 1860s onward accelerated the killing process.

More significantly, in the US a planned and catastrophic slaughter of the buffalo had begun. The carnage was the work of professional hunters and was aimed in part at supplying meat for rail workers and military men who were present in increasing numbers on the plains. But it was also a kind of backdoor rout on Indian culture and, in the long run, on the very presence of the tribes, who came frequently into conflict with US settlers. The latter had moved unannounced into tribal territory and were claiming land that once belonged to everyone. In protest, the Sioux and Comanche stole horses, robbed mail coaches and occasionally murdered those who had intruded onto land where their people once hunted freely. For this, they were punished with

For nearly a century between the mid-1800s and mid-1900s, the Hudson's Bay Company issued a variety of tokens representing the value or partial value of a beaver pelt. In 1854, a set of four brass tokens, one of which is shown above, was issued in denominations of ⅛, ¼, ½ and 1 "made beaver" or beaver pelt. The tokens were marked NB rather than MB for "made beaver" because of a stamping error in England where the tokens were minted, but they were used anyway.

While buffalo on the run can move at speeds of some thirty-five miles per hour (significantly faster than a human being), they tended to roam methodically and slowly across the prairie and plains. Because the thousands of buffalo in the herds of old ate so much grass, they had to move constantly so that all the animals could be fed.

For several years after he was forced out of Canada by the Dominion government, the legendary Sioux chief Sitting Bull was a somewhat unlikely feature of Buffalo Bill Cody's travelling Wild West show. Seen here in 1885 with Cody in Montreal, Sitting Bull was billed, quite accurately, as a fearless warrior and incomparable battle strategist.

vengeful brutality by the US Cavalry, which in the wake of the Civil War had advanced west to protect the settlers against those they perceived to be "gun-wielding and bloody-minded savages."

Governments and civilians alike endorsed the genocidal precept that "the only good Indian is a dead Indian." William Francis Butler claimed that a US colonel had once told him, "Kill every buffalo you see. Every buffalo dead is an Indian gone."

By 1870, the once-unified buffalo herd had separated into two parts. The northern herd roamed what is now the Canadian prairie and northern US plains, while the southern herd became sequestered in Texas, where within five years it was exterminated.

Buffalo Bill Cody, a one-time cavalry colonel and swashbuckling roughneck, was the most notorious of the American buffalo hunters. Under contract, Cody once killed nearly five thousand buffalo in eighteen months to feed the thousands of labourers building the Kansas Pacific Railway. On another occasion, responding to a taunt from a handful of Pawnees, who disputed his prowess, he shot dead forty-eight buffalo in fifty minutes and left them lying where they fell.

The result of this ruthless assault on the animal that had sustained ten thousand years of Indian life was to leave many tribes in near destitution. They were at war not only with the US Cavalry but increasingly with one another as they were forced to move farther for the hunt and to compete ever more aggressively for buffalo. Often they ended up shooting one another or stealing one another's horses, or plundering food when they were hungry.

The author of the infamous "the only good Indian" slogan was General Philip Sheridan, a ruthless military strategist who had achieved notoriety and success during the Civil War, and was in 1868 appointed by soon-to-be-president General Ulysses S. Grant to plan and implement the "pacification" of the tribes. In the winter of 1868–69, Sheridan and his forces attacked the Cheyenne, Kiowa and Comanche tribes in their winter quarters

Below: Buffalo bones gathered in carts by industrious Natives are seen here being loaded into box cars at Gull Lake, Saskatchewan, in 1891.

Right: Dealers such as B.M. Hicks of Minneapolis bought buffalo bones by the box car from Indians and Metis harvesters and sold them to manufacturers of fertilizer or porcelain, as well as to pharmaceutical makers, either locally or in cities such as Chicago and St. Louis.

The Wild West show became a popular form of entertainment for people east of the Mississippi and in Europe during the later nineteenth and early twentieth centuries. Buffalo Bill Cody, one of the most notorious of the government-sponsored buffalo hunters, oper-ated an extravaganza in which Native warriors recreated tribal battles, displayed their athletic horsemanship, and performed traditional-style dances. White hunters and plainsmen joined the act in mock warfare against the "hostile" tribesmen, often driving covered wagons and dis-playing their own brand of expert marksmanship. The circus-style poster below – a highly exaggerated depiction of what the audience might expect to see – shows Col. Cody himself at right.

The cartoon at right suggests something of the tragic and despairing confusion that befell the American Plains Indians who, during the latter half of the nineteenth century, were caught between the expansive plans of the US Department of the Interior, led by Secretary of the Interior Carl Schultz, and the annihilating plans of the US Army under General Philip Sheridan and General William T. Sherman, seen here peeking from behind the door. During the late 1860s, Sheridan, a Civil War hero, was given responsibility by the US government for eliminating the Indians from the plains. Realizing that wiping them out in battle would be too painstaking and difficult, this ruthless and relentless strategist decided instead to eliminate the buffalo, bringing the buffalo-dependent tribes to their knees.

on the north-central plains, stealing their supplies, horses and livestock, and slaughtering those who resisted, including women and children.

Realizing eventually that the plains were too vast a region for his war on the elusive Indians, Sheridan began instead to pour his energy into the slaughter of the buffalo, a more effective strategy, one that he believed would invite less scorn when the history books came to be written.

By 1874 in the US, hundreds of professional hunters, trespassing on land assigned by treaty to specific tribes, had killed more than four million buffalo, leaving the carcasses to rot on the plains. When the Texas legislature considered outlawing hunting on tribal lands, General Sheridan personally testified against the initiative, suggesting that rather than censoring the hunters, the legislature should give each of them a gold medal bearing the likeness of a dead buffalo on one side and a discouraged-looking or dead Indian on the other.

The newspapers took their own stance in the war against the Indians, as did farmers and townsfolk, many of them God-fearing people who believed that "the heathens should be taught a lesson." William Francis Butler spoke with particular abhorrence of the injustices practised against the tribes on US soil:

If on the long line of the American frontier, a single life is taken by an Indian, if even a horse or ox be stolen from a settler, the fact is chronicled in scores of journals throughout the United States. But the reverse of the story we never know. The countless deeds of perfidious robbery or ruthless murder done by white savages out in these Western wilds never find the light of day. The poor red man has no telegraph, no newspaper, no type, to tell his sufferings and his woes. My god, what a terrible tale could I tell of these dark deeds done by the white savage against the far nobler red man! From southernmost Texas to most northern Montana there is but one universal remedy for Indian difficulty – kill him.

"You take one barrel of Missouri River water, and two gallons of alcohol. Then you add two ounces of strychnine (poison) to make them go crazy – because strychnine is the greatest stimulant in the world – and three plugs of tobacco to make them sick – an Indian wouldn't figure it was whisky unless it made him sick – and five bars of soap to give it a head, and half a pound of red pepper, and then you put in some sagebrush and boil it until it's brown. Strain into a bottle, and you've got Indian whisky; that one bottle calls for one buffalo robe and when the Indian got drunk it was two robes."

E.C. "TEDDY BLUE" ABBOTT in *We Pointed Them North: Recollections of a Cowpuncher*

And kill him they did, if not with rifles then with starvation or poison. Butler relates with disgust the story of how one night several "starving Indians" in Helena, Montana, stole sugar from a storekeeper who, the next night, left the door to his store open, tempting the Indians to steal more. The sugar, now lethally poisoned by the merchant, left them in agony and then dead.

WORN DOWN by the war and at times half-starved, hundreds if not thousands of Natives, particularly the Sioux, began drifting north across the medicine line, seeking protection in territory that is now southern Saskatchewan and Alberta. Demoralized by the injustices perpetrated against them, and antagonistic toward anyone with a white skin, the drifters, in desperation, occasionally attacked settlers or traders, or stole cattle, horses or wagons. In their anger over the slaughter to the south – and the loss of the buffalo – they became a destabilizing influence on their northern cousins, imparting to them their profound dissatisfaction with the agenda of the rail builders and settlers, and with the government institutions that supported them.

More destabilizing yet to susceptible Blackfoot and Assiniboine – and to the itinerant Sioux from the south – was the growing number of whisky forts that had sprung up in territory just north of the border. Here hastily constructed stockades sheltered shady characters and even shadier activities, and thrived in the absence of any policing in the territory. They carried on a modicum of legitimate trade in guns, tack and flour. But their more lucrative business was providing distilled alcohol to the Natives, mainly in exchange for buffalo robes and pemmican. The booze – "whisky" only in name – was often rot-gut poison, containing anything from rubbing alcohol and leather dye, to rust, iodine and urine. Buffalo robes, which required days of effort to make, occasionally got traded for as little as a cup of contaminated whisky. Not that drinkers were entirely fooled by the traders. Indeed, the term "fire water" derived from the practice of spitting a mouthful of whisky onto a fire to see if it would ignite – proof of its alcohol content.

The most notorious of the whisky establishments, Fort Hamilton, better known as Fort Whoop-Up, was located at the forks of the Old Man's and St. Mary rivers, near present-day Lethbridge, Alberta. The place was run by an unscrupulous Montanan named John Healy, who it was said would trade coloured water to those drunk enough not to know it wasn't whisky. It is testimony to the ravages of the activities at Fort Whoop-Up that, in the vicinity of the fort during 1871, eighty-eight murders were committed by tribesmen in drunken brawls among themselves. Horse stealing was rampant in the area, as was fear among travellers and traders that they, too, would eventually be victims of the drunkenness.

The unruliness of the American wild west existed largely because settlement in the US had proliferated in the absence of any effective laws or institutionalized law-keeping. Sir John A. Macdonald, to

his credit, was determined to see some systematic means of control imposed before life in the Canadian west had a chance to descend into anarchy. Thus, during the summer of 1872, alarmed over reports of conditions around the whisky forts, he dispatched Colonel Robertson-Ross to investigate and to advise on the need for a national police force. The force, as Macdonald imagined it, would protect not just future settlers but the area's many peaceable Natives, and restore a measure of integrity to their villages.

Robertson-Ross was adjutant-general to the Canadian militia and a man known for his wisdom and perspective. But that perspective was challenged by what he found when he got onto the prairie – namely pockets of chaos and depravity that if left to fester would eventually have rivalled the uncontrolled wildness that characterized settlement to the south. He reported, for example, that during the weeks before his arrival in Edmonton a Metis by the name of Charles Gaudin had murdered his wife within sight of the HBC

Wa-Kan-O-Zahn-Zahn (Medicine Bottle), the chief of the Santee Sioux, fled to Manitoba in 1862 after the Minnesota Massacre, in which Sioux warriors in the southern part of the state slaughtered more than 400 settlers in response to ongoing treaty violations and brutal prejudices against them. In 1864, the chief was inveigled into drunkness by three Canadians who delivered him to the US Army at the border. He was executed at Fort Snelling on November 11, 1865.

fort and that the crime had gone unpunished. Just months earlier, the same man, in a fit of anger, had cut the tendons in a woman's arms, leaving her permanently unable to work or care for herself. A Cree man named *Ta-ha-kooch* had committed half a dozen murders at Edmonton and was, in the colonel's words, "walking free around the Post." Men had to be armed. Whisky flowed freely. Cattle and horse theft were regular occurrences. Settlers who had intended to farm were reluctant to do so for fear of losing their livestock.

Virtually everywhere Robertson-Ross went he found mayhem and fear, the result largely of a Native population deprived of its cultural and economic mainstay, the buffalo, and now in danger of losing its rights on the land. In his report to Ottawa, the adjutant-general recommended the establishment of "a chain of military posts from Manitoba to the Rocky Mountains" and the creation of a "small but effective Field Brigade" – a body of men with military authority and weaponry but with the mobility and regional awareness to be a functional local police force.

Robertson-Ross also suggested the appointment of an Indian commissioner. "The individual to fill this post," he said, "should, if possible, be known to the Indians, and a man in whom they have confidence." Ominously, he also recommended that the commissioner should at no time proceed into the field "unaccompanied by a military force."

In May 1873, Macdonald gave notice that he intended to introduce to Parliament a bill that would create precisely the force recommended by Robertson-Ross – a body of well-trained, decisive young men, between the ages of twenty-five and forty, all of whom could both ride and shoot. One of the sections of the bill declared that no person should be appointed to the force "unless he be of sound constitution, good character, and be able to read either the English or French language."

By the colonel's reckoning, anywhere from 50 to 150 of these hardy and intelligent young men should be stationed at each of eight posts stretching in a rickety line from Portage la Prairie in the east to Fort Porcupine Hills, near what is now Fort Macleod in southwestern Alberta.

Macdonald was determined that the force show no ostentation either in its dealings with the public or in its uniforms, which, according to the prime minister, were to display "as little gold lace and fuss and feathers as possible." The uniform was, however, to include a red tunic, with the hope that the goodwill and respect accorded the British military in most parts of Canada would be transferred to the lawmen in their frontier postings.

ALAS, BY OCTOBER 1873, the rapidly evolving police force had lost the support of Macdonald and his government. While the buffalo were disappearing and whisky was wreaking havoc on the prairie, the Macdonald government had been working to extend its national dream to the Pacific coast. And had done so, with alacrity, by successfully bringing British Columbia into Confederation in 1871.

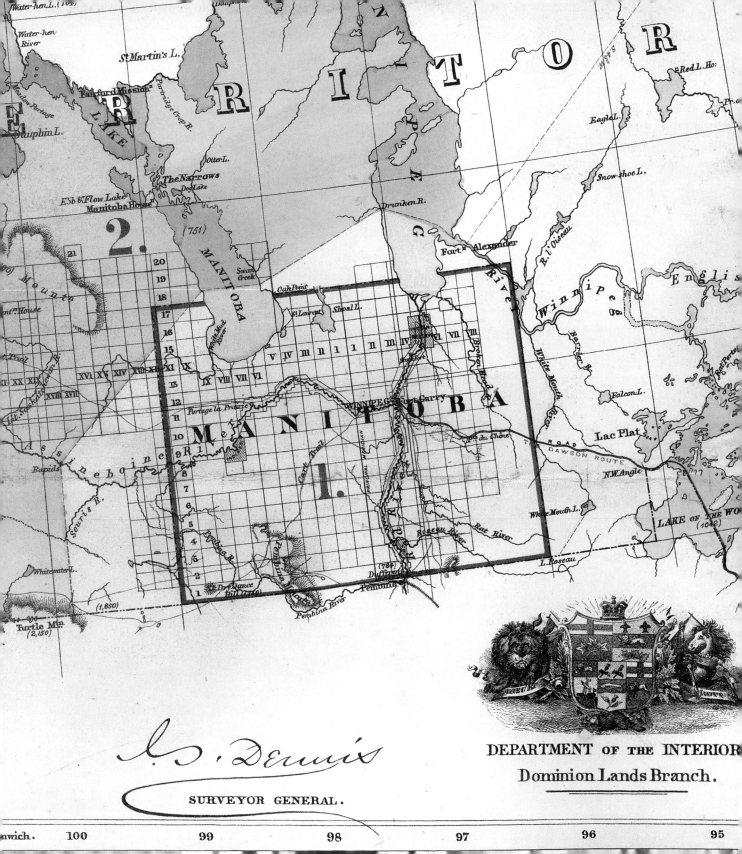

Water-hen L.

Water-hen River

St Martin's L.

Fairford Mission

Meadow Portage

Dauphin L.

Otter L.

The Narrows

Dog Lake

E.5b & Flow Lake

Manitoba House

(751)

2.

21

20

19

18

17

16

15

12

11

10

9

8

7

6

5

4

3

2

1

Mount...

...House

Assiniboine

Souris R.

Rapids

Whitewater L.

(1,850)

Turtle Mtn
(2,150)

St Laurent

Oak Point

Shoal L.

MANITOBA

Swan Creek

Whitemud River

XX XIX XVIII XVII XVI XV XIV XIII XII XI X

IX VIII VII VI

V IV III II I I II III IV V VI VII VIII

Broken Head R.

Portage la Prairie

MANITOBA

1.

Clark Trail

Pembina R.

WINNIPEG Fort Garry

R.I.

Dry Dance Hill (1,510)

Pembina River

Dufferin Emerson

Pembina

Roseau River

Rat River

L. Roseau

White Mouth L.

Principal Meridian

Pt du Chêne

DRITOBA

BRITOR

WINNIPEG

RIVER

Drunken R.

Fortᵗ Alexander

R. ĺ Oiseau

Winnipeg

English

Snow-shoe L.

Eagle L.

Red L. Ho:

Barren R.

White Mouth River

Falcon L.

Lac Plat

N.W. Angle

THE ROAD

DAWSON ROUTE

LAKE OF THE WO...

(1,042)

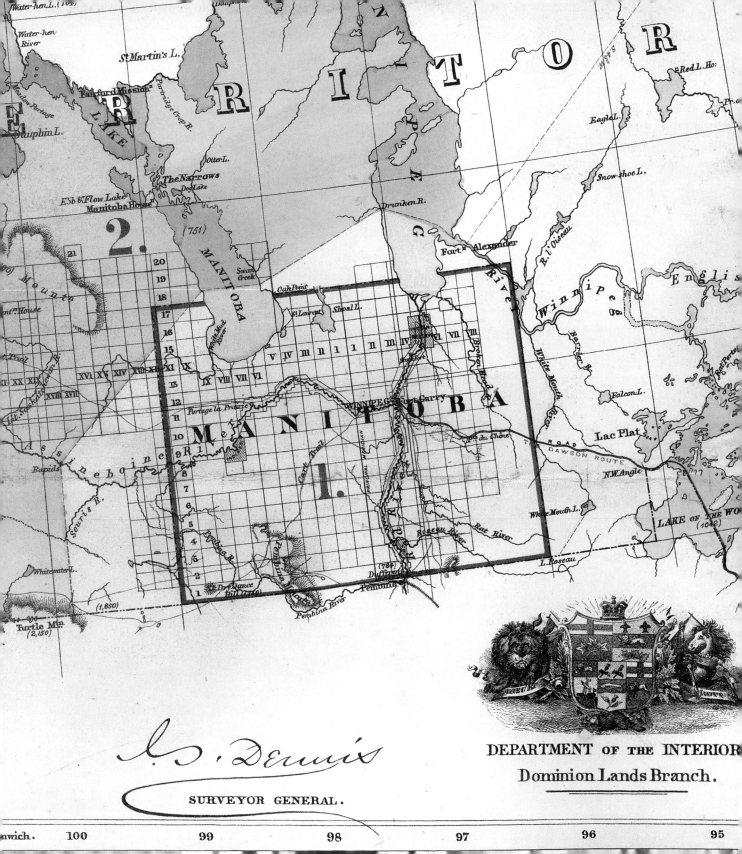

I. S. Dennis

SURVEYOR GENERAL.

DEPARTMENT OF THE INTERIOR

Dominion Lands Branch.

...nwich.   100   99   98   97   96   95

Below: Delegates from the legislatures of Canada, New Brunswick, Nova Scotia and Prince Edward Island met at the Convention at Charlottetown in 1864 to consider the union of the British North American colonies. Many of the delegates – George Brown, George-Etienne Cartier, D'Arcy McGee, Alexander Galt, Oliver Mowatt, Charles Tupper and of course John A. Macdonald – would eventually become famous across the country as Fathers of Confederation.

Right: The reverse side of the 1867 Confederation Medal is adorned with an allegorical depiction of Britain (in the seat of power) giving the charter of Confederation to Ontario (with sickle), Quebec (with paddle), Nova Scotia (with mining spade) and New Brunswick (with timber axe).

Sir Anthony Musgrave, one of the widest travelled of Canada's historic governmental figures, was born in Antigua and, as a young man, was governor of the Leeward Islands and then chief administrator of St. Vincent and the Grenadines in the British West Indies. He was appointed governor of the impoverished British colony of Newfoundland in 1864 and for half a decade attempted unsuccessfully to persuade Newfoundlanders to enter into an alliance with the evolving Dominion of Canada. Dispirited by his lack of success, he accepted Sir John A. Macdonald's request that he move to the opposite side of the continent as colonial governor of British Columbia and attempt to bring that colony into confederation. Musgrave quickly won the confidence of British Columbians and, knowing how badly Macdonald wanted BC in the fold, was able to negotiate for the colony a highly advantageous union with Canada. Among his demands was a railway that would reach BC from the east within ten years of the colony's joining the country in 1871. Musgrave eventually governed Jamaica and had two stints in Australia, where the dance music represented by the accompanying illustration was composed for him shortly before his death in 1888.

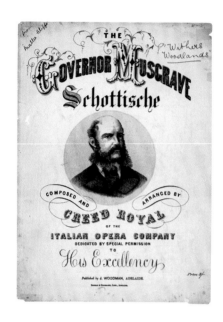

However, the cost had been steep – and for Macdonald would soon get steeper. Governor Musgrave of British Columbia and his legislative council were no fools. They knew well that Macdonald's dream of a dominion from sea to sea required a province on the west coast. They knew equally well that they had leverage with Ottawa because the Americans were as keen as the Canadians to annex their colony. Had the US indeed annexed British Columbia, it would have given the country control of the west coast from the Mexican border to the Beaufort Sea off the northern tip of Alaska. Not that the BC authorities ever thought seriously about joining the US. Far from it. But the ghost of the possibility that they would had nagged Macdonald for years.

Musgrave's team of negotiators travelled to Ottawa in early 1871 to present their demands for provincehood. They went by train through the US and, impressed by the luxury of the ride, had a bright idea en route. Perhaps such travel would eventually be possible across Canada, directly out of Vancouver. While a rail connection was not originally one of the demands they had in mind, when they got to Ottawa their requirements included a cross-country train track, linking them to the rest of British North America.

By the time the papers were signed and the *British Columbia Act* was passed in the House of Commons on July 21, 1871, some provinces thought Ottawa had been fleeced. And indeed there was reason for the government to feel shorn by Musgrave and his lieutenants. Among other things, Canada had assumed all of the British colony's debts, agreed to an annual subsidy of $1.60 per person, arranged to cover pensions for all former officials of the colony, and promised fortnightly mail service via San Francisco.

However, all the aforementioned largesse was pocket change compared with Macdonald's promise that if BC joined Confederation his government would build a railway to the coast. Construction would begin within two years and finish within ten. Impossible though it seemed,

Confederation: The Much-Fathered Youngster is cartooned here as a plump, ostensibly female child, surrounded by fretful "fathers," left to right: George Brown, Sir Francis Hincks, William McDougall and Sir John A. Macdonald.

the promise was right there in the act, in black and white.

As far as the Liberal opposition was concerned, Macdonald had lost his mind. And Canada was about to pay for it. How could three and half million Canadians finance such a project?

The truth was, they couldn't. Macdonald knew it and did the only thing he could in tough economic times – went directly for private help, in this case to Sir Hugh Allan, a man who could not only build the railway but finance it. Sir Hugh was an Ayrshire-born Scot, a cousin of the poet Robbie Burns, and believed to be the richest man in Canada. As a shipping magnate and railway promoter, he worked with a silent syndicate of wealthy financiers, including the American banker and railway builder Jay Cooke, who controlled the Northern Pacific Railway in the US.

Ever the shrewd businessman, Cooke possessed ideas of his own about how the Canadian railway should be built. In his version, it would cross the prairie and mountains to BC as planned, but would

connect to his own US system in such a way that he could delay indefinitely building the costly section of rail across the north shore of Lake Superior. Under the Allan-Cooke plan, people wishing to travel between eastern and western Canada, or to send freight to the west, would use a route that ran south of the Great Lakes on Cooke-controlled rail and came north into Canada near Winnipeg.

The Allan-Cooke blueprint was an appalling violation of Macdonald's promise to his electorate that he would build the entire railway on Canadian soil. If it went ahead, as it seemed likely to do, it would put all rail service to and from the Canadian west under American control.

Whether the prime minister knew about Cooke's role in the anticipated funding and building of the railway is still a matter of speculation. It is also unclear whether he knew what Allan's syndicate had in mind regarding a route.

What he did know was that when the Canadian election came along in 1872, his party received $300,000 in secret funds

from Allan's team, and that the source of the money was none other than the American Jay Cooke.

It was a bribe, plain and simple, intended to ensure the awarding of the contract. And it affected the outcome of the election.

In the wake of his victory, Macdonald claimed he had no idea about the US influence on his rail dealings or on the election. But the Liberal opposition knew otherwise, and within weeks produced proof in the House of Commons of the chicanery. That evidence included a telegram Macdonald had sent to Cooke's agent in the US "I must have another ten thousand," read the damning dots and dashes. "Do not fail me."

This stewpot of intrigue took the name of the ocean Macdonald sought to reach and became known as the Pacific Scandal. When Macdonald realized his government would be defeated over it in the House of Commons, he resigned, and the governor general, Lord Dufferin, invited the Liberals to form a government.

Prime Minister Sir John A. Macdonald and Lady Agnes Macdonald appear rather reticent in greeting prairie onlookers from the platform of their official railway car "Jamaica," on their way to Vancouver shortly after the Canadian Pacific Railway was opened to through traffic in the summer of 1886.

"ISN'T THAT A DAINTY DISH TO SET BEFORE A KING?"—Nursery Rhyme

This J.W. Bengough cartoon depicts the cabinet of Sir John A. Macdonald and a number of railway associates "cooked" into a pie over the Pacific Scandal. The "dainty dish" is being presented by Opposition politicians, including Sir Alexander Mackenzie at right, to an imperial figure presumably representing the royal commission struck in 1873 to look into the scandal.

In October 1873, they did so under the leadership of a gaunt-faced and humourless ex-stonemason, another Scot, named Alexander Mackenzie, who had once worked in construction in Kingston, Ontario, and had later been the editor of a Lambton, Ontario, newspaper. It was the new prime minister's misfortune to take office as an economic depression was settling on the country. As Macdonald had known, there was no money for railway building, and Mackenzie quickly curtailed rail and telegraph plans, at one point bringing BC to the brink of secession.

To his credit, Mackenzie had the foresight to advance Macdonald's plan to create the North West Mounted Police (NWMP) as recommended by Robertson-Ross.

For the settlers, the NWMP would, in years to come, be a significant factor in bringing peace and prosperity to the west. But for Canada's western Natives, life was already in tatters and would improve little with increased policing. No lawman could bring back the buffalo or restore the freedom of the land and hunt – or reverse the process that was putting many Native people on reserves and depriving them of their culture and language.

What the force could do, with persistence, was put the cork back in the whisky bottle – and, with luck, chase away the bartenders. And this they intended to do.

In 1880, the year Commissioner James Macleod retired from the NWMP, George B. Crozier, the father of Inspector Lief Crozier, published a book of waltzes that he composed especially for the Mounties and their dances. The book, whose cover is emblazoned with scenes from the early days of the NWMP in the west, was dedicated to Macleod "by his brother officers."

Chapter Two

THE TRUTH ABOUT THE GREAT MARCH WEST

IN THE END, IT WAS INDEED whisky that pushed the government to create the North West Mounted Police and send the new force west. The tale has been told from numerous perspectives of how, in late May 1873, a gang of American-based "wolfers," drunk on homebrew near Abe Farwell's trading post in the Cypress Hills, advanced on an Assiniboine camp and indiscriminately opened fire, killing twenty or more unsuspecting members of the tribe and leaving dozens more wounded.

The Cypress Hills massacre, as this alarming incident has come to be known, was the outcome of events that began two weeks earlier near Fort Benton, Montana, where a group of Cree stole forty horses from wolfers who had finished their season's work and were returning home with their furs. The wolfers were a kind of lesion on the proud trapping profession – men who poisoned the carcasses of newly felled buffalo so that wolves that ate the meat would die, making an easy harvest of their pelts. Unfortunately

for the tribes, this inhumane practice also killed dogs, which were valued as pack animals, and sometimes killed tribe members who, unaware of the poison, would eat the meat of recently skinned buffalo.

The wolfers in question were led by Missouri-born Thomas Hardwick, also known as the Green River Renegade, who had gained a reputation for meanness during his years in the Confederate army. Hardwick was married to a Blackfoot woman but was nonetheless an "Indian hater" who a year earlier had been involved in the slaughter of a number of Assiniboine in northern Montana, and a couple of years hence would lead a lynching of two Sioux men at Fort Benton.

Realizing that their horses had been stolen they set off north, tracking the thieves, intent on applying their own brand of rough justice. When they lost the trail in the Cypress Hills, in what is now southwestern Saskatchewan, they settled instead into a night of hard drinking, briefly at Farwell's trading post,

В.ШТЕЙНБЕРГЪ.   ДИНАБУРГЪ.

Left: A rare photo of the gun-toting Moses Solomon, a durable Russian Jew whose trading post in the Cyress Hills supplied both legitimate goods and bad liquor to the local Assiniboine and Sioux. Note that the writing along the bottom of the photo is in Russian, while the note on the box is in Hebrew.

Opposite: In the absence of the buffalo, which had been wiped out by the US government in a calculated attempt to drive the tribes into extinction, Assiniboine families such as this one were gradually herded onto reserves — or "reservations" as they are called in the US.

then at that of another trader, Moses Solomon, just two hundred yards away.

Farwell himself was a crafty scoundrel, thirty-one years of age, who had at least two wives, including an eighteen-year-old Crow woman named Horse Guard. If he respected the tribespeople, however, it was not on Horse Guard's account but largely because without the Crow he would have had no trade.

When Hardwick arrived, thinking perhaps that a band of Assiniboine camped nearby had his horses, Farwell assured him that the local Assiniboine were poorly organized and had most certainly not sent horse thieves to Montana in recent weeks. The Assiniboine had, in fact, arrived just months earlier, hungry and destitute, believing that the area would provide better game than their previous hunting grounds nearly three hundred miles to the north.

As Hardwick and his boys worked themselves into a drunken frenzy at Solomon's, the Assiniboine were coincidentally doing the same thing just a few hundred yards away, consuming whisky that had been given to them in exchange for returning a horse they had "borrowed" from one of Farwell's assistants, George Hammond.

The drinking at Solomon's continued unabated into Sunday morning, Hardwick and his men riling themselves with tales of Indian atrocities against traders and settlers. A few months earlier, Natives had in fact killed a trader just west of the trading posts in present-day Alberta.

One of two Assiniboine chiefs, *Inihan Kinyen*, had been at Farwell's the previous day when Hardwick and his wolfers arrived. He had warned his encampment that there could be trouble and that he thought they should strike camp and move farther away. But his suggestion had been laughed off by the already drunken tribesmen. At about noon Sunday, when George Hammond couldn't find his horse and assumed that the group had stolen it again – presumably so they could return it for more whisky – he went to Solomon's in a rage and exhorted Hardwick and his

Below is D.W. Davis's hand-drawn (perhaps booze-stained) map of what he called Whisky Country, drawn in 1875 and including Fort Macleod and the surrounding territory. Known as Otahkee-wa or "drink givers" by the Niitsitapii, whisky traders like Davis gave diluted whisky to the Natives in exchange for buffalo robes. Eighteen robes for nine gallons of whisky was a typical deal at Fort Whoop-Up, which Davis operated during the early 1870s for his employer, Healy and Hamilton, of Montana. Known as a fair trader, Davis was well paid for his work – $150 per month plus accommodation and board. In a letter home to his family, Davis wrote, "My work is not without danger as it is trading with the Indians, altho I have never been hurt or scared yet had to kill 2 last winter on act. of stealing horses." The lawless whisky trade flourished in southern Alberta for five years. When the NWMP arrived in 1874, D.W. Davis obeyed the Mounties' laws, leaving his days as a whisky trader behind. He finished his days as a trader running a legitimate post at Fort Macleod for the US firm I.G. Baker and Co. This map features significant places in Davis's life on both sides of the border.

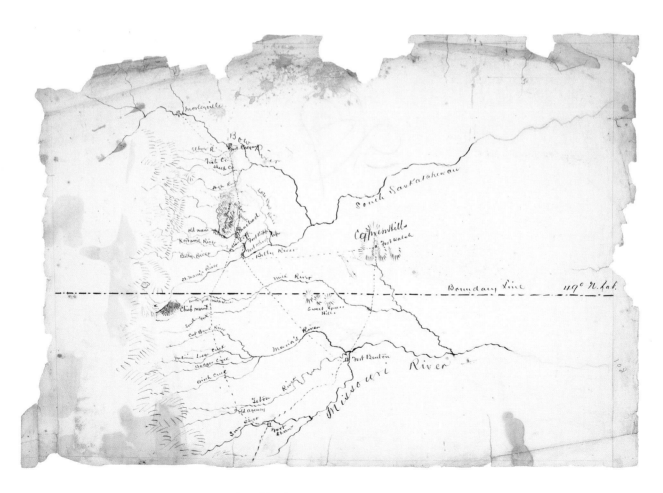

Judging by appearances and the standards of the day, the log buildings at right might well have been a small prairie cattle or chicken farm. They were in fact the NWMP posting at Farwell Coulee, ten miles east of Cypress Lake, Saskatchewan, and were typical of the many small police posts constructed in the vast distances between the main NWMP forts. The Coulee and posting were named after Abe Farwell, the whisky trader whose tavern was a kind of launching pad for the Cypress Hills massacre.

men to accompany him to the Assiniboine camp to seize horses in retaliation.

The wolfers needed little encouragement and, grabbing their rifles, headed off accompanied by a number of Metis "freighters" (Red River cart drivers) who had been drinking with them. Meanwhile, at Farwell's, Alexis Labombarde, another employee of the post, discovered that Hammond's horse had merely wandered off, and called to the wolfers to stop. However, by this time they were too enraged to do so, and they continued to the banks of the river that separated the trading posts from the encampment.

Farwell later claimed that he had urged the wolfers to be reasonable. What's more, he waded across the river and tried to persuade the Assiniboine to give him two of their own horses as a deposit until the matter of the stolen horse could be settled. But upon entering the camp, he was met by an armed warrior who summarily rejected his plea. A Metis freighter who had been drinking at Solomon's followed Farwell into the camp, urging the people to scatter.

By this time, Hardwick and his wolfers had crossed the river. As they sheltered unseen in the willows along a nearby coulee, someone, possibly Hammond, fired a shot, and within seconds the wolfers were pouring round after round from their repeating rifles into the camp.

With their poor single-shot weapons, the Assiniboine were helpless. Men, women and children fled into an adjacent woods. Many, including *Inihan Kinyen*, were shot as they ran. The wolfers, according to Labombarde, "pushed into the tents and lodges," killing anybody they could find. Another chief, Little Soldier, was shot and beheaded, his head impaled on a lodge pole. As the wolfers gave chase to those fleeing, one of them, a Canadian named Ed Legrace, became the only wolfer casualty when he was shot dead by an Assiniboine hiding in the undergrowth. When the shooting ended, the wolfers proceeded to loot the camp.

Later, at trial, Labombarde would report that he saw four women dragged from their tents and led away to Solomon's fort, where Hardwick and his thugs sexually assaulted the captives throughout the night. An Assiniboine man who returned to the camp just after dark reported that he found a woman with her back broken lying amidst the corpses but not yet dead.

At some point in the pre-dawn hours, a group of the routed Assiniboine crept back into camp and gathered the band's belongings. Because their pack dogs had run off or been killed, the men loaded what was salvageable onto their shoulders and onto travois, and set off for a nearby Metis settlement.

It was only in the morning that Farwell's teenage wife, Horse Guard, revealed her considerable character by negotiating with Hardwick's brutes for the release of the four women, none of whom had expected to live.

The wolfers hastily packed up and set off to continue the search for their horses – but not before they had burned to the ground first the Assinboine camp and then Solomon's trading post. Infuriated

WANTED IMMEDIATELY BY GOVERNMENT.

20 Active, Healthy Young Men, for service in the Mounted Police Force in the North West Territory. They must be of good character, single, between the ages of 20 and 35 years, capable of riding. They will have to serve for a term of 3 (three) years. Their pay will be 75 cents per diem, and everything (uniform, rations, board, &c., &c.) found, and on completion of service will receive a free grant of 160 acres of land, with right of choice. For further particulars, apply without delay to Captain C. Young, Halifax Hotel.   3t pd   sept30

Ottawa July 9/76

Col Richardson

Sir   Hearing that you are sending a staff of Mounted police to Manitoba i would like to be one of the number that is going being raised on a farm i am used to horses in most all shapes

G E Cusick
Brockville

Please send me through if possible

Height —   5: 8
Weight   140. —
Chest —   38 —
Age   25

NWMP recruitment notices such as the one above from the Halifax *Chronicle* in October, 1873 called for men of "good character" who were "capable of riding." However, the first contingent of Mounties into the west included many who had never been on a horse and a number whose character was questionable to say the least.

Little is known about George Cusick's career as a Mountie, but his letter of application, seen here, was sufficient to get him into the force as a constable at Fort Walsh. He served there from 1876 to 1879, when, honourably discharged, he received the standard departure grant of 160 acres of land in what is now southern Saskatchewan.

survivors later burned Farwell's post too, leaving the valley deserted except for the dead Assiniboine, who lay on the blood-soaked ground where they had fallen.

On June 1, a Montana newspaper, the Helena *Herald*, praised the American "trappers" for gallantly standing up to the "depraved and heathen savages." News of the slaughter did not reach Ottawa until August, when Canadians read in their newspapers of "innocent Indians" being mown down by "drunken US border ruffians."

Canadians, for all their own delinquency toward Native people, were scandalized. The government quickly made plans to have Hardwick and his gang extradited to Canada to stand trial. But it was not until 1875 that five of the wolfers were arrested and brought before an extradition hearing in Helena. There they claimed that it was Farwell who had led them to the Assiniboine camp and that, until fired upon, their intentions had been "entirely peaceful." In the end, the extradition order was dismissed, although two of the wolfers were subsequently arrested in Canada

and tried in Winnipeg. But witnesses were scarce and there was not enough evidence to convict them.

A MORE IMMEDIATE and lasting effect of the massacre was that the Canadian government passed an emergency Order-in-Council creating the first six divisions of the NWMP. Peace would be restored. While overall plans called for a force of 300, it was decided that, for the time being, 150 men would be sufficient.

Recruitment began without delay. The hope was that the men could be in Manitoba before winter made travel through the wilderness impossible.

Of the first 150 men who signed on, 46 gave their occupation as clerks, 39 as tradesmen, 9 as soldiers, and another 9 as farmers. The rest were a mix of telegraph operators, policemen, sailors, bartenders, gardeners, students, lumberjacks, surveyors and adventure-seekers. One was identified as a French "professor of history."

The haste with which recruitment was carried out was not clear until three

Despite her significant referential role in the settling of the west and her ubiquitous image on the documents of the day, Queen Victoria –"the Great White Mother"– never visited the Canadian prairie. The certificate shown above – government-issued "scrip" – indicates that the Canadian Department of the Interior (on behalf of Queen Victoria) deeded 160 acres of land to Constable William Johnston for his years of contracted service to the NWMP.

This hand-painted lead toy Mountie from the late 1800s stands three inches tall and was one of the first in a long line of NWMP and RCMP toys that has included wooden Mounties, paper cut-out Mounties, wind-up tin Mounties, plastic Mounties, play-time Mountie hats, and, more recently, teddy-bear Mounties, all in the sartorial style of their era.

months later when medical examinations revealed that two of the "healthy" young men were in fact blind in one eye, five were suffering from serious heart ailments, one had tuberculosis and another had been recruited with a broken leg. One had advanced syphilis.

Originally, the plan had been to train the men in eastern Canada. But on September 20, the new lieutenant-governor of Manitoba, Alexander Morris, who had been nagging Ottawa to "hurry up" with its police force, sent a telegram to the prime minister insisting that any further delay in the arrival of police in the west would lead to "grave disaster."

So off the recruits went – first to Collingwood on the south shore of Georgian Bay, then in three divisions of fifty or so, up the Great Lakes to Port Arthur. From there, their route took them west through the forests along the Dawson Route, a preposterous series of bogs and impasses masquerading as a road.

The first two divisions enjoyed relatively clear sailing to the Lakehead. The

third, however, encountered Lake Superior storms of a sort that over the centuries have littered the bottom with sunken ships and drowned seamen. The division reached Port Arthur exhausted, hungry and happy to be alive.

From there, conditions deteriorated. Struggling through freezing rain and occasional blizzards, the men reached Lake of the Woods in a snowstorm so severe that they could not unpack their frozen tents. They had not yet been issued winter uniforms. Some had no hats. Most were without gloves. Others had boots so saturated with water that they froze solid and were unwearable. On the last difficult stretch to Lower Fort Garry (north of Winnipeg), many of the men had nothing more on their feet than bundled underwear and rags. The meals, meanwhile, consisted largely of rotting pork and mildewed hardtack, although according to one of the recruits, James Fullerton, there was at least one decent meal: "The officers had several boxes of beef for their personal use," wrote the young Englishman

THE FIRST weapons issued to the NWMP were the single-shot .577 Snider-Enfield carbine Mark III and the Adams Mark I long-barrelled handgun – a five-shot revolver. The former, which was generally carried in a saddle bucket behind the right leg, was a British-made breech-loader that, in many cases, had been converted from its original form as a muzzle-loader. The revolver was carried in a holster on the left hip.

The word "carbine" described a rifle with a somewhat shortened barrel, ideal for easy transport and for use while riding a horse. However, the single-shot gun took time to reload and was therefore not ideal for the Mounties, especially as their responsibilities and need for firepower increased.

Native hunters, both north and south of the medicine line, were, by the mid-1870s, carrying lever-action repeating rifles obtained from American traders. In 1878, to compensate, the Mounties were issued with Model 1876 Winchester .45-75 lever-action carbines. The Winchester held a cartridge containing eight rounds that could be popped into the chamber one at a time with the simple flick of a six-inch lever located behind the trigger. Winchester advertisements of the day claimed that the gun could fire two rounds a second. The lever was easy to work with either hand and from either a standing position or on a horse. Typically, however, the gun was not popular with the military because the lever was difficult to work from the prone position.

The Mounties used a variety of sidearms during their developmental years, including the .476 Enfield Mark I and II revolvers, the first of which were issued in 1882. Officers and constables were also trained in the use of the battle lance while on horseback, but in reality lances were never used for anything more significant than holding a flag aloft or for show purposes in the famous Musical Ride, begun in 1887.

Beyond small arms, the Mounties employed a range of light artillery, including a pair of nine-pound cannons that they hauled with them on the march west.

The force later acquired other artillery items and Gatling machine guns. However, it was the Canadian military forces, not the NWMP, that used the Gatling gun with debatable results at Fish Creek, Cut Knife Hill and Batoche during the Rebellion of 1885. The Metis referred to the Gatling gun as *la rababou* ("the noisemaker"), claiming that it made a lot of noise but did little real damage.

Overall, however, it was the reliable Winchester repeater that carried the day for the NWMP in their occasional confrontations with unruly traders or Natives, in their battle with the Metis during the North-West Rebellion and, later, during the gold rush. Indeed, the Winchester repeater remained standard issue for the Mounties until the beginning of World War I.

THE MOUNTIES AND THEIR GUNS

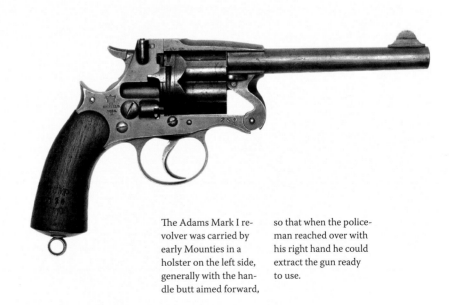

The Adams Mark I revolver was carried by early Mounties in a holster on the left side, generally with the handle butt aimed forward, so that when the policeman reached over with his right hand he could extract the gun ready to use.

At the time this photo was taken, in 1894, Arthur H. Griesbach (mounted) was a senior officer in the NWMP. But he started in 1873, in Manitoba, as a staff constable in charge of teaching recruits discipline and the use of firearms. On one occasion he is reputed to have advised newcomers (perhaps sarcastically) that discipline meant "never drinking more than twelve ounces of liquor at a sitting or firing a gun in anger or indoors." Griesbach is seen here with Sergeant Major J.T. Flintoff.

in his diary. "One dark night we reached a portage and in unloading the canoe, by some 'accident,' those boxes were broken. Bivouac fires that night gave off a delightful aroma of roasting beefsteaks."

On another occasion, it was discovered that the officers' twenty-gallon keg of "fine whisky" had mysteriously been drained and filled with water.

At Lower Fort Garry, where the men were to be housed and trained, Lieutenant-Colonel Osborne Smith, commander of the Manitoba militia, was placed in charge of the largely disheartened force. He had plenty to accomplish before the constables and officers could be sent further west. Horses had to be bought, clothing upgraded, better barracks constructed. The winter uniforms were frozen in the ice somewhere back in the wilderness.

One of the best of the force's recruits, Staff Constable Arthur Griesbach, who had served in South Africa with the British army and had come west with the Wolseley Expedition, was placed in charge of teaching foot drill, discipline and the use of arms.

The inimitable Sam Steele, another star recruit, was given the responsibility of breaking the horses and teaching the men to ride – exasperating work that went on seven days a week from 6 a.m. till well after dark. Steele would eventually write:

With very few exceptions the horses were broncos which had never been handled, and none but the most powerful and skillful dared attempt to deal with them. Even when we had them "gentled" so as to let recruits mount, the men were repeatedly thrown with great violence to the frozen ground; but no one lost his nerve…I drilled five rides per day the whole of the winter in an open ménage, and the orders were that if the temperature were not lower than thirty-six below zero the riding and breaking should go on.

BACK IN OTTAWA, the force's first commissioner had been appointed in the person of Lieutenant-Colonel George Arthur French, an Irishman and British

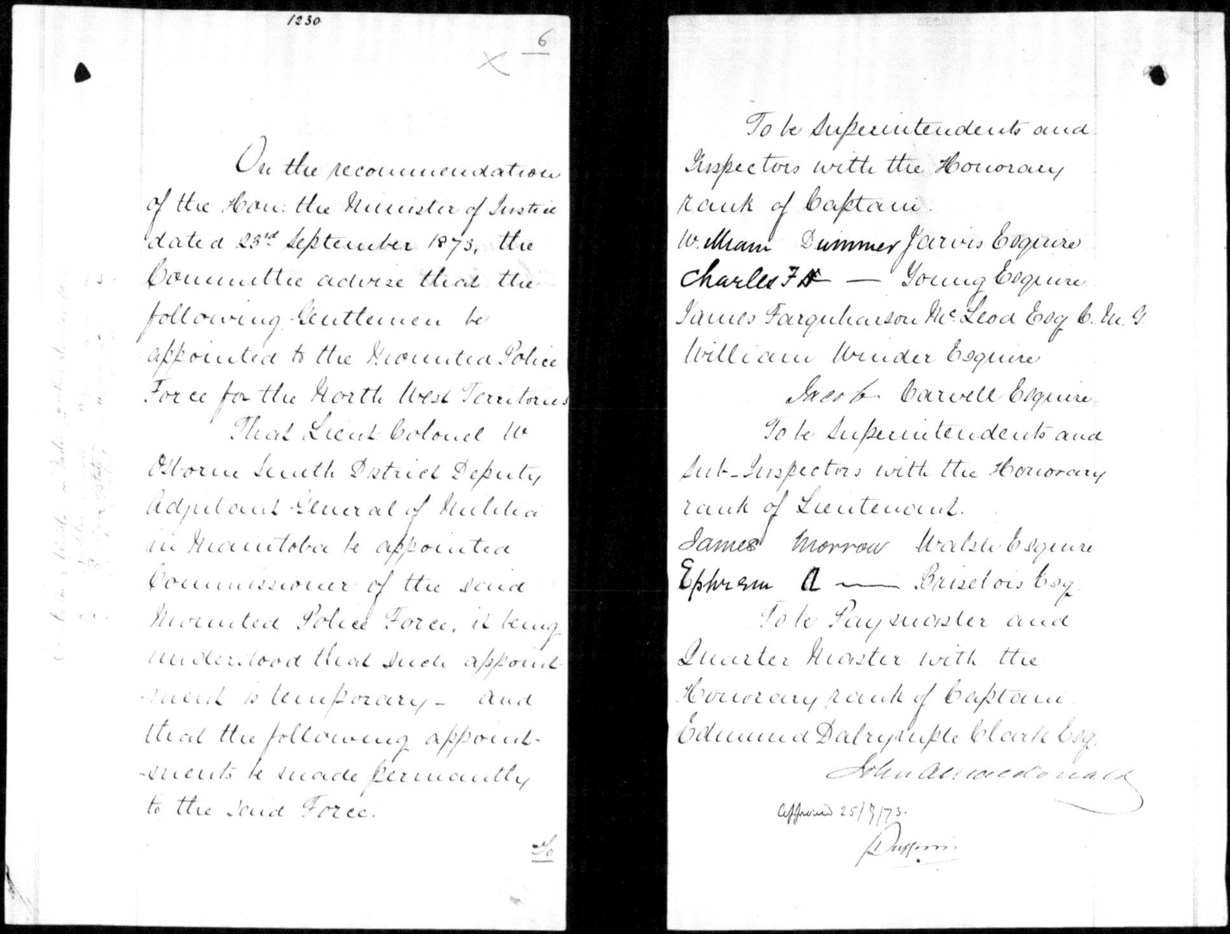

On the recommendation
of the Hon. the Minister of Justice
dated 23rd September 1873, the
Committee advise that the
following Gentlemen be
appointed to the Mounted Police
Force for the North West Territories

That Lieut Colonel W
Osborne Smith District Deputy
Adjutant General of Militia
in Manitoba be appointed
Commissioner of the said
Mounted Police Force, it being
understood that such appointment is temporary – and
that the following appoint-
ments be made permanently
to the said Force.

To be Superintendents and
Inspectors with the Honorary
rank of Captain.
William Dummer Jarvis Esquire
Charles F. — Young Esquire
James Farquharson McLeod Esq C. M. G
William Winder Esquire
Jacob Carvell Esquire
To be Superintendents and
Sub-Inspectors with the Honorary
rank of Lieutenant.
James Morrow Walsh Esquire
Ephrem A — Brisebois Esq
To be Paymaster and
Quarter Master with the
Honorary rank of Captain.
Edmund Dalrymple Clark Esq
John A. Macdonald

Approved 25/9/1873.

The original Order-in-Council for the appointment of officers to the NWMP, dated September 23, 1873, included the names of a number of men who would achieve legendary success in the force – among them, William Jarvis, James Macleod and James Walsh. It also includes names such as Charles F. Young, who was fired for poor performance after just a year, and Ephrem Brisebois, who disgraced himself somewhat by lobbying unsuccessfully to have the as-yet-unnamed Fort Calgary named Fort Brisebois.

Below: This photo shows Upper Fort Garry in 1871, seven years before the removal of the walls. The steam vessel *Dakota* is docked in the foreground on the Assiniboine River.

Right: Lower Fort Garry, North America's oldest still-standing stone fort, was built in 1830 by the HBC as an administration and trading centre. On November 3, 1873, the first 150 NWMP members were sworn in there. The new recruits had arrived in late October to be trained through the winter; the standing order was that riding drills would go on unless the temperature dipped under −36 degrees Fahrenheit.

soldier, a mere thirty-two years of age, with a reputation for discipline and competence, and perhaps more important to the recruits, for hating incompetence. French had been in charge of the gunnery school at Kingston, and when he arrived at Lower Fort Garry nine days before Christmas in 1873, he was mortified by what he saw. Hardly any of the men could yet ride, and even the officers were dressed in a hodgepodge of ill-fitting uniforms that appalled a man schooled in British decorum and discipline. "The rank and file looked like prisoners of war!" he complained.

When the recruits griped about saddle sores or bruises, French ordered an extra ration of salt for them to scrub into their wounds. An anonymous letter from one of the recruits appeared in the Toronto *Globe* in early January 1874, slagging everything at Lower Fort Garry from the clothing to the beds to the food: "We get dry bread and bad coffee for breakfast, boiled meat and worse potatoes for dinner and real bad tea and dry bread for supper…I'd as soon be in a penitentiary as in this corps."

Fortunately for the men, bad meals and large bruises were not the sum of barracks life – as evidenced by the recollections of Sam Steele:

During the winter a grand ball was given by the sergeants of Lt.-Col Irvine's corps at Winnipeg, to which I was invited – marvelous affair, with fine music…And when the Queen's birthday came round, athletic sports were held in a pleasant little park not far from the Stone Fort… There was a Quadrille Club for the NCO's and men, but I never attended, as I much preferred an evening either with the old settlers, who could tell me something about the country, or in attending their dances and weddings.

Throughout the winter, no one at the fort was more active than Commissioner French, who was doing everything possible to learn more about the west – in particular about the tribes and whisky traders and what sort of resistance the force might expect from them. At the time,

The artisans of Fort Macleod are shown above by the fort's barracks in 1894. A close look reveals indications of some of the men's trades – hammers, harness, leather aprons, and so on. Carpenter Ernest Haug is on the extreme right, while blacksmith Alex Alexander stands fourth from right. The others are unidentifiable.

Competition for the dwindling numbers of buffalo was responsible for some fierce battles between prairie tribes of the mid-nineteenth century. One of the other causes of inter-tribal violence was the presence of whisky brought north of the medicine line by American whisky traders. The photo above shows the remains of Crow people slaughtered by Blackfoot tribesmen near Sweetgrass, Alberta, during the early 1870s.

there were five main whisky forts along the border, one of which was rumoured to house a hundred or more outlaws with mounted guns, including a cannon or two, stolen from a US army supply train. Tribal war parties were a less knowable threat, and when French learned from the lieutenant-governor that the Blackfoot alone could send two thousand armed warriors into the field, he sent word to Ottawa demanding that the force be increased to three hundred men. Approval came quickly, and in late winter the commissioner travelled to southern Ontario to recruit the men he needed.

This time it was easier. The newspapers had been full of stories of the NWMP's romantic and adventurous mission to the west. Illustrations showed men wrestling grizzlies while fetching young Native women peeked out at them from the mysterious recesses of their teepees. In Stratford, a single advertisement drew two hundred young men, all of whom were reported to be "literate, healthy, and over six feet tall."

While adventure was the goal for most, at least a few joined for moral or social reasons. A young Quebec priest, Father Antoine Legault, wrote on his application that he was "sworn to temperance" and that his aim was "to help put an end to liquor traffic in the west."

The recruits took crash training in Toronto. In a naive and now famous letter to his mother, recruit William Parker, who had come from England, wrote, "I rather suspect we shall have pretty good times in the West. We shall camp out in the prairies all summer. There is most splendid shooting up there and from what I hear there is magnificent fishing, so we ought to live well."

On June 6, more than two hundred men and officers boarded trains that would take them through the American Midwest to Fargo, North Dakota, from where they would march north to Fort Dufferin on the Canadian side. There they would meet the hundred or so men who remained from the original force at Lower Fort Garry, which by this time had been trimmed

Dᴜʀɪɴɢ the early days of the ɴᴡᴍᴘ, the roles and responsibilities of the officers and men were not always well defined. Commissioned officers were occasionally called upon to do relatively menial work or make basic arrests, while constables and corporals were often given a great deal of independence and authority in defining and enacting the laws of the frontier.

If the duties were vague, the structure of the force and the chain of command were well understood. At the time and throughout the early years, the ɴᴡᴍᴘ was divided into six divisions lettered A to F. The entire force was headed by a government-appointed commissioner (originally George Arthur French), whose rank was lieutenant-colonel and who was backed by an assistant commissioner – originally James F. Macleod.

At the next level of authority were superintendents who commanded the force's divisions. They were in charge of their divisions' administrative and operational needs. Commissioners Macleod and Irvine were both superintendents before their elevation to the top rank.

The entry-level rank for most commissioned officers was inspector. These men assisted superintendents with operational matters within a division and often took on special duties. Promotion to a higher rank was never guaranteed, since superintendents were few in number. Of the twenty inspectors

appointed between 1886 and 1891, only five reached the rank of superintendent.

At the non-commissioned level, all recruits entered the force as constables. Through hard work and good conduct, they could move up through the non-commissioned ranks, from corporal to sergeant to staff-sergeant. The rank of sergeant major was first created in the mid-1870s. The sergeant major's role was to ensure that recruits received sufficient training and drill, and that discipline was maintained.

With the opening of the ɴᴡᴍᴘ's training facility in 1885, a regimental sergeant major was appointed to ensure that new recruits were trained to a high standard and that they were instilled with the traditions and practices of the Mounted Police.

As in the modern era, the force always had an administrative command, several divisional headquarters, and any number of detachments and sub-detachments spread first across the west in the early days, and now across the country.

An ensemble of sergeants with their sabres and pill-box hats at Fort Walsh, Saskatchewan, during the late 1870s.

This fanciful European depiction of nineteenth-century Native women, with its none-too-subtle hint of seductive sexuality, was a kind of soft pornography aimed clearly at male fantasies. The styles of clothing and footwear, and the depiction of the female form and attitude, are closer to what was seen in the fashionable salons of Paris and Berlin during the late 1800s than anything even remotely representing the realities of the rural Canadian west. But there is also an inherent sense of irony in the painting: the women are clearly toying with the tiny male animals, which appear in semi-human guise.

significantly of men in poor health or with bad attitudes.

The Manitoba contingent would be travelling to Fort Dufferin under the command of James Macleod, a tall, bearded thirty-seven-year-old, who had accompanied Colonel Wolseley on the Red River Expedition, and who had recently been appointed assistant commissioner. Macleod had been a bulwark of the force since its inception and was admired by his men for his toughness and intelligent decision-making, as well as for his sense of fair play and his two-fisted drinking in off-hours.

Nine wagonloads of supplies were added to the recruit train in Sarnia, Ontario, and at Detroit several dozen extra horses were herded into boxcars. Newspaper reports claimed that several men travelled with shaved heads, or shaved their heads en route, in order to make it harder for warriors to take their scalps.

As the recruits rolled west, Commissioner French continued to work feverishly, assembling supplies, pack animals and wagons – everything that would be needed to send the force on its long march into the west. Provisioning was complicated by the fact that some four thousand pounds of flour and two thousand pounds of oats had been destroyed by water as supplies were brought down the Red River by barge from North Dakota.

The arrival of the easterners in Fargo was a predictable fiasco. Many of the men had never pitched a tent or even slept out of doors. Some had never been bitten by a mosquito, billions of which now buzzed around them in the heat as they attempted to make sense of their surroundings. Henri Julien, a young journalist and artist who had accompanied the recruits as a reporter for *Canadian Illustrated News*, wrote that the pestilence of mosquitoes was "thick enough to put out a fire, or tear a protective net to pieces."

Farce turned quickly to calamity. On the five-day march north to Fort Dufferin, several of the men were felled by heat stroke. Others were treated for dust inhalation or suffered blisters so severe

Right: The bugler had an important role with the early Mounties – rallying the men, sounding alarms, or just announcing wake-up, curfew or the changing of the guard. The bugle was also a key aspect of all formal police ceremonies and formalities.

Above: Constable Fred Bagley was the Mounties' first bugler – a youthful stalwart of the march west – and would be an NWMP musician of note for many years thereafter.

that they could barely walk. Four men contracted typhoid from bad water, and two of them eventually died. Many of the horses had been chosen for looks rather than an ability to haul loads, and two died of fatigue en route. Others resisted the harness and stampeded, overturning wagons, in some cases seriously injuring their keepers.

Several of the men questioned Commissioner French's wisdom in moving his forces so quickly under the conditions. French would later write that he "feared the Sioux" and was "determined to get back on Canadian soil." He also knew that if he was to get his men to the Rockies before winter, he had best make haste.

The mustering at Fort Dufferin was as chaotic as the arrival at Fargo. The tents were bulky, the food barely edible, the heat oppressive. The horses were corralled in a field enclosed by a loose line of wagons and tents. The "fencing" proved a disaster on the second night, when a wind and hail storm rattled the heavens, sending down what French described as "one incessant sheet of lightning from 10 p.m. to 6 a.m."

At about midnight, an immense bolt of electricity exploded above the wind-flattened tents, sending the horses into stampede – out through the gaps between the wagons, off across the prairie. Fifteen-year-old Fred Bagley, a recently recruited bugler from England, sounded the alarm, rallying the men, some of whom believed they were under attack from the Sioux.

Crazed with fear, 250 of the force's 310 horses ran, some as far as 40 miles into North Dakota, before collapsing of exhaustion on the plains.

Young Sam Steele witnessed it all and, with the others, laboured through the night to calm the horses that remained in camp. At dawn, a contingent set out to recover the runaways, travelling more than a hundred miles during the next twenty-four hours, anxious to get to their animals before they were claimed by the Sioux. Miraculously, the posse brought back all but one horse, which was thought to have drowned in the Pembina River.

Stop-action photography did not yet exist during the 1870s. In order to record the movement and events of the march west, an imaginative young sketch artist named Henri Julien travelled with the Mounties, sending both words and pictures back to Montreal for publication in the *Canadian Illustrated News.* Below is his meticulously energetic drawing of the storm and subsequent stampede that befell the untested policemen as they camped briefly at Fort Dufferin, south of Winnipeg, where the great march began.

For several decades the white dress helmet was a staple of the NWMP uniform. However, with its weight and the awkwardness of carrying it when it was not being worn, it was not popular. Constable Alfred Aspinall, an artist of decidedly modest talent, chose to decorate the cotton interior of his hard hat with an ink drawing probably of Fort Macleod, with its flag, fences and backdrop of poplar trees. Aspinall served in the NWMP from 1896 to 1900, much of that time in Calgary.

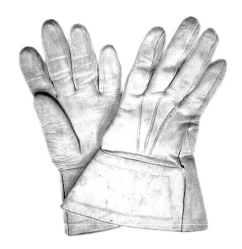

Steele wrote that the "stampede had such an effect on the horses that for the remainder of the summer they were ready to repeat the performance on hearing the slightest unusual sound. Every thunderstorm brought us out of our tents at night, and in the daytime we had to be amongst them to calm their fears."

Meanwhile, reports of Sioux atrocities – nearby scalpings – sent some of the recruits into private panic. "The proximity of the border was just too tempting," wrote the historian A.L. Haydon some thirty years later. "And one by one the chicken-hearted slunk out of camp and headed south." In all, fifteen men deserted the force the night before departure for the west. Luckily, the commissioner had anticipated their leaving and had had the foresight to bring with him twenty spare men, so the force was not short-handed.

THE GREAT MARCH WEST began on July 8 with the NWMP's first ever full-dress inspection on the dusty parade grounds of Fort Dufferin. Fred Bagley, the force's youngest member, wrote in his diary that "the parade was an inspiring sight with every man in new scarlet tunic, grey riding britches, gleaming black boots, white buckskin gauntlets and white cork helmets with brass-link chin straps."

At 5 p.m. French gave the signal and, to an assorted chorus of bellowed commands, the long line of troopers moved out onto the prairie. French himself called the departure an "astonishing" scene:

First came A Division, with their splendid dark bays, and thirteen wagons. After them followed B Division, with dark brown horses; C, with light chestnuts, drawing the guns and ammunition; D, with their greys; E, with their black horses; and lastly F, with their light bays.

Behind the six divisions came a motley string of ox carts, wagons, cattle for slaughter, cows for milk, and a variety of mowing machines and agricultural implements and appliances. In all, there were 21 officers, 254 constables, 310 horses,

Among the grace notes of the early NWMP uniform were the white buckskin gauntlets seen first at Fort Dufferin as the Mounties departed on their great march west. Worn chiefly for dress, gauntlets were also worn on duty in the days when every member of the force rode a horse.

> "We have along with us ten days rations hard tack pork tea & sugar, with a few boxes of sardines, and a gallon of whiskey. Chapman takes this along and he ought to know what to take – it is vile stuff."
>
> R.B. NEVITT, Assistant Surgeon, North West Mounted Police 1874

20 guides, 2 field guns, 2 mortar cannons, 142 working oxen, 93 head of cattle, 73 wagons, and 114 Red River carts.

It is an intriguing bit of symmetry, perhaps irony, that the lead guide on the expedition was one Pierre Leveille, a three-hundred-pound Metis, all muscle and sinew, who had been a lieutenant of Riel's during the Red River Rebellion, and had been instrumental in persuading the Metis leader to cede Manitoba to Confederation.

As harmonious and unified as everything appeared when the column left Fort Dufferin, weaknesses quickly began to show. The first of many horses to die perished on the second day. Heat and dust continued to cause fatigue for the men. Carts broke down. Oxen and horses strayed. Storms created mud in which wagons sank to their axles. Further west, grasshoppers were so thick they blotted out the sun and ate the paint off the wagons and machinery. Amidst the endless clouds of these voracious insects, the men were unable to erect tents for fear the canvas would be consumed.

In some places, prairie fires had left no fresh forage for the cattle and horses. Water holes had dried up, or were so foul the men got dysentery. Inexplicably, canteens had not been included in the equipment.

Two days into the march, another twelve men deserted into the US The next day, Inspector Theodore Richer, appalled by the pace at which Commissioner French was moving the force, informed French that he would tell authorities in Ottawa about the commander's deplorable bad judgment. Richer was immediately arrested and sent back to Dufferin.

Originally just a mile and a half long, the parade was soon spread out over five or six miles. Supply wagons fell so far behind that often there was no food for the men at supper hour. On July 14, Constable James Finlayson wrote in his diary: "Camped on the open plain near a swamp. No water, no wood, no supper. The supply wagons did not get in till after midnight, therefore no provisions."

The men were often up as early as 3 a.m. and were marching by 5 a.m. without breakfast. On July 20, the commissioner's diary read: "Two days of rest at Souris. Many horses so exhausted they were unable to proceed. Two more left behind, and two died. It was rumoured that a war party of Sioux was in the vicinity."

The next day, fifteen sick horses failed to reach camp at nightfall and were abandoned. Two days later, thirteen more were left behind. Constable Pierre Lucas became so frightened when his exhausted horse lagged miles behind the column that he shot it, caught up to the others on foot, and explained to the commissioner (who remained unconvinced) that he had been attacked by a Sioux war party.

French's chosen route led pretty much due west along the US border on the road built by the Boundary Commission. But at La Roche Percée, 270 miles from Dufferin, the road veered south into the US, forcing French and his charges to make a road of their own as they continued toward the Cypress Hills and Fort Whoop-Up.

T HE RED RIVER cart – the Model T of its day – was an indispensable part of Metis life throughout the nineteenth century. So closely were the carts identified with their Metis inventors that the Plains Indians' hand sign for "Metis" was "half-cart half-man."

While the inspiration for these simple conveyances came from European carting traditions, the design and materials, like those of the birch bark canoe and the snowshoe, were indigenous to a people and a locale. The main components were a high-sided wooden box, about six feet long and three feet wide, and two enormous spoked wheels, sometimes standing nearly six feet high.

The carts were drawn by horses or oxen and, with their huge wheels, could carry loads of up to a thousand pounds through virtually any morass of mud or swamp without getting stuck. They often broke down, but because they were constructed entirely of wood, held together with strips of raw buffalo hide and wooden pegs, a driver en route needed only a saw, a drawknife and an auger to construct a replacement part out of wood carried for such purposes – or, in forested areas, of an available tree. At river crossings, the cart could be removed from its wheels, wrapped in buffalo hide, and floated across with its load.

Twice a year brigades of as many as six hundred carts would make the journey from Red River to St. Paul, Minnesota. Once a year, a smaller contingent would make the five-hundred-mile trip on the Carlton Trail to Fort Edmonton.

For all their fine features, the carts had one significant drawback: the terrible squealing of their wheels as they rolled along. When travelling in numbers, they could often be heard for miles across the prairie. The cause of the noise was the wooden axles and hubs, which were unlubricated to prevent any greasy buildup of dust and dirt that would quickly have worn down the hubs and immobilized the cart. Sam Steele of the NWMP compared the "hideousness" of the sound to "a den of wild beasts."

Fur traders and settlers of various nationalities used Red River carts, but first and mainly it was the Metis who drove them back and forth across the prairies, hauling their goods from camp to camp, or often the goods of others, on well-established commercial trading routes.

The coming of the steamboats during the 1870s and then the railway in the 1880s put an end to the use of Red River carts for transportation. However, to this day, these marvellous devices are identified with Metis hardiness and ingenuity.

IN PRAISE OF THE RED RIVER ROLLERS

This photo of a Metis family camp on the prairie west of Red River shows both the covered and uncovered versions of that most versatile of ox-drawn vehicles, the Red River cart.

If the International Boundary Commission had used Red River carts rather than these more conventional fourwheeled covered wagons as they surveyed and marked the Canada-US border during the early 1870s, they might well have altered the persistent series of breakdowns and delays that characterized their slow trek across the prairie to the Rockies.

IT WAS AT LA ROCHE PERCEE, on July 29, that French decided to break up the column and send the dozen men remaining from A Division, plus a dozen Metis guides and six invalids, directly northwest to Fort Edmonton.

And so the small group departed, under Inspector William Jarvis and Constable Sam Steele. The main party pressed on through what is now southern Saskatchewan, where they encountered wood and then food shortages. Sugar, bread and cooking grease were rationed. One constable found a tin of machine oil abandoned by the Boundary Commission and began putting a few drops on his meals, refusing to share it with the others.

By early August, as a result of drinking brackish water, twenty-two men had dysentery, including the bugler, Bagley, whose lips were so swollen and blistered that he could not blow a single note. Horses were dying at the rate of nearly six a day.

One day in mid-August, a flurry of excitement spread among the men when advance scouts reported a Sioux camp ahead at Old Wives Lake, just east of the Cypress Hills. A powwow of sorts was arranged for the following morning, and at about nine o'clock some two dozen dirty and dejected Sioux – members of the Sisseton tribe who had sought refuge in Canada after a massacre in Minnesota in 1862 – shuffled into the NWMP camp, the women following the men in single file. The appearance and bearing of the Natives created palpable disappointment among the constables and officers, who had been hoping for a party of "noble savages," perhaps in ceremonial clothing. Nevertheless, anxious to make a good impression, the commissioner and his adjutants smoked the traditional peace pipe with the Sioux and gave them trinkets and tobacco as gifts.

If first impressions were poor, they were even worse a few days later when every man in the column realized he had picked up fleas and lice from the woebegone visitors. The grumbling and discomfort ended only when the men were ordered to line up, disrobe and rub themselves

1

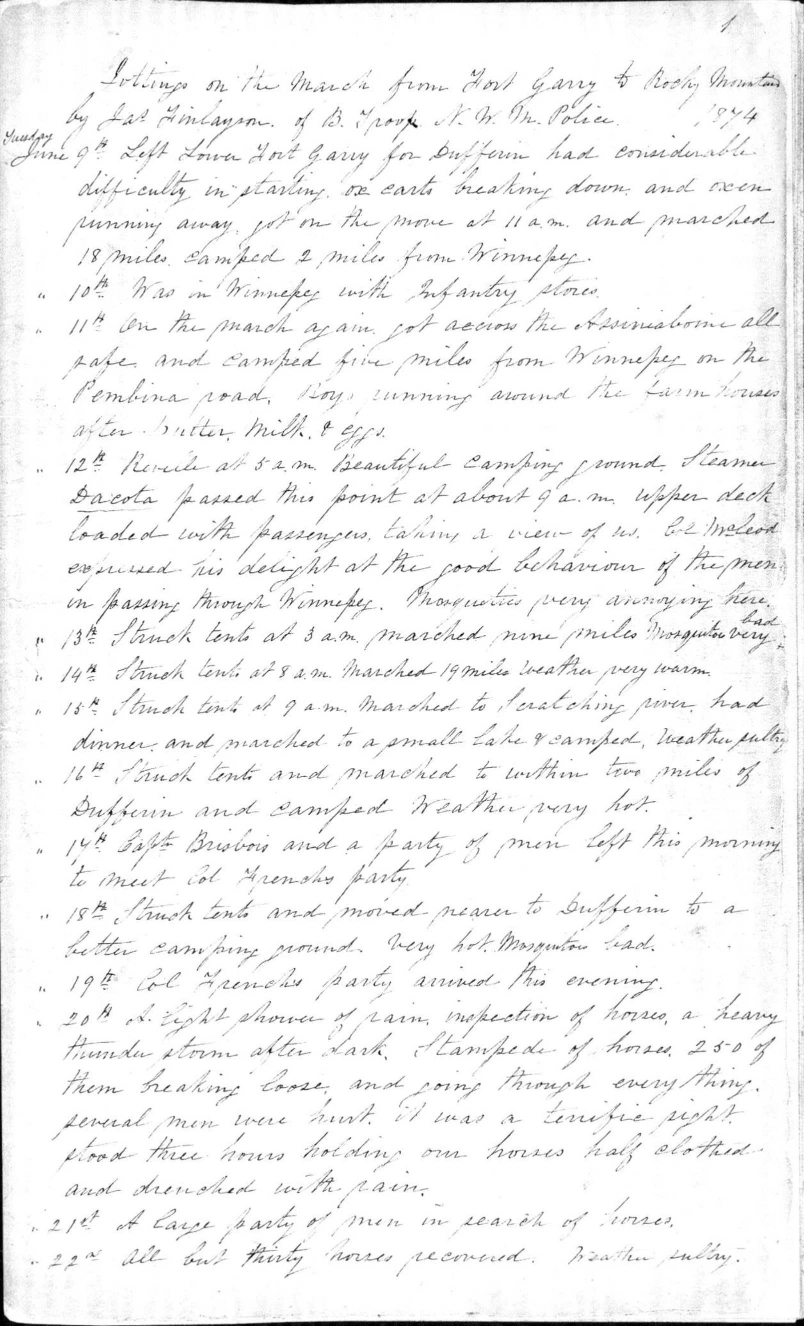

Jottings on the March from Fort Garry to Rocky Mountains
by Jas Finlayson of B. Troop N. W. M. Police. 1874

Tuesday June 9th Left Lower Fort Garry for Dufferin had considerable difficulty in starting, ox carts breaking down and oxen running away, got on the move at 11 a.m. and marched 18 miles, camped 2 miles from Winnipeg.

" 10th Was in Winnipeg with Infantry stores.

" 11th On the march again got across the Assiniboine all safe and camped five miles from Winnipeg on the Pembina road. Boys running around the farm houses after butter, milk & eggs.

" 12th Revelie at 5 a.m. Beautiful camping ground. Steamer Dacota passed this point at about 9 a.m. upper deck loaded with passengers, taking a view of us. Col McLeod expressed his delight at the good behaviour of the men in passing through Winnipeg. Mosquitoes very annoying here.

" 13th Struck tents at 3 a.m. marched nine miles Mosquitoes very bad.

" 14th Struck tents at 8 a.m. Marched 19 miles weather very warm.

" 15th Struck tents at 9 a.m. Marched to Scratching river had dinner and marched to a small lake & camped, weather sultry.

" 16th Struck tents and marched to within two miles of Dufferin and camped Weather very hot.

" 17th Capt Brisbois and a party of men left this morning to meet Col Frenchs party.

" 18th Struck tents and moved nearer to Dufferin to a better camping ground. Very hot. Mosquitoes bad.

" 19th Col Frenchs party arrived this evening.

" 20th A light shower of rain, inspection of horses, a heavy thunder storm after dark. Stampede of horses, 250 of them breaking loose, and going through every thing. several men were hurt. it was a terrific sight. stood three hours holding our horses half clothed and drenched with rain.

" 21st A large party of men in search of horses.

" 22nd All but thirty horses recovered. Weather sultry.

A page from Corporal James Finlayson's diary, written during the march west in 1874 and replete with revelations of weariness, danger and privation. Had the NWMP recruited its men from the west, instead of from predominanttly English-speaking segments of eastern society, the early Mounties would have known the territory far better than they did and would undoubtedly have had an easier time on the march west.

THESE DAYS, we take the border between Canada and the US for granted. But earlier generations of Canadians and Americans did not. Beginning with the Jay Treaty in 1794, a total of twenty agreements, conventions and treaties were negotiated by four nations (the United States, Canada, the United Kingdom and Russia) to define adjacent US and Canadian territories.

In 1846, the British and Americans decided that the border separating each country's territory across the west should run along the 49th parallel of latitude.

Sappers of the North American Boundary Commission are seen here building a boundary cairn, one of thousands that were the earliest markers along the Canada – US border.

The construction of these mounds, of either rock or earth, frequently required blasting – hence the sappers, military engineers who specialized in land mines and explosives.

But it was not until 1872, as the west opened to settlement, that a decision was made to mark the exact location of the international boundary from Lake of the Woods in the east, across the prairie, to the pinnacle of the Rocky Mountains – a distance of nearly nine hundred miles.

The chore fell jointly to "Her Majesty's North American Boundary Commission" and the "United States Northern Boundary Commission."

The Canadian team included some 300 men – engineers, surveyors, Metis scouts on horseback, carpenters and provisioners. The US contingent brought together 250 civilians, escorted by several troops of cavalry and infantry.

Field work commenced in September 1872 at Fort Dufferin, in what is now southern Manitoba. By pre-arrangement, the line was first surveyed eastward from the Red River to Lake of the Woods. Because of the severity of the winter of 1872–73, the US party immediately took several months off. But because the swamps west of Lake of the Woods were accessible only when frozen, the British party worked on through even the coldest months.

Over the next two years, the large body of men and horses endured snowstorms, blackflies and flash floods, as well as stupefying transport difficulties in bad weather and over rugged terrain. At times, they suffered severe shortages of water, wood and forage for the horses. The threat of smallpox

was never far off, and rumours of the Indian Wars just to the south caused some men uneasy days and sleepless nights.

Along the way, the teams built shelters, supply depots and crude roads that would occasionally be used by the Mounties during their great march west – and later in patrolling the border. But for the surveyors themselves the main business every day was applying their scopes and measuring devices to a variety of maps and landmarks, and to the stars, in the all-consuming process of defining an invisible line. As each new mile of terrain was surveyed, a cairn of either earth or stone, depending on the materials available was erected. (The original markers were replaced with tapered iron posts in 1874 and 1875)

As the teams moved into the Sweetgrass Hills below the Rockies during July 1874, they comprised the greatest accumulation of scientists, teamsters, scouts, cooks and soldiers to be seen in the west prior to the arrival of the railway. They finished on August 20 of that year when they located a marker that had been placed high in the Rockies by an earlier group of surveyors who had moved eastward from the Pacific.

In drawing what the Sioux referred to as the "medicine line," the combined commissions helped define the final shape of both the US and Canada. At the same time, they brought a rigorous finality to any surviving notion of the open west.

down with juniper oil. The Metis guides showed the men how to delouse their garments by putting them on ant hills and allowing the ants to go to work.

In an attempt to alleviate the growing feed shortage, Assistant Commisioner Macleod led a foray south to the Boundary Commission depot at Wood Mountain where he was able to purchase fifteen thousand pounds of oats, with the promise of another twenty thousand to be delivered to the "cripple camp" that French decided to establish at Old Wives Lake. There, amidst forage and good water, he left behind all the sick horses and cattle, seven sick men, and provisions that could be used by those of his force who would be returning that way in autumn.

On August 24, the column reached the Cypress Hills, site of the massacre that had spurred the force west and where persistent rumours of war parties and grizzly bears tended to rattle the discouraged policemen.

The force was now entering the last great buffalo range, and while signs of buffalo were everywhere in the form of cropped grass, trampled ground and droppings – "buffalo chips" – there were still none of the legendary animals. Hungry for fresh food, the men did discover plentiful blueberries and saskatoon berries, and excited marksmen were able to bring down a few antelope and deer, providing fresh meat for the first time since the column had left Fort Dufferin six hundred miles back.

The men's pleasure and excitement were all the greater a few days later when, just west of the Cypress Hills, they spotted buffalo for the first time. According to Constable Cecil Denny, "Cries came down the column, and guns began popping in every direction."

Buffalo fell – five of them in all – one brought down by Commissioner French himself. In total, the downed animals yielded nearly half a ton of meat. However, the anticipated feast was a disappointment when the meat, mostly that of grizzled old bulls, turned out to be so tough that even the youngest constables were unable to gnaw through it.

Having reached the area west of the Cypress Hills during the great march west, the officers and constables of the NWMP got their first taste of buffalo hunting…and of badly needed buffalo meat. That awkward and disorganized first hunt, depicted here by artist and journalist Henri Julien, produced five fallen buffalo and at least an equal number of significant sprains and bruises as men fell from horses and flailed about among the huge prey.

"I have been examining the water that we are forced to drink – with a microscope & there are animals in it that look like huge fleas – nice it is not – Some of them are not animal culae but are visible individually to the naked eye. However when boiled and tea made with them you can't distinguish the animals from tea leaves so it don't matter…"

R.B. NEVITT, Assistant Surgeon, North West Mounted Police, 1874

Communication with those back home was anything but easy for the Mounties as they staggered westward en masse in 1874. Letters such as this one from Assistant Surgeon R.B. Nevitt to his sweetheart, Lizzie Beaty, in Toronto were carried on horseback from the NWMP column to a "convenient" town in the northern US, and sent from there, perhaps by steamboat, to St. Paul, Minnesota, and from there by boat or train to their destinations in eastern Canada or elsewhere. Dr. Nevitt's letter therefore bears a St. Paul postmark and US postage stamps.

However, the men quickly became adept at killing younger animals, especially cows, which provided the best meat. But the buffalo were not universally a boon. For one thing, they had eaten every blade of grass in the territory, leaving none for the horses and cattle. And they trampled the watering holes into mud pits, contaminating them with feces and urine. So thirsty were the men after their long days of marching that, despite the pollution, they boiled up the evil-smelling sludge, made it into tea, and drank it down, sometimes regurgitating it as quickly as they had consumed it.

As the column continued west toward the headwaters of the South Saskatchewan River, the herd increased. Constable Denny wrote: "There were places where, as far as the eye could reach, untold thousands were in sight, the country dark with them."

So impressed was Assistant Commissioner James Macleod by the appearance of the animals, particularly their giant heads, he suggested that the policemen's brass buttons, which till then had borne a version of the royal crest, be decorated instead with a likeness of the head of a buffalo – and that the force's official badge be similarly emblazoned. His suggestion was soon after adopted, and the insignia has been standard ever since.

But all thoughts of heraldry and show had evaporated by early September when the first signs of winter moved in. By the time the men reached what is now the Alberta border, they were saddle-sore and filthy. Many of them had worn out their boots and were patrolling camp with gunny sacking wrapped around their feet. The commissioner's diary for September 10 read:

I had a blanket taken from every officer and man last night so that each horse was covered and protected from the cold rain and wind. I began to feel very much alarmed for the safety of the Force. If a few hours' cold rain kills off a number of horses what would be the effect of a twenty-four-hour snowstorm?

In the nineteenth century, brass buttons mattered, not only sartorially but as symbols of the honour and history of an institution. This button, on one of the early tunics of Corporal Fred Bagley, marks not only a connection to the Crown, to the White Mother, but also to the new Dominion and to the life of the old west and the Natives, as exemplified by the likeness of the buffalo. The image of the great mammal is also a reminder of the more sobering history of a territory and a lost culture.

Below: A group of rather forlorn-looking Natives poses by the door of Fort Whoop-Up, where their buffalo robes and pemmican, the staples of their existence, were traded away for the contaminated whisky that in the last days of the buffalo was likely seen as a form of escape from the harsh realities of their lives.

Right: Bull teams such as this one, belonging to merchant J.G. McLean of Fort Benton, Montana, were used to haul industrial, military, building, and agricultural supplies across the plains and prairie to where settlement and construction were taking place. Their cargoes included doors, windows, construction hardware, cement, bulk food, clothing, armaments and seed.

The following day, Constable James Finlayson noted: "We are lost on the prairie. No one knows where we are. Horses and oxen dying fast, provisions getting scarce, things looking very dark."

Unfortunately for the force, Colonel Patrick Robertson-Ross's report of the previous year had wrongly identified the location of Fort Whoop-Up as being at the junction of the Bow and South Saskatchewan rivers (whereas in fact it was at the confluence of the Old Man's and St. Mary, seventy-five miles to the southwest). French had hoped to clear the fort of any remaining whisky traders before establishing headquarters in the area, and he was stupefied to find that it was not where he had expected it to be. He was doubly chagrined because the terrain, which was supposed to be rich in grass and water, was an infertile expanse of dust, offering no support to men, horses or cattle. In frustration, French ordered his men to prepare to march south into the Sweetgrass Hills near the American border.

And so they marched, through winds and light snow, losing another nine horses en route. Toward the end of the five-day march, Fred Bagley made the mistake of taking his boots off to treat his blistered and bleeding feet and then could not get the boots back on. Consequently, he had to finish the march on the back of Inspector James Walker, who volunteered to carry him. Bagley recorded in his diary that the force en route looked like "the popular image of the outlaws they were supposed to be chasing."

At the border, French wasn't about to rest and, with a small detachment and the reliable Macleod, struck out immediately for Fort Benton, Montana, eighty miles away, where he hoped to replenish supplies. The detachment was slowed by having to thread its way through a herd of buffalo numbering some eighty thousand animals.

French's first task on reaching Fort Benton was to telegraph Ottawa, from where he got surprising news – that the force's proposed headquarters at Fort Ellice in western Manitoba had been shifted

The miseries of the great march west were extraordinary – for both men and livestock, particularly horses. This drawing by artist/journalist Henri Julien from September 1874 records the death of several horses, and the pathetic state of those still alive after ten weeks of privation on the trail. It also records the despairing response of at least one member of the force, or perhaps a guide or groom, who sought comfort in the bottle and was scolded for his conduct.

Blackfeet
Migrating

Copyright Secure
By Prof Buell

With the buffalo all but gone in 1885, Blackfoot families who refused to settle peaceably on reserves were forced to migrate further and more often in the interest of survival. This family is undoubtedly carrying its entire earthly wealth, as well as its children, on simple travois, which were dragged along the ground like sleds, by either horses or people. At settling places, the long, straight poles were often used in tee-pee construction.

Above: Jerry Potts with a group of Peigan tribesmen and Mounties at a Peigan sun dance ceremony in southern Alberta in 1886. Standing, left to right: NWMP Sergeant Gaigen; Runs Among Buffalo; Kidney; Crow Shoe; Running Wolf; Jerry Potts; remainder of row unknown. Front, seated, left to right: Good Young Man; Little Plume; Running Eagle; and Shining Double.

Opposite: It was common practice among the prairie tribes to wrap their dead in blankets and place them in trees or on scaffolds where their elevation would allow them easier transit into the spirit world. Here, NWMP Sergeant G. Rolph, left, and a police scout examine the "burial" site of a Sioux warrior who is reputed to have been wounded at the Battle of Little Big Horn and later died in Canada near Eastend, Saskatchewan, circa 1878.

north to Swan River because the railway was to run that way. Barracks were under construction and would be ready when French got there with D and E Divisions in October.

French decided to leave for Swan River immediately, putting Divisions B, C and F, some 150 men, under Macleod, who would proceed to Fort Whoop-Up, clean up the mess, and build a post in the area from which the rule of law could be dispensed.

While French hurried back to the Sweet Grass Hills with blankets, clothing and food, bought on credit in Fort Benton, Macleod hired a bow-legged American scout named Jerry Potts – the squat, hard-drinking son of a Scottish clerk and a woman of the Peigan tribe – a man who spoke in monosyllables and was reputed to be the most knowledgeable guide in the territory. Potts's father had been shot to death by a Peigan marksman when Jerry was a boy – a killing avenged personally by Potts – and he had spent much of his youth in the camps and war parties of the Blackfoot, Peigan

and Blood. As a teenager, he led a war party of the Blackfoot Confederacy into a murderous battle against invading Cree, cementing his fame as a warrior by returning to camp with nineteen scalps, an arrow lodged deep in his body and a cavernous bleeding head wound, which he is said to have wrapped in rawhide until it healed. He later worked in the whisky forts, where he developed a taste for booze and learned the tragic price of unregulated liquor when his mother and half-brother were shot dead in a pointless fracas along the border.

Potts knew French, Cree, Sioux and Blackfoot, but was all but tongue-tied in English – and had little use for words anyway. One day an NWMP officer rode up to Potts on the trail and inquired impatiently, "Jerry, what do you think we'll find over this hill?"

"Nudder hill," Potts is reputed to have answered.

But he was a brilliant guide and a respected go-between, and for the next twenty-two years he would be an indispensable part

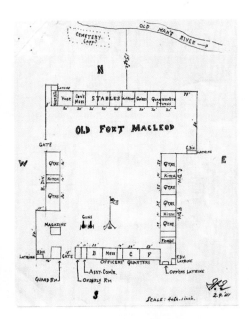

Stuart Wood, who was commissioner of the NWMP from 1938 to 1951, drew the layout plan at right, as well as others like it, from various eras, in order to provide a record of the evolving physical history of Fort Macleod. The presence of a cemetery by the river, even in the fort's earliest days, is a stark reminder of the dangers and diseases faced by the first generation of Mounties in the west.

A S THE GREAT march west moved into the hills of what is now southern Alberta in the autumn of 1874, the job for Superintendent James Macleod was to build the first NWMP fort. Within a matter of months, the force would also erect forts at Calgary and Edmonton and in the Cypress Hills. But it was that first fort on the Old Man's River – eventually named Fort Macleod – that would be the model for them all.

The specifics of construction depended on what materials were available – trees, rocks and earth, but also pre-manufactured windows and hardware, which in remote areas were more difficult to come by.

Fort Macleod was 200 feet square, and construction began with the digging of a three-foot-deep trench along the entire eight-hundred-foot perimeter. Meanwhile, more than two thousand poplar logs were cut in twelve-foot lengths and sharpened on one end. These were posted upright in the trench and plastered with clay to form both the stockade and the outer walls of certain buildings within the fort.

Out of concern for the well-being of the horses, the stables were constructed first, then the constables' barracks and the officers' quarters.

On the east side were the barracks of Divisions C and F and the blacksmith shop. On the west, beside a gate, were B Division's barracks. On the north side were the stables, stores, and hospital while the south wall backed the officers quarters, guard room, and the main gate.

The bare ground provided natural flooring, and local stone was used for fireplaces, chimneys and any other masonry that was required. Windows and doors were hauled on wagons from Fort Benton, Montana. Finally, the Union Jack was raised on a seventy-foot flag pole above the fort.

"It wasn't much," as one constable noted in his diary. But for the most part the fort was warmer and drier than the tents in which the men had been living for months. More significantly, it was a protected base from which to begin the complex business of bringing law to the west.

Field guns such as these, seen at, NWMP barracks in Regina in 1885, had been brought west by the Mounties as early as 1873. But apart from their use at Batoche against Riel and his insurgents during the North-West Rebellion of 1885, and in incidents such as the last stand of Almighty Voice in 1895, there was little real need for them. Note the extensive array of well-built frame houses and barns at NWMP headquarters in Regina.

of the NWMP's hard-working operation in what is now southern Alberta.

Potts's value was demonstrated a week hence when he and Macleod set out for the elusive Fort Whoop-Up with Divisions B, C and F. On his first day of guiding, Potts rode on ahead. When the divisions caught up with him during the late morning, he had already killed a cow buffalo and had it butchered in preparation for a noon banquet. The following day, he led the men and horses to the purest spring they had drunk from in weeks.

On October 9, Potts, Macleod and the men made their way quietly up a grassy incline, and from several hundred yards away gazed down on the notorious Fort Whoop-Up, site of endless nights of drunkenness, debauchery and violence – the "evil rendezvous," as it was called by John Peter Turner in his 1948 history of the NWMP.

From this perverted "hang-out" sprang the traffic with which the Montana freebooters in their greed for buffalo robes debauched the wild hunters of the Canadian West. Words fail utterly to depict the extremes of degradation that here awaited the arrival of the Benton caravans with their vile canteens… From tubs of raw liquor, potations in tin cups would be pushed through the trade opening in return for robes and other coveted articles. Hour after hour, with briefest interruptions, the greedy business would go forward. And at last, a savage mob, bared of its wealth, would surge at the bolted gates.

Preparing for the worst, the constables and officers of the NWMP unlimbered their field guns and mortars, and trained them on the fort. Macleod and Potts then rode down the embankment, up to the palisade and, having dismounted, entered the open main gate and knocked on the door of the first building they came to. A couple of Native women and a number of dogs were afoot in the fort, and a few ponies grazed on the nearby flats.

Eventually, a grey-haired Civil War veteran named Dave Akers answered the door, explained that he was merely a caretaker, and surprised his visitors by inviting them in for a lunch of fresh vegetables and buffalo steak, the vegetables pulled from a flourishing garden along the south outer wall of the fort. Akers told Macleod that his bosses, the agents of the Fort Benton owners, were away on business and that their return date was uncertain.

In reality, the fort's head trader had received a warning from itinerant buffalo hunters of the coming of the redcoats and had shrewdly pulled out, hauling wagonloads of liquor, perhaps into hiding in Canada, perhaps back to Fort Benton where it had come from. A thorough search of the interior revealed no liquor, although it was later rumoured that barrels of whisky were stored underground within the palisade.

Ever a practical man, Macleod eyed the fort and, impressed by its comforts and warmth – and especially by its solid construction – offered to buy it as a winter quarters for his men. But Akers did not have the authority even to consider the offer.

Mounties and their horses at ease by a poplar-log outbuilding at Fort Macleod some two years after the construction of the fort. By this time, 1876, virtually every Mountie was wearing the soft brown Stetson originally affected by the dashing NWMP inspector, James M. Walsh.

For the battle-ready police, their arrival at the "evil rendezvous" was something of an anti-climax after the tensions and anticipations of the long and grinding march west. When, they wondered, would they encounter real action? Certainly not at Fort Slideout a few miles away, where, again, there were neither people nor whisky.

JERRY POTTS, who knew the area intimately, had been given the task of finding a suitable site for a fort. And three days later, at a deep-cut river gorge, fringed with poplar, Potts halted the cavalcade and explained that it was here, in a broad loop of the Old Man's River, that he had decided they should build the fort.

The site was ideal, with its dense pasturage and deep nearby forest. Deer, elk and smaller game frequented the surrounding brushland, and the foothills were still home to buffalo. From a policing point of view, the site overlooked a well-used north-south whisky traders' trail.

In accordance with hastily plotted ground plans, hundreds of twelve-foot-long poplar logs were placed upright in trenches and were plastered with clay to form the outer walls. As at Fort Whoop-Up, crossbeams piled with sod formed the roofs. Windows and doors were already on order from Montana, and there were plenty of stones in the riverbed for fireplaces and chimneys.

By unanimous decision of the men, the fort was named for Assistant Commissioner Macleod who, true to character, mandated the construction of stables for the horses and a small heated shelter for the sick before the buildings proper went up. When a snowstorm hit at the end of October, he ordered that all the horses be herded into the protection of the nearby woods, wrapped in blankets and fed liberal helpings of oats and corn. Hay was scarce, and would be until spring.

By the beginning of December, everybody was out of tents and under roofs, although the officers were still sleeping dorm-style in the kitchen. Within weeks, a general store and "eating place" opened outside the walls. A log pool room appeared,

Never has the romantic image of the Mounties been so burnished or exaggerated as it was by Hollywood during the 1930s, '40s and '50s. In films such as Cecil B. DeMille's *North West Mounted Police*, the villain was invariably a "hellbent rogue," the heroine a "sizzling beauty" (or in this case a "little wilderness spitfire") and the Mountie a "son of courage," a "sculpture in sinewed steel."

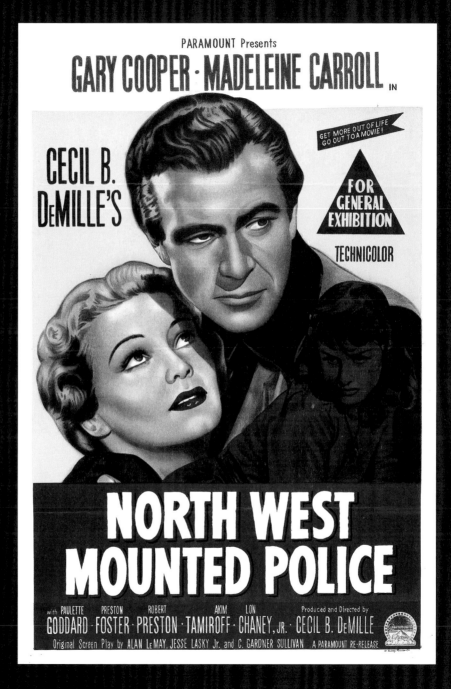

PARAMOUNT Presents

GARY COOPER · MADELEINE CARROLL IN

CECIL B. DeMILLE'S

GET MORE OUT OF LIFE
GO OUT TO A MOVIE!

FOR
GENERAL
EXHIBITION

TECHNICOLOR

NORTH WEST MOUNTED POLICE

with PAULETTE GODDARD · PRESTON FOSTER · ROBERT PRESTON · AKIM TAMIROFF · LON CHANEY, JR.   Produced and Directed by CECIL B. DeMILLE

Original Screen Play by ALAN LeMAY, JESSE LASKY Jr. and C. GARDNER SULLIVAN   A PARAMOUNT RE-RELEASE

It was in the shelter of this wooded ravine at Pine Coulee, Alberta that the Mounties made their first-ever arrest, bringing in a quintet of scofflaw whisky traders along with two wagonloads of booze. Inspector James Macleod ordered the illegal sap spilled, disappointing those of his men who thought they might at least merit a party for their valiant efforts.

and a cemetery – where Constable Godfrey Parks, who had contracted typhoid in the Sweetgrass Hills, became the first occupant on October 26. The constable was the first member of the force to die since leaving Fort Dufferin nearly four months earlier.

Large quantities of meat were laid in by hunters led by Pierre Leveille, and bull teams arrived regularly from Fort Benton, laden with oats, flour, sugar, tea and canned goods.

WHILE CONSTRUCTION was still going on, the great chief Crowfoot sent his foster brother, Three Bulls, to let Macleod know that at Pine Coulee, fifty miles to the north, he had been sold two gallons of whisky in exchange for his two best ponies – and furthermore that the whisky had been contaminated. The ringleader of the operation was an American named William Bond. On hearing this news, ten Mounties, led by Inspector Lief Crozier and guided by Three Bulls and Jerry Potts, immediately set off for Pine Coulee. There

they surprised five whisky traders and made their first arrests in the west, returning to Fort Macleod with ten smuggled guns, more than one hundred illegally acquired buffalo robes (which were promptly converted to coats for the Mounties) and two wagonloads of whisky (which, to the chagrin of the men, Macleod ordered spilled onto the ground).

Macleod, who had at one time been a lawyer and had the foresight months earlier to have himself sworn in as a justice of the peace, tried the men, convicted them, and fined the three leaders $200 each. Since none of them could pay, Macleod put them in jail, from which Bond eventually escaped.

It was the post's first call to action and, from Crowfoot's perspective, was a test of whether the NWMP planned to make good on its promise of protection for the tribes. And they had passed with honours. Several more arrests brought the whisky trade to a trickle in the area, and on December 1, 1874, Macleod, perhaps prematurely, penned the following message and

Below: Chief Crowfoot was successful not just in battle but in procreation, as evidenced by this 1884 photo of the great leader and his family. Sadly, a significant number of Crowfoot's sons and daughters had already been lost to smallpox.

Right: Three Bulls, Chief Crowfoot's foster brother, seen in this studio portrait dressed in an iconic Hudson's Bay blanket coat, succeeded Crowfoot as head chief of the Blackfoot in 1890.

"The Colonel went ahead the other morning and got 32 ducks for the mess. It was a very great change from the salt pork…Our tea last night consisted of tea – (no sugar, no milk) bread (no butter) molasses – fried duck, & fried pork."

R.B. NEVITT, Assistant Surgeon, North West Mounted Police, 1874

dispatched it to Commissioner French: "I am happy to report the complete stoppage of the whiskey trade throughout the whole of this section of the country, and that the drunken riots, which in former years were almost a daily occurrence, are now entirely at an end."

For French, who by this time had reached Swan River in what is now Manitoba, the news was a welcome antidote to the report he had just received from Fort Edmonton. Division A, under Inspector Jarvis, had recently staggered into the fort after an eighty-eight-day endurance test that by rights should have defeated even the toughest of the force's constables and officers. Division A had begun its trek at La Roche Percée with the force's poorest horses (the best having been taken by French for his own trip west with the other divisions) and some of its poorest cattle and draft animals – hence earning the nickname "the Barnyard Division."

In the end, the trek to Fort Edmonton killed most of the division's horses and left the men sick, hungry and in rags.

Of the horses that did survive, several had to be propped up as the division limped in, while others had to be carried on slings between poles.

If there was a positive element to the trek, it was that both men and horses had had access to uncontaminated water along much of the route, and game and wildfowl had been plentiful. At one point near the Saskatchewan River, one of the officers is reported to have brought down eleven geese with a single round of buckshot. And the division had been able to follow the reasonably well-worn Carlton trail used over the years by trappers, traders and tribesmen.

Perhaps most important to the march's completion was Inspector Jarvis's thoughtful and compassionate leadership – noted upon arrival by Constable Jean D'Artigue (with an implied swipe at the tactical and disciplinary skills of the commissioner):

Jarvis was as fond of short marches as French was of long ones, and he was right, for the proverb "slow but sure" is always the safest to follow in long marches. Since we were detached from the main column we were living together like a family. No more of this quasi-discipline. We performed our duties not only for our country's sake but to please our commander. If Jarvis had asked us to follow him, even to the North Pole, not one of us would have refused.

Jarvis, in turn, appreciated his men, as evidenced by his report to the commissioner a few days after arrival:

Had it not been for the perfect conduct of the men and really hard work, much of the property would have been destroyed. I wish particularly to bring to your notice the names of Troop-Sergeant-Major Steele and Constable Labelle. Steele has been untiring in his efforts to assist me and has performed the manual labour of two men. The attention paid to the horses by Constable Labelle has saved many of these unfortunate beasts.

The comfortable and serviceable California saddle, seen here, was adopted by the NWMP in 1878. The British military saddles used by the Mounties during their earliest years tended to slip from side to side and incorporated steel buckles and stirrups that rusted and were unbearably cold during the fierce prairie winters. The Winchester Model 1876 .45-75 lever-action repeating carbine, seen atop the saddle, became NWMP standard issue in 1878, replacing the single-shot English Enfield carbine. Patrol field notes were immediately accessible in the saddle pouches shown below.

The ill-fated NWMP post at Swan River was an architectural and functional nightmare compared to the Hudson's Bay Company's legendary settlement of Norway House on the Nelson River at Little Playgreen Lake. Seen here, Norway House was named for Norwegian axemen hired by Lord Selkirk during the early nineteenth century to clear a road from York Factory on Hudson Bay to the northern end of Lake Winnipeg. Until the late 1870s, when the settlement's significance began to decline, it was a fur trade supply and administration centre known, among other things, for its production of the famous York boats so important to the opening of the north.

By the time Division A reached Fort Edmonton, the men had travelled 1,255 miles from their starting point at Fort Dufferin in just over three months.

COMMISSIONER FRENCH'S march northeast to Swan River with D and E Divisions had been a breeze by comparison. Free of ox carts, cattle and cannons, and with freshly purchased horses, the divisions had averaged twenty-five miles a day, largely in weather described by French as "Indian summer." Occasional prairie fires had created shortages of fresh forage, although men and horses alike had eaten well en route, had experienced little sickness and had travelled through territory where trees and firewood were plentiful. At one point French noted in his diary:

The men could not build their campfires big enough; whole trees were chopped down and placed on the fires, as if to make up in some measure for the deficiency in fuel for the last thousand miles we had marched.

The divisions' difficulties started when, on October 21, the commissioner rode on ahead of the column, excited by the prospect of a first glimpse at the new headquarters and barracks that he was told had been erected by the federal department of public works.

What he found frustrated and infuriated him. The barracks, at best half completed, were of flimsy construction and had been built in a long open line, vulnerable to the north wind, on treeless land covered with immense boulders infested with garter snakes. Moreover, prairie fires had burned every morsel of fresh browse for miles around, right up to the barracks doors.

In a subsequent letter to Ottawa, French reported that "the buildings, put up with spruce boards which were growing in the forest in the same month as they were framed, presented an airy, sieve-like appearance which would have been more enjoyable in July than as prospective winter quarters, say 500 miles north of Kingston."

Adding to the sorry picture, Sub-Inspector Thomas Shurtliffe, who had come north from Fort Ellice, informed French that half the winter's supply of fresh hay had been consumed by fire. Hudson's Bay Company traders at nearby Fort Pelly were unable to replace the hay because they themselves had lost three hundred loads to local fires.

Fires were still burning in the vicinity, and French immediately sent a message back to his column to find any convenient pasturage. He also sent several officers to help the contractor in charge of construction fight a fire that was threatening the local sawmill.

Beyond the immediate difficulties, Swan River was simply too remote, both from the Canadian capital and from the far west where the presence of the NWMP was most needed. Fort Macleod, which had contact with Ottawa via the telegraph line in Montana, would have been a far more intelligent choice as headquarters.

Deeply disturbed that this abominable site had been chosen without his approval, the commissioner gathered several of the best men from Division E, plus all of

This photo of the officers and constables at Fort Macleod in 1879 seems to capture almost perfectly the mixture of rigidity and insouciance – discipline and laxness – that characterized the force during its early years in the west.

Division D, and, leaving the rest under Inspector Jacob Carvell, set out for Fort Ellice to the south, where he would make his objections known.

The march south was a nightmare. Freezing rain and snow threatened the health of men and horses alike. Grass was hard to find. At the half-way point, the convoy met a drove of eighty-four cattle en route to Swan River for the force. French turned them back.

A few days later he turned back another northbound expedition that included Constable William Parker, who recorded in his diary that the horses in French's column were as "thin as lathes, swaying and wobbling…every once in a while falling down." The men he said "were in rags," many without hats and boots.

By November 7, French and Division D were back in southern Manitoba, from where the commissioner began bombarding Ottawa with complaints about Swan River. To make his point, he refused to use Swan River as a headquarters, instead establishing temporary command in Winnipeg

and Fort Dufferin. His tirade, understandably, made him exceedingly unpopular with the government.

If French was gracious, it was in praise of his men, about whom he wrote in a letter to a friend:

Notwithstanding all the difficulties, we have performed a march that all the croakers said was impossible. For hundreds of miles we went over country never traversed by white men; we cut down banks, made roads and crossings of streams and coulees, and by the mercy of Providence survived it all… Two thousand miles is a long march for a force of recruits to make in a summer. Hunt up your history and let me know if there is anything ahead of this on record.

By the end of 1874, the NWMP had been established, as planned, in six posts scattered across the west. Sixty men were at Dufferin with French, fifteen at Winnipeg, thirty-eight at Swan River, twenty-two at

Edmonton, and six at Fort Ellice on the Assiniboine River. At the key post, Fort Macleod, one hundred and forty men and four officers were on the job.

The NWMP had not only been born but had been tried and found ready to serve.

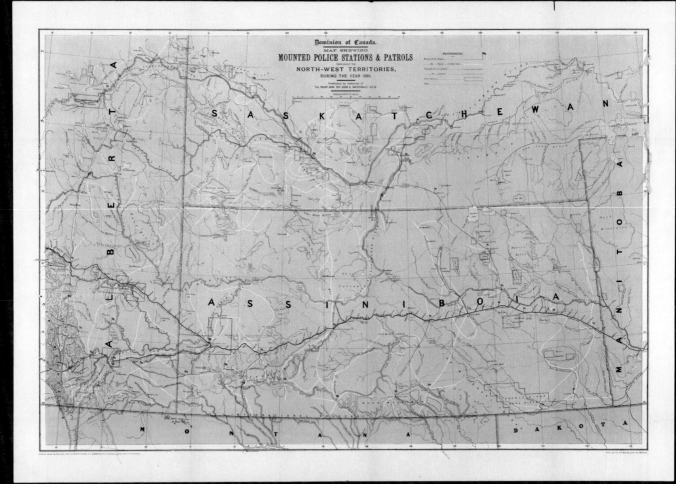

This map, published by the federal Department of the Interior in 1886, shows pretty much everything of geopolitical significance to those in the Canadian west at that time: the rail line, the telegraph line, the provincial and territorial boundaries, treaty boundaries, reserves, judicial districts, and NWMP patrol routes and stations, the last of which are marked with red flags, concentrated mainly along the border and the Canadian Pacific Railway line.

Chapter Three

THE LAST OF THE MIGHTY CHIEFS

ONCE THE NWMP HAD built its first forts and organized its food supply, its most significant ambition, particularly in its westernmost precincts, was to establish trusting relations with the prairie tribes, many of whose people were still deeply suspicious of the police. For Assistant Commissioner James Macleod, this meant meeting and parlaying with a succession of chiefs from the eight-thousand-strong Blackfoot Confederacy. The latter brought together four tribes who occupied what is now southern Alberta and the foothills of the Rockies: the Peigan, the Blood, the Sarcee and the Blackfoot.

Such meetings required infinite tact and good judgment. Macleod would invite one or two chiefs at a time to Fort Macleod and, having formally shaken hands and invited them to seat themselves on buffalo robes, would have his interpreter Jerry Potts light a pipe of tobacco, which was passed first to the chiefs and then around the room.

As these small conclaves sat in silence, Macleod would explain the presence of the "White Mother's" troops, then outline the laws and the penalties for breaking them, emphasizing that there would be no penalty for unintentional infractions. The Confederacy's land, he said (somewhat prematurely), would not be taken from them.

The chiefs would in turn stand, shake hands with everyone and respond, often thanking the force for being there, and proceeding to explain the woes of their tribes: how they were being robbed and ruined by whisky traders, how their horses, women and possessions were being taken from them, how their young men were being killed in brawls. If this flow of catastrophes prevailed, they believed, they would soon have no horses or equipment – or perhaps even men – to hunt the buffalo. Their hope, they invariably said, was that all this would change with the arrival of the police.

On the first day of December 1874, the great eminence of the Confederacy, Chief Crowfoot, whose word was law and whose authority was undisputed, walked up to the fort gates with a contingent of

The chiefs of the Blackfoot Confederacy carried eagle wings as symbols of their power, which was considerable in the foothills of the Rockies and east onto the prairie and plains for generations before the arrival of the Europeans. This group made its dramatic first visit to Fort Macleod in early December 1876. Back row, left to right: Jean L'Heureux, Chief Crowfoot's secretary; Red Crow, Blood chief; Sergeant W. Piercy, North West Mounted Police. Front row, left to right: Crowfoot, Blackfoot chief; Eagle Tail, minor chief of the Peigans; Three Bulls, Blackfoot.

warriors. Barely contained excitement pervaded the place as the forty-three-year-old chief entered bearing an eagle's wing, the symbol of his office. Otherwise, he was dressed simply in a buckskin shirt and beaded moccasins, with a Hudson's Bay blanket draped around his shoulders. A crucial moment in the history of the Canadian west was at hand, and with formal courtesy Assistant Commissioner Macleod stepped from his quarters to meet the man with whom he would have to get along or else.

At that point, nothing could be taken for granted. As a boy during the 1830s, Crowfoot had been told, apparently in a dream, that he was to become a great chief by caring for his people and waging war on their enemies (chief among them being the Sioux). As a young man, Crowfoot had fought with legendary bravery in battle, and he carried the same courageous attitude into his dealings with the newcomers. For years, he had known that his hunting grounds would increasingly be invaded, that the buffalo would not last, and that when the buffalo were gone his

people would have to establish some sort of peaceable relationship with the settlers. In that light, he was ready and willing to acknowledge the white man's laws – especially since those laws were a means to eradicating the whisky traders, for whom Crowfoot had as deep a contempt as did James Macleod. But Macleod knew well that a false move or any indication of antipathy could be fatal to whatever truce he and Crowfoot might establish.

Fortunately for everyone, the meeting went well. The orations were translated by Jerry Potts with uncharacteristic thoroughness and sensitivity, and from that point forward the police had Crowfoot's co-operation and respect. In the months to come when the Sioux contacted Crowfoot seeking his help in fighting the US Cavalry, promising in return to help Crowfoot eliminate the police and settlers north of the border, Crowfoot responded that he wanted no part of the Sioux's plan, that the police were his friends, and that the feeling was mutual.

In particular, the chieftain admired Macleod himself – indeed he bestowed on

Chief Crowfoot, seen here in 1885, was given his name, *Isapo-muxika* (Crow Indian's Big Foot) when as a teenager in battle he kicked over an enemy teepee in a hostile Crow camp. He was known for his courage, and once attacked and killed a grizzly bear with a lance. His name was shortened to Crowfoot by interpreters like Jerry Potts.

the assistant commissioner the flattering Blackfoot name, *Stamix Otokan* (Bull's Head), in part because of Macleod's significant brow and full beard, but perhaps also because Macleod had hung in his office an immense buffalo head, stuffed and presented to him by his unofficial right-hand man, Jerry Potts. Macleod is said to have told Crowfoot at that first meeting that he was "a very fine Indian" and that his chiefs were "a very intelligent lot of men."

If the NWMP's relationship with the Sioux and Cree had been even half as conciliatory as it was with the Blackfoot Confederacy, the force's struggles over the next few years would have been considerably lighter. However, south of the medicine line events were already taking shape in the form of bloody battles between the Sioux and the US Cavalry that would eventually send nearly six thousand warlike Sioux into Canada. Their arrival would create for the NWMP a challenge that would see the Mounties, as they were now commonly known, increase the size of their force, shift their headquarters

to Fort Walsh in the Cypress Hills, and develop obsessive caution and diligence in their dealings with the unpredictable itinerants.

Meanwhile, 1875 opened tragically for the force when two constables, Frank Baxter and Thomas Wilson, who had been manning Fort Kipp, a former whisky post east of Fort Macleod, got lost in a snowstorm while picking up mail at Fort Whoop-Up, and froze to death on the trail. Their partner, Constable Cecil Denny, later reported that he stayed alive on the trip by dismounting each time he felt the cold beginning to paralyze his limbs, and running alongside his horse for twenty minutes "in order to keep warm."

As the winter deepened, Macleod's men settled into an eventful and draining routine, taking long patrols in search of contraband liquor and repeating rifles, returning livestock to its rightful owners, delivering mail and, when the spring came, fighting occasional prairie fires. Wherever possible, they worked with the Natives to improve sanitation in the interest of quelling diseases such as smallpox, which had

"I went to the Blackfoot Crossing with Mr. Dewdney and didn't we just delight the heart of our old friends the Blackfoot with the meat and flour tea sugar and tobacco we took them. They have suffered awfully this last Winter and it is wonderful how well they have behaved. Crowfoot appears to have kept them all in check. We went thro' their camp and I rec'd a perfect ovation. Men women and children flocked round to greet me and shake hands. The women brought their children on their backs to shake hands and held out the tiny little skeleton hands for me to shake."

JAMES MACLEOD, Lieutenant-Colonel, North West Mounted Police, 1879

Above: Pair of North West Mounted Police long shank spurs, 1880s type, worn by Sergeant Fred Bagley. Although they were essential for policing duties on the vast prairie, horses were always in short supply and on occasion were loaned from division to division.

Left: Two NWMP constables on patrol on cultivated land near Fort Walsh in what is now southern Saskatchewan. These patrols regularly covered hundreds of miles of prairie. In this case, the anonymous riders appear to be riding Hanoverian horses, famous with the NWMP for their strength, agility and stable temperament.

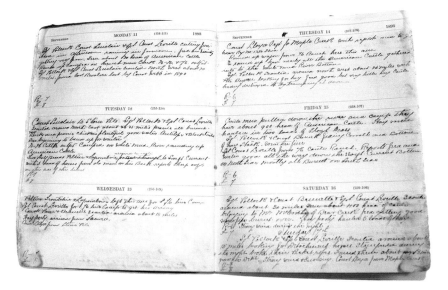

Just as Mounties do to-day, early NWMP officers and constables penned observations on every significant move they made and occurrence they encountered while on duty. The record from notebooks such as those seen here often became significant evidence in court and is, of course, an important part of the historical record.

left so many dead and many more scarred both physically and psychologically.

In broad terms, a new order of life had dawned in the sparsely populated west. The Natives were now freer to hunt and trade in peace. A new confidence had been born among the mixed-bloods and missionaries, and among the scattering of settlers who now appeared on a landscape that until recently had been considered too dangerous for travel, let alone permanent habitation.

BUT IF THE BLACKFOOT were happy in the presence of their new neighbours, the troops themselves were less sanguine about being where they were. The daily foot and rifle drills were exhausting, and as late as March 1875, the men had not been paid for their months of commitment to the cause. Most owed small fortunes to the traders. Moreover, the fort diet was a repetitious round of buffalo patties, beans and tea. One outspoken constable complained that "the food in Hell could not be a greater punishment than the meals at Fort Macleod." Another suggested that,

Fort Macleod was not generally a comfortable or luxurious place in its earliest days. By contrast, the office of Inspector James Macleod, seen here in 1875, seems extraordinarily well furnished, with its hardwood desk, oil paintings, rugs, lamps and substantial wood stove.

for variety, the cooks might consider "roasting up" some of the hundreds of mice that infested the fort, sometimes moving so noisily through the walls and over the floors that they kept the men awake at night. Constables and officers alike were wearing uniforms patched beyond recognition. Or they had switched to buffalo skins, tanned rawhide, canvas – any available material. Most wore moccasins, bought or traded from the Natives, or simply wrapped long strips of crudely tanned hide around their feet when they went on patrol.

Whatever "comforts" could be found in the spacious new quarters were by no means obvious or compelling to the men. The barracks were drafty and damp; wash water froze solid overnight; and when the warming chinook winds blew down out of the foothills, they melted the snow on the sod-topped roofs, sending cascades of mud through the rafters into the barracks and mess hall. Many of the men slept with oil cloths strung above their beds.

While the police were duty-bound to protect the Natives from the ravages of alcohol, a growing portion of the constables

themselves took to booze. Many of them regarded it as the sole escape from the tedium and loneliness of life on the frontier. A so-called whisky made of raw alcohol and Jamaica ginger was readily available to them on the sly through American traders – or through confiscation, which was not always officially reported. The price was $5 a bottle, roughly a week's pay, and when the smuggled (or confiscated) booze was unavailable, the most persistent drinkers resorted to liniment or bay rum, a popular aftershave of the day. Or they drank medicinal alcohol stolen from the surgeon's supplies. In one noted case, several non-commissioned officers at Battleford drank ether, prompting the post commander to report that his sergeant "was for the time being a regular lunatic."

At Fort Macleod, eighteen men, more than a tenth of the detachment, went AWOL during that first hideous winter, disappearing across the Montana border to work in the mines, where they would at least be paid for their efforts. The ever-judicious Macleod allowed that the men had a legitimate complaint, given that they

had not been paid since they marched out of Fort Dufferin amidst a pestilence of mosquitoes and dust the previous summer.

At the news of these desertions in early March, Ottawa telegraphed Macleod, advising him that $30,000 was available to him at a bank in Helena, three hundred miles to the south, and that he should go there immediately, get the money and pay his men.

Macleod would not normally have undertaken such a journey in winter. But, placing his trust in the matchless Jerry Potts, he set out in clear weather on March 15 with three of his finest officers and seven horses selected especially for their toughness and staying power.

By the time they reached Fort Whoop-Up, however, the weather had turned. Their host at the fort, Dave Akers, whom they had met before on the original march west, advised against continuing until the advancing storm passed. But Macleod was anxious to keep moving.

Two days later, snow-blind and in the grip of a harrowing blizzard, they made camp beneath the cut bank of the Milk River, where hundreds of buffalo were also

sheltering for the night. As the storm about them intensified and the threat of being trampled by the milling animals increased, Potts, using his knife to cut blocks of snow, dug a deep cave in the drift-covered banks where the group holed up, frostbitten and starved, for two days.

On the third day, desperate for food, they resumed their journey. But only Potts possessed any sense of direction in the driving snow. As the little party blundered forward, the extraordinary guide grew morose and silent, refusing to answer questions, knowing that survival depended entirely on his almost mystic capability to focus his intuitions and keep moving in the right direction.

After sixteen hours on the trail, when the men had all but given up, Potts shouted that they had reached the springs he had been heading toward all along. He knew of a shanty nearby, and within minutes the horses were watered and fed and the fortunate five were inside, with a fire going, thawing their fingers and toes, preparing morsels of food that, mercifully, had been left in the shelter.

Morning broke clear and, with the help of men at various military and trading posts along the rest of the route, the officers rode into Helena a week later and checked into the St. Louis Hotel where, over a period of three weeks, two of them recovered from snowblindness, one had a gangrenous toe removed and Macleod allowed his severely frozen face to heal. Potts, it is said, spent much of the three weeks drinking happily in the local saloons.

Apart from picking up the cash, Macleod completed two important transactions in Helena before returning home: he rehired seven of the deserters who had left the NWMP for the mines (which, it turned out, were even less attractive than life at Fort Macleod), and he began extradition proceedings against Thomas Hardwick and his wolfers, who had killed more than twenty Assiniboine at the Cypress Hills massacre.

At the force's headquarters in Swan River, conditions were every bit as bad as at Fort Macleod. Meals throughout the winter consisted largely of "preserved" pork – or, more accurately, pork fat that in its state of decomposition glowed in

No fewer than seven of the officers and constables grouped outside the impressive barns of the NWMP barracks in Regina appear to be smoking pipes. While just one Mountie is wearing a full beard (beards were later banned by the NWMP), at least a dozen are wearing the droopy moustaches made popular by Inspector James Walsh. The barracks at Regina were the first to have a bar for the men, as well as a pool room and library.

STEELE & WING'S
Photographic and Art Rooms,

474 MAIN STREET,
WINNIPEG, MAN.
NEGATIVES PRESERVED.

"There is a carelessness manifested in every thing connected with the force even the placing & posting of the guard around the camp & of the picquet around the horses. A band of Indians could easily rule the camp and scalp us all before we knew it. More stringency in this respect will now be enforced as we are about to enter a territory swarming with Indians who will never refuse a scalp when offered to them."

R.B. NEVITT, assistant surgeon, North West Mounted Police, 1874

colours ranging from green to pale yellow to iridescent blue. Those who couldn't stomach it got by on a diet of bread and tea. Clothing was a wretched assortment of skins and rags, and so much snow drifted through cracks in the buildings that after snowstorms almost as much shovelling was required indoors as out. The stables had no roofs, the barracks no indoor toilets, and there were two-inch gaps between the shrunken timbers of the hospital. On several occasions the men suffered frostbite in their sleep.

Commissioner French continued to battle Ottawa over the choice of Swan River as a headquarters and over his own decision to spend the winter at Fort Dufferin and Winnipeg, from where he had been running the force, if inadequately. A government memorandum in March described French's attitude and criticisms as "most unfortunate," in particular because they fed the opposition Conservatives' scathing attacks on Prime Minister Mackenzie over his operation of the police force. The prime minister himself wrote, "We have had a great deal of trouble with

French, his general mismanagement being very bad indeed." The commissioner lashed back that his support from Ottawa had been deplorable, that he had been the victim of "brainless and profiteering" practices by the government-hired contractor at Swan River and that he had been kept in all but total ignorance of government policy regarding the NWMP.

While the insults were flying, French accused his own assistant, James Macleod, of woefully inadequate reporting from the west. News of the deaths of the two constables on New Year's Day and of the desertions of eighteen Mounties to the US had reached French, he said, not through official channels but via the newspapers and gossip in the barracks.

In spring, the commissioner was ordered back to Swan River, where he was greeted in early June by a welcoming parade of men dressed mostly in tattered buckskins and fox-fur hats with tails hanging behind in the style of American frontiersman Davy Crockett. French is said to have taken one look, exclaimed "Good God!" then wheeled his horse and ridden off.

A week later, the post commander, Inspector Jacob Carvell, took leave for a much-needed vacation in the US. He never returned.

Earlier in the spring, French had asked that a "competent and independent" person be sent to investigate the sorry state of affairs at Swan River, including the utter ineptitude and dishonesty of the contractor who had constructed the barracks, stables and administration buildings. Thus it was that Major-General Edward Selby Smyth, the government's choice for the job, arrived in late June at the post – one of many stops on an impressive inspection of the force that would ultimately cover eleven thousand miles and take in all NWMP facilities and men.

Smyth's report to Ottawa on arriving back in late November stated that the force was "in very fair order" considering its circumstances and the haste with which it had evolved. The report tended to vindicate the commissioner, who again took up his assault on Ottawa, concentrating now less on government ineptitude than on the deprivations suffered by the

Above: During the early years of the force, every NWMP base had a veterinarian and at least one surgeon, the latter doing everything from setting broken limbs to extracting teeth to treating riding sores and sunburn. Assistant Surgeon Charles Selby Haultain, who apparently also doubled as a model, is seen here, in Regina, in full dress (left), mess uniform (centre) and patrol uniform (right).

Right: The extensive gold braid seen on this 1876 NWMP dress uniform was something of a sartorial overstatement amid the rough conditions that surrounded the Mounties in the west, and was eventually toned down. The equally ostentatious top plume was also eliminated, although the helmet, which the men found heavy and cumbersome, survived for decades as part of the officers' dress uniform.

men, and on how they might be corrected. He demanded, for example, that a piano and orchestral instruments be sent to Swan River so that the men could have music – and that a library be installed and the buildings be improved.

Among Smyth's recommendations was that the Mounties' uniforms be updated – that the red frock coats, for example, be replaced with tunics "because they are more dressy."

> And I would suggest that officers should wear swords, which have a great effect upon the Indian mind, and a shoulder belt with a pouch for field glasses. Indeed, I think constables, too, should have field glasses, as they are absolutely necessary on the prairie; a great number of Indians now wear them, and the police are therefore at a disadvantage without this aid.

Shortly thereafter, in accordance with Smyth's recommendations, additional gold finery was added to the officers' uniforms, as well as decorative belts and an impressive new helmet with drooping plumes of horsehair. A blue "undress" jacket was provided for the officers, while the constables continued to wear dowdy brown cotton for daily business.

FRENCH AND THE MEN endured a ferocious winter at their Manitoba headquarters, and in March 1876, the commissioner asked the government if he could come to Ottawa and discuss the ever-deteriorating situation in which he found himself. His request was refused, and on July 22 he was fired as commissioner (but ultimately allowed to submit his resignation, in the interest of his dignity).

Although many of the men had disliked French, particularly for his impetuous ways during the march west, his work on behalf of the troops at Swan River had won him popularity there, and on the eve of his departure his charges entertained him with a banquet and music and presented him with a gold watch and his wife with a silver tea service, said to be valued at $300, representing more than a year's pay for some of the constables.

In his inspection of NWMP bases in 1875, Major-General Edward Selby Smyth recommended that officers and constables be equipped with field glasses so that, tactically, they could keep up with Native hunters and scouts, who already had such glasses, obtained from US traders. At least one constable with poor eyesight is said to have used his binoculars as crude reading glasses in the dim winter light at Fort Walsh.

Four elaborately dressed Cree warriors, including the great chief Big Bear, or *Mistahimaskwa*, fourth from left, are seen here trading beaver pelts at Fort Pitt, Saskatchewan in 1884. In exchange, the Cree undoubtedly received guns, traps, dry goods or tools – but not whisky, thanks to the arrival of the NWMP in the west a decade earlier. The young Cree man seated in front is Sky Bird or King Bird, the third son of Big Bear. Within a year of this photo being snapped, both would play a significant role in the North-West Rebellion under Louis Riel.

French's replacement, not surprisingly, was the capable if overworked James Macleod, perhaps the most important non-Native man in the west at the time. Macleod was a natural choice because his sound relations with the Blackfoot Confederacy would be needed in negotiating the treaty that the government now required if a more comprehensive truce was to be won with Crowfoot and his people. Macleod had temporarily quit the force in order to work as chief magistrate in the area of Fort Macleod, but immediately rejoined when appointed commissioner, taking on double duty.

French, who had battled the government for months over the location of the force's headquarters, must have found it ironic, if not infuriating, that the new commissioner was immediately able to persuade Ottawa to move NWMP headquarters to Fort Macleod. The move was predicated not on the poor conditions at Swan River, however, but in a roundabout way on the fact that General Custer of the US Cavalry had been annihilated at Little Big Horn by Sitting Bull and the

Sioux. Fearing retaliation, the Sioux – or the Dakota as they are sometimes called – had begun a massive migration toward the forty-ninth parallel, with the intent of moving north into "the land of the White Mother," where they would be safe from the cavalry. Clearly, the mounted police were needed in the area, as was their command, in order to maintain the peace and keep their eyes on the movement and ambitions of the Sioux.

From Ottawa's perspective, the move to Fort Macleod also put the police in a better position to supervise existing treaties and to establish those that were still pending. To date, five treaties had been signed with western tribes. But shortly after the shift of headquarters, the sixth and most extensive treaty was enacted with the Plains Cree, who, in signing, gave up control of some 120,000 square miles of land along the north and south branches of the Saskatchewan River. If there was a hitch in proceedings, it was that the great Cree chief, Big Bear, refused to sign, believing correctly that the treaty was fundamentally unfair to

Inspector Francis Dickens was born in London in 1844, the fifth child of the renowned English novelist, Charles Dickens. As a young man he studied medicine in Germany and spent seven years in India with the Bengal Mounted Police. In 1874, after the death of his father, Francis's aunt used her influence with family friend Lord Dufferin, then governor general of Canada, to get Francis a commission in the North West Mounted Police. He was a capable rider and, during postings at Swan River, Fort MacLeod and Fort Walsh, spent long hours in the saddle. He was present at Blackfoot Crossing for the signing of Treaty Seven in 1877, and in 1883 was placed in charge of Fort Pitt on the North Saskatchewan River. In histories of the Mounties, Dickens is sometimes described as a tragic character, struggling to live in the shadow of his great father. Charges against him included drunkenness, laziness and recklessness. Whatever the truth, he held up well during the Rebellion of 1885, and throughout his 12-year career maintained both his commission and his loyalty to the NWMP. The sword shown here is said to have been used by Dickens during his years with the Bengal police in India.

Inspector James M. Walsh exerted the first real fashion influence on the NWMP, impressing constables and officers alike with his widely emulated moustache, his buckskin jacket and his soft Stetson hat, which, while not official gear, was comfortable, protective and, in the eyes of most of the men, dashing. A less sporty version of the Stetson was eventually made the official headgear of the force.

CHICAGO.

his people. But the signing went ahead without him, completed with great pomp at Fort Carlton and Fort Pitt, attended by territorial officials in cocked hats and gold braid and by lesser Cree chiefs in quasi-military uniforms given to them by their governmental co-signatories. In exchange for their land, the Cree were given reserve land (160 acres for each family of five) as well as horses, wagons and agricultural implements. They were also given a promise of aid and rations in the event of "pestilence or general famine" – a promise that would come due in ensuing years when the buffalo disappeared and starvation became an all but annual threat. In addition, each family was awarded $12 a year, in perpetuity.

IN THE MEANTIME, three new and important NWMP forts had been constructed across the west. With the area around Fort Macleod free of whisky peddlers, and friendly relations established with the tribes, Ottawa had decided during the spring of 1875 to reduce personnel at Fort Macleod and extend the force's influence and authority back along the border in an easterly direction. In May 1875, Inspector James Walsh, accompanied by the indispensable Jerry Potts, led the entire B Division, some thirty men, on a 160-mile trek east into the Cypress Hills. There, near the site of the famous massacre, the group took six weeks to erect a fort in a verdant mile-wide valley, beside Battle Creek.

The constables and officers named the place Fort Walsh, in honour of their popular commander, a dashing thirty-four-year-old graduate of the Royal Military College in Kingston. Walsh had been a champion lacrosse player in his home-town of Prescott, Ontario, and could ride as well as anyone in the force. He affected a wide-brimmed hat and fringed buckskin jacket, and wore a goatee and moustache, which was copied by so many of his men that almost anyone from B Division was immediately identifiable by his beard. As at Fort Macleod, a community soon grew up around Fort Walsh – stores, a hotel, a restaurant, and inevitably a loose community of itinerant Natives.

This large group of Mounties was camped near Fort Walsh, probably on manoeuvres, during the summer of 1878. For veterans of the detachment, the bell tents must have been an echo of the perilous march west five years earlier, although by this time the force was better trained, better equipped and significantly better organized to be camped on the open prairie. A police brass band warms up in the foreground, watched by dozens of Mounties and tribesmen.

Inspector William D. Jarvis argued with his NWMP superiors and with Ottawa over his use of contractors to build Fort Saskatchewan, near Edmonton, in 1874. However, of all the force's early inspectors, he was perhaps the most popular with his men, whom he treated with genuine consideration and who are said to have felt comfortable enough with him to call him by his first name.

In August of the same year, twenty-five-year-old Ephrem Brisbois led F Division north from Fort Macleod into the heart of Blackfoot country. There, at the junction of the Bow and Elbow rivers, the division founded and built Fort Calgary, the name of which was an adaptation of the Gaelic word *Calgarry*, meaning "clear running water."

Further north at HBC Fort Edmonton, Inspector William Jarvis and A Division were soon at work building Fort Saskatchewan, although not without controversy. Early in the year, Jarvis had received instructions from Commissioner French to select a site for a new post, to build it and to fence the surrounding land and sow crops. When the orders became known in the vicinity, a group of Edmonton settlers approached Jarvis, aggressively demanding that the fort be built at Edmonton for their protection. Their demands antagonized Jarvis, who immediately chose a site at Sturgeon Creek, some twenty miles away across the Saskatchewan River, where he believed (wrongly) that a railway crossing would one day be built. Sam Steele wrote,

"I have no doubt that if the settlers had let him alone he would have chosen a site on the opposite side of the river exactly where they wanted it." As it turned out, the site was inconveniently distant from well-travelled trails. Moreover, in the months leading up to construction, Jarvis's men had grown unhappy about having to buy their own clothes and supplies at expensive prices from the Hudson's Bay Company trading post. As a result, when Jarvis asked them to become builders and farmers, they refused. In response, the commander rashly promised to pay the men an extra 15 cents a day, and then contracted some of the work to local labourers. When his largesse became known to French, the infuriated commissioner wrote reminding him that the contracting out of work did not have official approval and that Jarvis himself would be responsible for the costs if approval was denied (which fortunately for Jarvis it was not).

For the men at Fort Saskatchewan, life was a daunting succession of hardships, particularly in winter. On one infamous fifteen-day trek in search of a group of

whisky traders near Belly River, Sam Steele reported that daily temperatures ranged between −42°F and −56°F.

We took no tents and no stoves, such luxuries being unknown in the west. Our halts for the night were made about an hour before dark, so that the ponies could be made snug and a large quantity of firewood cut. The snow was then shoveled away, a large fire built, buffalo robes laid down, and after a supper of buffalo steaks, bread and tea, we lay in front of the fire like herrings in a barrel and slept.

The hardships were not unmitigated. On the same trek, the men enjoyed the hospitality of Mr. and Mrs. John Ashon, who owned Ashon's Store at Buffalo Lake. Steele recorded that as he, Jarvis and their group of constables searched out the store, "we heard the sound of dance music and directed our steps to a large log cabin in which a lively wedding dance was going on."

For four days, Mrs. Ashon, a young woman about twenty years of age, took

THE STRONGEST and most aggressive Natives on the Canadian prairie in the middle of the nineteenth century were the Blackfoot, whose territory stretched from the Rocky Mountains in the west to present-day Saskatchewan in the east, and south from there to the upper Missouri River in the American Midwest.

The Blackfoot Confederacy encompassed a number of tribes, including the Northern Blackfoot or Siksika, the Peigan or Piikani, and the Blood or Kainai. At different times, both the Sarcee and the Gros Ventre were also part of the Confederacy. The Assiniboine or Stoneys to the east were sometimes friendly to the Blackfoot, but usually were not.

The social organization of the Confederacy brought together complex warrior societies that participated in joint religious ceremonies and acted together to mount hunting or battle expeditions. Great value was placed on the bravery of warriors in battle, and descent was traced through the male line only.

Each spring the scattered bands united for the great Sun Dance festival, which often lasted four or five days and allowed the bands to plan for the summer hunt and other social and religious gatherings. The sacred medicine-bundle was a central and indispensable talisman at many of the ceremonies held at these gatherings. The Blackfoot spoke different dialects of the musical Algonkin language rich in vowel sounds and devoid of the harsher consonants.

At the time of contact with the Europeans, the Confederacy was expanding rapidly. However, beginning in the nineteenth century, smallpox, typhus, tuberculosis and other diseases brought by explorers and traders swept through the tribes. The illnesses left thousands dead in their teepees. In some camps, no one remained even to wrap and place the remains on scaffolds, as custom required.

Contact with Europeans also brought horses and firearms to the Confederacy, two rather mixed blessings. Both acquisitions contributed to a new way to hunt buffalo, and horses in particular became a new medium of exchange. As feats of valour went, it was almost as honourable to steal an enemy's horses as to kill him in battle, and raids for this purpose were a constant feature of camp life. By the middle of the nineteenth century, when nearly all tribes possessed firearms as well as horses, war was all but constant, and peace a rare interlude in the lives of prairie Natives.

After Treaty Seven was signed in 1877, most of the Peigan people settled on a reservation in Montana, while the Northern Blackfoot and Blood, as well as the remaining Peigan, settled on separate reserves in southern Alberta.

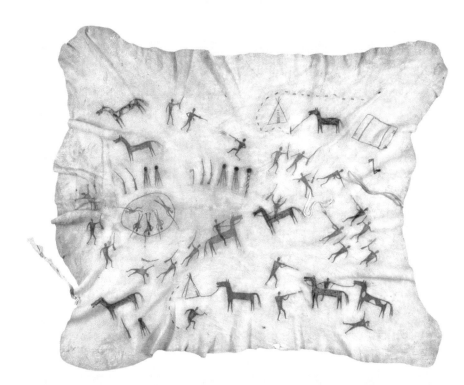

Raw Eater, a respected leader among the Blackfoot during the late nineteenth century, used a traditional style of painting, with natural pigment on buffalo hide, to record some of the important events of his life and the life of his tribe. The artist invariably painted himself in red — stealing horses, fighting enemies, and taking scalps and guns.

This small, thread-bound notebook stamped "Peigan Indian Agency, April 29, 1904," was used briefly by an unknown member of the Peigan tribe as a winter count or calendar of events on the Peigan reserve southwest of Fort Macleod, near Brocket, Alberta. Each of the small vertical lines between the x's or crosses appears to represent a day, while each cross represents a week.

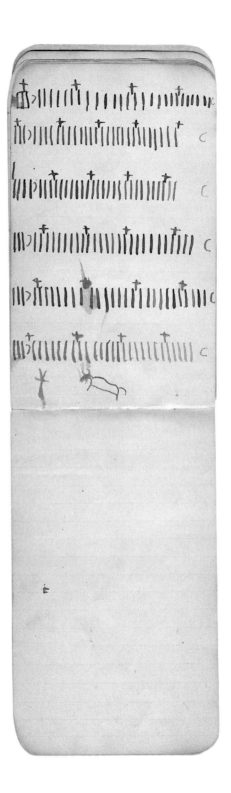

> "Just fancy seeing 100 miles without a piece of wood so large as a lead pencil, we are now approaching the buffalo country. Living animals are beginning to be seen. Buffalo skulls & skeletons more numerous & apparently fresher than they were."
>
> R.B. NEVITT, assistant surgeon, North West Mounted Police, 1874

good care that we should not suffer from starvation, for she kept the fire going and the pot boiling the whole time. The intervals between meals were very short, for every now and then we would be asked to "draw in" and eat buffalo tongues, bannocks, strong tea and tinned fruits.

The buffalo were crucial to the survival of everyone in the area, and one of Steele's most telling descriptions of the activities around Fort Saskatchewan was that of the contrasting methods of the Native and non-Native buffalo hunters:

Whites were few in number, but when they went to hunt for the purpose of obtaining a supply of fresh meat, they committed the most wanton destruction, killing enough for a whole settlement or regiment of soldiers. They were, as a rule, poor horsemen, and did their hunting on foot. Concealed in a bluff of timber, or behind a snow drift, they would shoot down hundreds of animals without the poor beasts having a chance to see the direction from which the shots came.

The Metis and Indians gave the buffalo a chance for its life; they were splendid horsemen, the equal of any in the world, and killed the game from the saddle, a dangerous operation in the winter, owing to the numerous badger holes concealed by the snow. The most successful of the half-breed hunters during that winter was Abraham Salois, who killed six hundred animals. In one run, thirty-seven fell to his rifle, no doubt the best on record.

BY THE SPRING OF 1877, with Treaty Six in place, only the Blackfoot Confederacy retained the rights to its ancestral lands – some fifty thousand square miles of the most fertile territory between the Cypress Hills and the Rocky Mountains, in what is now southern Alberta. Commissioner Macleod, who was responsible for bringing the Confederacy to the treaty table, trusted that his ally, Crowfoot, would be a support to him in the process. What he hadn't reckoned with was that the Confederacy's long-time enemies, the Stoneys, were among the occupants of the territory and were not likely

to come amiably into league with Crowfoot and the other chiefs.

Macleod had also overestimated the political authority of a single chief. Crowfoot, while powerful, had no direct control over, say, the Bloods, whose chief, Red Crow, was Crowfoot's brother-in-law and in fact resented being treated as the great chief's subordinate.

Crowfoot complicated the situation by insisting that the treaty conference be held in his own territory, at Blackfoot Crossing, some eighty miles north of Fort Macleod. This meant a long journey for the Bloods and Peigans, who lived south of the fort. Red Crow immediately refused to make the trip, and Macleod had no reassurances that other dissatisfied chiefs would attend.

Nevertheless, in early September while some tribespeople were still out hunting buffalo, the intrepid commissioner called the tribes together – at least those willing to attend. Within days they began to assemble in an open meadow along the banks of the Bow River at Blackfoot Crossing. On one bank stood the tents and flags of the

Blackfoot Crossing, on the Bow River, seen here in 1900, was the site of the September 1877 conference that brought together the Canadian government and the Blackfoot Confederacy to discuss the terms of Treaty Seven. In all, it was a rueful couple of weeks for the tribes who, fearing a future without buffalo and the impositions that would come with European settlement, accepted the modest rewards of the reserve system in exchange for the freedom to be at large on land that had sustained them for ten thousand years.

government treaty team, led by territorial Lieutenant-Governor David Laird, accompanied by Commissioner Macleod and a Mountie escort of 108 men and officers. For ceremonial purposes, the sizable NWMP contingent included a small artillery unit and the military band from Swan River (bearing instruments ordered for them by the departed George French).

Laird was, in effect, Queen Victoria's representative. A forty-four-year-old native of Prince Edward Island, the one-time journalist stood six feet four inches tall and so impressed the Indians with his honest manner that they eventually named him "The Man Who Talks Straight" and trusted his every utterance.

During the first couple of weeks of September, the Indian encampment grew along both sides of the river until more than four thousand Blackfoot, Bloods, Peigans and Sarcees were present with their horses and dogs. The Stoneys were nowhere in sight. Nor was Red Crow of the Bloods. In a now-famous description of the scene, Inspector Cecil Denny recorded in his diary:

There must have been a thousand lodges. Their horses covered uplands to the north and south of the camp in thousands. It was a stirring and picturesque scene; great bands of grazing horses, the mounted warriors threading their way among them and as far as the eye could reach the white Indian lodges glimmering among the trees along the river bottom. Never before had such a concourse of Indians assembled on Canada's western plains.

Finally, on September 19, with anticipation building, the Mounties sounded a cannon blast, and the chiefs began parading to the treaty tent. Suddenly, on the hilly skyline, a thousand Blackfoot warriors charged into view on horseback, whooping and firing their rifles. Laird later described the scene as one that would "strike fear into any man's heart." But the police honour guard stood unfazed behind the treaty table as the warriors descended and reared to a halt by the big tent.

At this dramatic signal, Crowfoot strode forward, hand raised in peace, took his

In an age of consultation and consensus, it is perplexing to consider that the text of Treaty Seven, the Blackfoot Treaty, was presented to the Blackfoot Confederacy pre-written, either to sign or not to sign. What's more, the treaty was presented in English only, which the members of the Confederacy could not read, and in legalese that could barely be understood by most of the non-Natives present at the signing. Below is page one of the eleven-page handwritten text of the treaty.

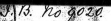

I.B. No 9020.

Articles of a *Treaty* made and concluded this twenty second day of September in the year of Our Lord One thousand eight hundred and seventy seven, *Between* Her Most Gracious Majesty the Queen of Great Britain and Ireland by Her Commissioners the Honorable David Laird, Lieutenant Governor and Indian Superintendant of the North-West Territories and James Farquharson Macleod C. M. G. Commissioner of the North-West Mounted Police, of the one part, and the Blackfeet, Blood, Piegan Sarcee, Stoney and other Indians, inhabitants of the Territory north of the United States Boundary Line, east of the Central range of the Rocky Mountains and south and west of Treaties numbers Six and Four, by their Head Chiefs and Minor Chiefs or Councillors chosen as hereinafter mentioned of the other part.

Whereas the Indians inhabiting the said Territory have pursuant to an appointment made by the said Commissioners been convened at a meeting at the "Blackfoot Crossing" of the Bow River to deliberate upon certain matters of interest to Her Most Gracious Majesty of the one part and the said Indians of the other

And whereas the said Indians have been informed by Her Majesty's Commissioners that it is the desire of Her Majesty to open up for settlement and such other purposes as to Her Majesty may seem meet a tract of Country bounded and described as hereinafter mentioned, and to obtain the consent thereof Her Indian subjects inhabiting the said tract, and to make a Treaty and arrange with them so that there may be peace and good-will between them and Her Majesty; and between them and Her Majesty's other subjects; and that Her Indian people may know and feel assured of what allowance they are to count upon and receive from Her Majesty's bounty and benevolence.

And whereas the Indians of the said tract duly convened in Council and being requested by Her Majesty's Commissioners to present their Head Chiefs and Minor Chiefs or Councillors who should be authorized on their behalf to conduct such negotiations and sign any Treaty to be founded thereon and to become responsible to Her Majesty for the faithful performance by their respective Bands of such obligations as should be assumed by them; the said Blackfeet, Blood, Piegan and Sarcee Indians have therefore acknowledged for that purpose the several Head and Minor Chiefs and the said Stoney Indians the Chiefs and Councillors who have subscribed hereto; that thereupon in open Council the said Commissioners received and acknowledged the Head

This Cree identity card (No. 65) was required by its owner, a member of the Little Pine Band in southern Saskatchewan, in order to collect the Crown's annual payment under the Treaty Six agreement. It was apparently used successfully in 1883 and 1884.

seat among the other chiefs and lighted a peace pipe, which he puffed on and passed to the lieutenant-governor.

"The Great Mother loves all her children," Laird began, proceeding into a somewhat inflated account of what an honourable and magnificent advantage it had been to the Natives to have the Mounties arrive in the west. They had driven out the whisky traders, punished criminals, fought disease and put out grass fires. From afar, the, Great Mother, appreciated the tribes for "taking the Mounties by the hand" and obeying their laws.

"In a few years," continued Laird, "the buffalo will probably all be destroyed, and for this reason the Queen wishes to help you live in the future in some other way. She wishes you to allow her white children to come and live on your land."

The details proposed by Laird were along the lines of previous treaties: 160 acres of reserve land for each family of five; $12 a year in treaty payouts; hunting rights on "government" land; ammunition for hunting; education; the means for agriculture; and so on.

The chiefs eventually withdrew to their encampment to discuss the proposal. Eagle Calf, chief of the Many Children band of the Blackfoot tribe, believed the treaty should be accepted, since the settlers were coming anyway. Eagle Ribs, who led the Skunk band, threatened to withdraw from the proceedings if better terms were not offered. Some wanted no treaty at all.

Amidst conflicting views, the chiefs eventually looked to Crowfoot for wisdom. Until this point, Crowfoot's brother-in-law, Red Crow, had not appeared. But Crowfoot believed he would come and now refused to speak until his relative arrived – which he did two days later, as yet undecided about which way to vote.

After an all-night council on September 21, Red Crow made his decision. The treaty, he told his fellow chiefs, was preferable to the bloody and futile war that would certainly ensue if the Native people were to attempt to retain their land and exclude the newcomers from occupying it.

The next morning, the chiefs and government officials reconvened, and Crowfoot rose to speak. He began by begging the government's indulgence:

We are the children of the plains, it is our home, and the buffalo has been our food always. I hope you look upon the Blackfeet, Bloods and Sarcees as your children now, and that you will be charitable to them. If the police had not come to the country, where would we all be now? Bad men and whisky were killing us all so fast that very few, indeed, of us would have been left today. I wish them all good and trust that all our hearts will increase in goodness from this time forward. I am satisfied. I will sign the treaty.

Red Crow rose next (translated, as were all chiefs and officials, by the multilingual Jerry Potts):

Three years ago, when the Mounted Police came to my country, I met and shook hands with Stamix Otokan at the Belly River. Since that time he has made me many promises and has kept them all...I trust Stamix Otokan and will sign with Crowfoot.

Left: The Eagle (also called Little Bull) was one of the Blackfoot signatories to Treaty Seven, for which he undoubtedly received the chief's coat and hat that he is seen wearing in this photograph.

Below: This 1887 document alleges that promises were made by Sir John A. Macdonald to supply canvas for tents to the bands of chiefs Crowfoot and Red Crow and to have a house constructed for the Peigan chief North Axe. The promises, made during the three chiefs' trip to Ottawa several months earlier, were apparently never fulfilled.

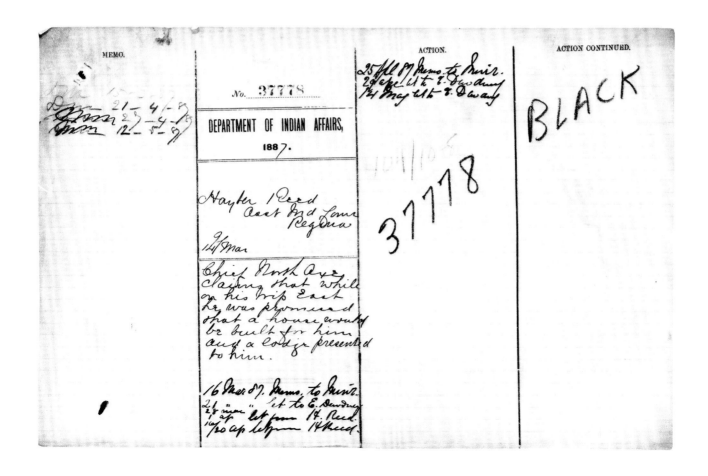

Below left: On the signing of a treaty, the leaders of the assembled tribes were each given a medal. One side of the metal disk bore a likeness of Queen Victoria, while the other showed an image of the treaty commissioner shaking hands with a lightly clad Native man. At the bottom of each medal, somewhat obscured, there was a depiction of a peace pipe crossed over a war club, the ironic suggestion being that peace would now replace hostile relations, when in fact the treaties themselves led to numerous antipathies and disputes.

Below right: Native signatories to the treaties were also given decorative frock coats such as the one shown here belonging to Old Sun, who signed Treaty Seven, the Blackfoot treaty.

Chief Red Crow of the Blood tribe is seen here in 1895 wearing his treaty coat and hat and a number of medals dispensed by the treaty commissioner.

When everyone had spoken, the chiefs filed forth, each making his mark on the treaty document. The Canadian delegates added their signatures, and the chiefs were presented with red coats, flags and medals commemorating the occasion. For the government, it was a great victory – no blood had been shed. For the Confederacy, it was an act of perilous and unprecedented faith.

Three additional days were required to make treaty payments totalling $52,000 to 4,392 men, women and children from the assembled tribes. To keep things simple, the money was paid in $1 bills, brought from a bank in Fort Benton because there was no bank west of Winnipeg at the time. It bespeaks the vulnerability of the Natives that when they spent their treaty money on goods offered by traders who had gathered for the signing, the traders often gave them their change in bits of newspaper or jam bottle labels that the Natives then tried to spend with other traders.

IF THE CANADIAN authorities were pleased with the signing of the treaty, Chief Crowfoot was at this point doubly pleased. His long-time enemies, the Sioux, whom he had refused to help in their mortal struggles against the US Cavalry, were about to arrive in Canada in numbers. Without the Mounties and government on his side, Crowfoot would certainly have had more than liquor and the disappearing buffalo to worry about. Indeed, small parties of Sioux began slipping north across the border almost immediately after Treaty Seven was signed.

Numbering inthe tens of thousands, the Sioux were North America's second largest tribal group after the Algonquians – and were by far the most warlike and feared. By 1876, hunting grounds ceded to them by treaty with the US government had been trespassed upon repeatedly by road and telegraph builders and by the gold rush into the Black Hills in 1874. The Sioux, under Chief Sitting Bull, had defended their lands aggressively, creating a backlash against them led by American Brigadier-General Alfred Terry.

In late June 1876, Terry and his forces orchestrated a pincer movement against thousands of Sioux and Cheyenne in the

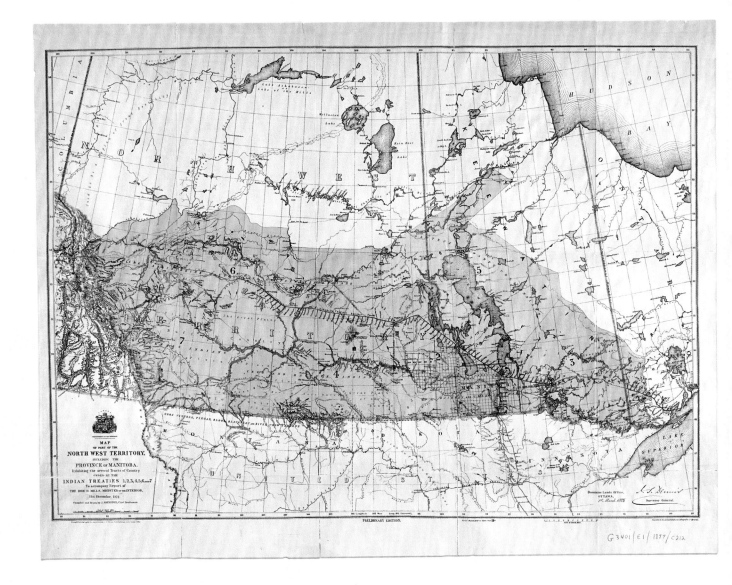

J. Johnston's map of the North-West Territories depicts the seven immense tracts of land ceded to the government by the Natives via Treaties One through Seven. The map would have been considerably more revealing had it also shown the tiny acreages onto which the various tribes would be confined from that point forward.

THE FIRST SEVEN numbered treaties between the Canadian government and the Native people were signed between 1871 and 1877. Their purpose, from the point of view of the government, was to secure land from the tribes so that settlement, railway building and industrial and agricultural development could proceed across the west. Notably, the government provided farm supplies and new clothes to help transform the Native societies from hunters and gatherers into farmers like their European counterparts.

Treaties One through Five, signed between 1871 and 1875, involved the Cree, Ojibwa and Assiniboine and took in territory that today includes much of northwestern Ontario, most of Manitoba, and southern Saskatchewan.

In return for giving up their land rights, the Natives received, among other things, cash, farming assistance, schools on reserve land and, from Treaty Three forward, the right to hunt and fish on all ceded land not used for settlement, lumbering or mining. They also, of course, received reserve land to live on — usually just 160 acres for each family of five.

In return for the aforementioned items, the Natives promised they would keep the peace and maintain law and order, and would never possess liquor on the reserves.

At a glance, Treaty Six, signed by the Plains and Woodland Cree, and taking in much of central

Saskatchewan and Alberta, is very similar to the first five. By the time it was signed, however, the government faced more resistance from the Natives, who had some very serious and justifiable concerns. One of these was that European settlers were moving onto the prairie at an alarming rate, displacing the Natives from their land; another was that the buffalo had virtually disappeared from the region, so that more and more Natives were facing starvation. A third pressing anxiety was that diseases such as smallpox were wiping out thousands of Natives across the west.

Treaty Six was also unique because it was the only treaty of its sort with a provision for health care. One clause obliged the local Indian agent to keep a medicine chest in his home where it would be perpetually available to the local people. In the years since, many activists have felt that the provision for local and immediate health care should have been extended, and should extend today, to every tribe that signed the numbered treaties, or indeed every Native person in the country.

Treaty Seven with the Blackfoot Confederacy took in the southern Alberta prairie west to the Rockies and was signed by the Blackfoot, Blood, Peigan, Sarcee and Stoneys. Treaty Seven was similar to the treaties that preceded it, with the exception that the Confederacy was more successful than other tribes had been in negotiating for

money and supplies, and there was no local health care provision as there had been in Treaty Six.

In the end, the treaties deprived the tribes not only of their freedom on the land but, eventually and indirectly, their languages, culture and spiritual practices. While in some ways the government of Canada has honoured the treaties, in many ways it has not — at least in spirit. Dozens of today's reserves are impoverished, even destitute. For most of the tribes, it has taken the better part of a century to begin reclaiming what was lost.

The negotiating of treaties in Canada did not stop with the numbered treaties signed in western Canada during the 1880s. Treaties Eight to Eleven were signed during the years from 1899 to 1921, and negotiations, both old and new, continue to this day. The photo shows several Metis men with members of the Scrip Commission, working out the details of Treaty Eight in 1899 at Fort Dunvegan, Alberta.

Valley of the Little Bighorn some three hundred miles south of Fort Walsh. However, General George Custer, unwilling to wait for the strategy to unfold, attacked Sitting Bull and the Indians prematurely. The result was that Sitting Bull's men annihilated over two hunderd and fifty cavalrymen, including Custer himself, bringing down upon the Sioux the wrath of the entire US Cavalry.

While renowned as a strategist and warrior, Sitting Bull knew at this point that his war with the Cavalry was over and that he and his people could do little more than seek asylum north of the medicine line if they were to survive. And so he gave his blessing to the northward migration.

A French-Canadian trader named Jean-Louis Legard, who had a store at Wood Mountain, was the first to encounter the hungry and disinherited migrants, a disturbing experience that he recorded years later in an account of his life in the west:

On the afternoon of 17 November the weather was cold and I was in my store with two of my men when a dozen Indians on horseback arrived and, without dismounting, came directly to the window and started looking in at us. They were completely clad in buffalo hides. They kept inspecting us that way for at least half an hour. Finally, Little Knife, their leader, came in, left the door open and watched us for a long while. Thereafter, just ignoring us, he advanced quietly to the middle of the room, sat down on the floor and called his companions one after the other.

As for me, I took care not to say a word nor to make a gesture, peacefully waiting for what they were going to do. The scene lasted two hours. All of a sudden, Little Knife jumped to his feet, came to us to shake hands and returned to his place. One of them called Crow was the speaker of the band. After turning to the four cardinal points, he said, "We have come from the American border because we could not sleep in peace there and also because we heard that the Great Woman was kind to her

Chief Sitting Bull was one of the most respected and, in his youth, most feared of the great nineteenth-century chiefs. Assistant Commissioner Irvine of the NWMP at Fort Walsh described him as a "man of somewhat short stature but with a pleasant face, a mouth showing great determination and a fine, high forehead. His speech showed him to be a man of wonderful capacity."

children." Thereafter he explained that they were in great need, which was obvious. They told me that if I would give them ammunition for hunting purposes, powder caps, tobacco, they would trade for me. In order to get rid of them without offending them I gave them merchandise for the amount of $30 and they went away.

Having evaded the US troops, Sitting Bull, too, moved north toward Canada, with his thousand-strong group.

The Mounties were on nervous alert. In the late autumn, Inspector Walsh, who had been on leave in Hot Springs, Arkansas, recovering from a severe skin inflammation, was recalled. His deputy, Inspector Lief Crozier, began patrolling the border with small groups of constables. A number of log buildings at Wood Mountain, 150 miles east of Fort Walsh, were hastily converted into an NWMP post. To assist with intelligence and communication, Walsh hired Joseph Morin, a Metis interpreter, and stationed him at Wood Mountain.

SITTING BULL.

The women of the nineteenth century tribes could make an object of beauty out of almost anything: shoes, gloves, hats, toys, jackets, harness, teepees, tools, robes. The quirt or riding crop shown here, with its bright armour of beads and its heavy ball, was used to urge a horse along, without causing it undue discomfort.

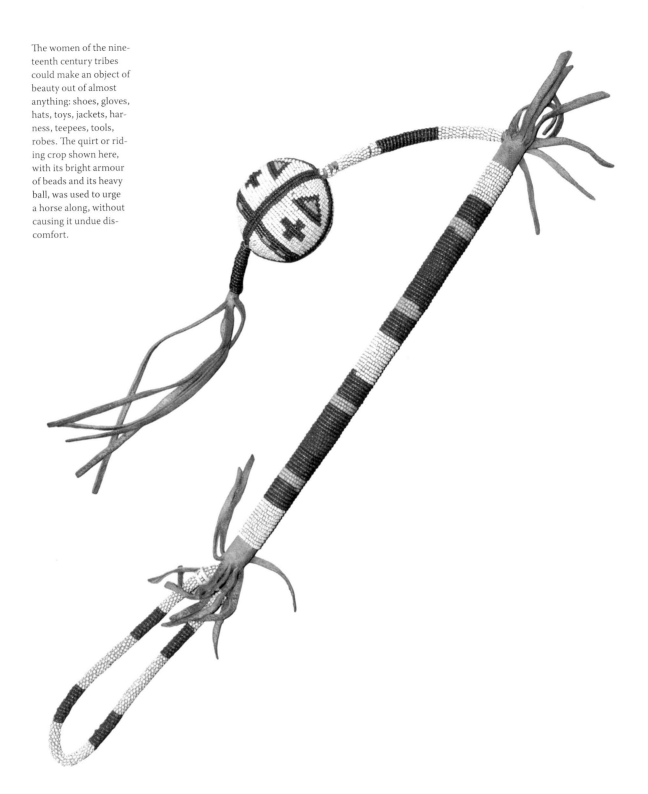

The early Mounties adapted quickly to the frigid prairie winters, as well as to available resources, and by the mid-1870s they were wearing standard-issue buffalo hats and cozy buffalo coats with collars that turned up around their ears. Moccasins were at first worn unofficially as an alternative to stiffer, colder footwear, but eventually also became standard winter garb. The dashing figure at right is Constable Alfred Aspinall, who served in the NWMP from 1896 to 1900.

THE ARRIVAL of the Sioux was no simple matter for Walsh or for the Canadian government. First, the Sioux were traditional enemies of the Saulteaux and Plains Cree, as well as the Blackfoot, which raised the spectre of conflict, especially if the tribes found themselves competing for the same scarce resources (fortunately, in the winter of 1876, there were plenty of buffalo in the Wood Mountain area). The mass arrival also had the potential to bring US troops into border skirmishes with either the Mounties or the tribesmen north of the medicine line.

Beyond all of this, the Mounties were concerned about Sitting Bull's capacity to unite a range of tribes, even his enemies, into an alliance that he would lead on raids back across the border before returning to Canada for protection. The more remote possibility was an alliance between the disaffected tribes, including the Sioux, and the Canadian Metis under Louis Riel, who was living in Montana and was believed still willing and able to strike out at the authorities he had battled in the past on behalf of his people.

Early in December, word reached Fort Walsh that some three thousand Sioux had straggled across the border and had established camp near the trading post at Wood Mountain. They had with them a remarkable thirty-five hundred horses, many of them bony from hunger, and thirty recently captured US Army mules.

Accompanied by a mere twelve constables, Inspector Walsh departed immediately on horseback for the area – a nine-day trip under difficult winter conditions. On arrival, four days before Christmas, Walsh and his officers, who were clad in buffalo-hide coats, rode straight into the great Sioux encampment where Walsh went at once into solemn council with the chiefs. The Sioux, he told them, were now in the country of the White Mother, and that while they remained here they must obey the laws. There would be no fighting, no horse theft and no raids back across the border.

The chiefs assured Walsh that they were tired, starving and sick of war. In the interest of assuring sanctuary, they reminded the Mounties of their historic ties to the British Crown and thereby to

Canada. They had fought with the British in the War of 1812, and for their loyalty they expected to be protected in the land of the Great Mother.

Throughout the winter of 1876–77, Walsh and his scouts kept up a constant reconnaissance along the border, as well as through the badlands that surrounded the valley of the Whitemud River.

More Sioux arrived – all of them hungry, some of them sick, most of them discouraged and in rags. When a band of Teton Sioux arrived in mid-winter, Walsh noted in his report that "the warriors were silent and solemn; the mothers' hearts were beating; the maidens' eyes were dim. War had made the children forget how to play." Moved by their condition, Walsh arranged to supply the Indians with ammunition for hunting and a limited amount of food.

Then late in May, a message reached Fort Walsh that another group of Sioux had entered Canada at Pinto Horse Buttes and had camped about sixty miles southeast of Fort Walsh. Their leader was none other than Sitting Bull himself.

In the days following the Duck Lake Massacre, Chief Big Bear's son Little Bear led a band of his father's followers out of Saskatchewan, across the US border and eventually to Havre, Montana, where they were safe from reprisals. Little Bear is seen here in Havre in 1896 standing above the remnants of Big Bear's band as they await deportation to Canada. Most returned to Montana and, having been denied a home for several years, settled in 1914 southwest of Havre on the Rocky Boy Reservation, created especially for the wandering Chippewa and Cree by President Woodrow Wilson.

Sitting Bull was a stocky, bow-legged medicine man, scarred by smallpox, who had gained his name after a teenage knife fight left him permanently lame. While he was often carried around in a chair, he could nonetheless ride and shoot – in fact he was renowned for his marksmanship and hunting capabilities, as well as for his courage, intelligence and indomitability.

When Walsh arrived in his camp a few days later, he shook hands with the great chief, sat down with him on the floor of his lodge and, in straight, clear language, dictated the usual terms concerning obedience to the law. In response, Sitting Bull declared that his band had buried their weapons before crossing into Canada and wanted only peace and prosperity. He then vehemently denounced the US Cavalry for all they had done to destroy his people. While the meeting was not exactly sociable, it was in fact the beginning of a trusting and supportive friendship between Walsh and Sitting Bull.

Curious about the Sioux, Assistant Commissioner Acheson Irvine decided

a week later to visit Sitting Bull himself. However, on the eve of his departure, three of Sitting Bull's warriors arrived at Fort Walsh with news that a trio of Americans had entered their camp and been taken prisoner. Sitting Bull, who was furious over the incursion, wanted advice from the Mounties about what to do about the intruders. Irvine, accompanied by Walsh and a small escort, left immediately to sort out the impasse.

Having greeted them, Sitting Bull protested the ill-treatment and lies his people had suffered in America and then verbally abused his prisoners in front of the police. Irvine, however, was not about to see the captives harmed, and recommended that they be released, which they were, lucky to be alive.

As the conclave broke up, Sitting Bull asked Irvine if the White Mother would protect the Sioux as long as they remained on Canadian soil. "As long as you obey the law," responded Irvine, "you will be safe and unmolested in Canada."

The police party spent the night in the Sioux camp – the first time in the history

...from
...F. Mac-
...sioner
...West
...e, to his
...ed Octo-
...d sent
...sh.

"My Dearest Mary,
I have just got back to this place with Sitting Bull and a lot of his Chiefs. It was quite a job getting them this far they are so very suspicious. However here they are safe within the Fort about 25 of them. I expect Genl. Terry at the Boundary on Sunday and am going out to meet him myself. I hope to get this done with them on Tuesday or Wednesday and then if possible, I will start for home. How I do look forward to getting there day and night. Winder writes by Mr. Powers that you were not well. I sincerely hope it was only that cold you spoke about. Perhaps you will see me before you see this. The messenger is waiting for my dispatches so good bye my own darling. I am as ever your own Jim."

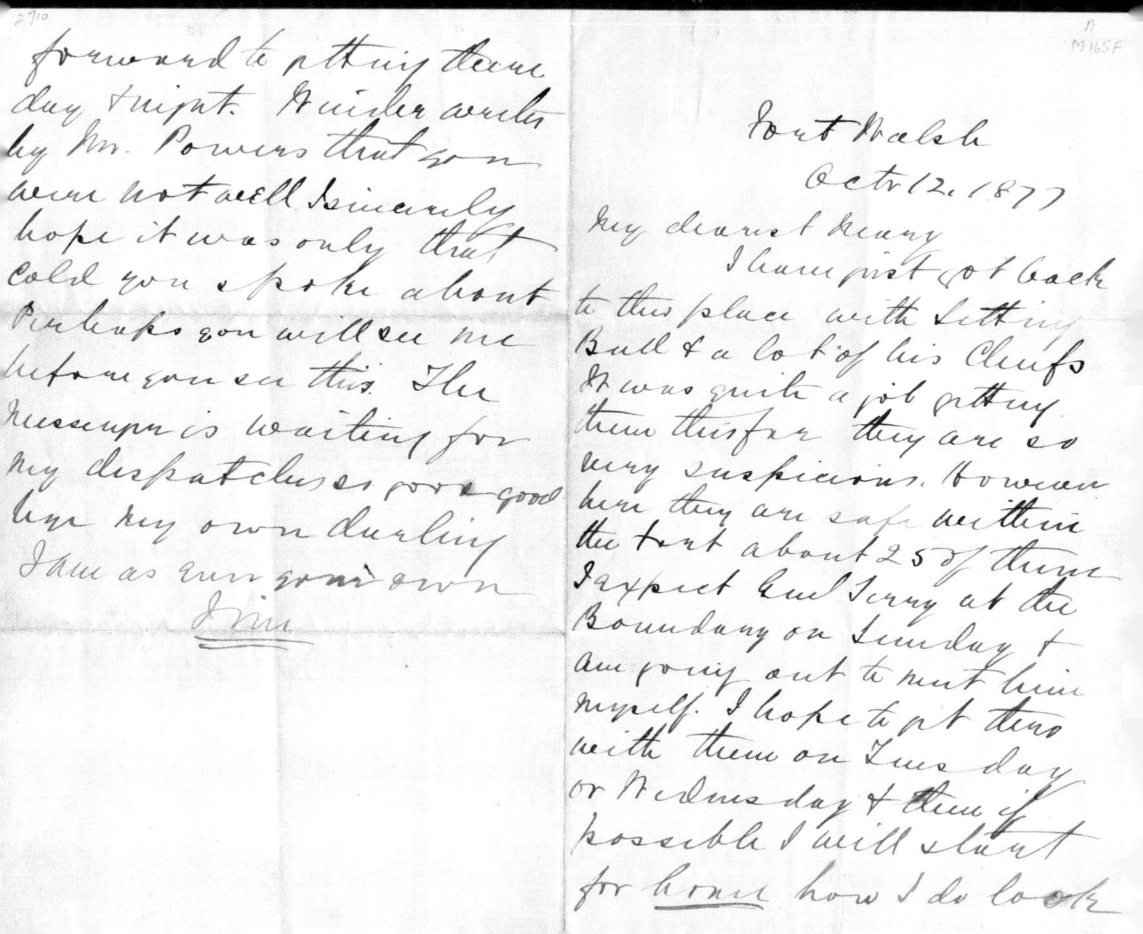

Fort Walsh
Octr 12. 1877

My dearest Mary

I have just got back to this place with Sitting Bull & a lot of his Chiefs It was quite a job getting them this far they are so very suspicious. However here they are safe within the Fort about 25 of them I expect Genl Terry at the Boundary on Sunday & am going out to meet him myself. I hope to get thro with them on Tuesday or Wednesday & then if possible I will start for home how I do look forward to getting there day & night. Winder writes by Mr. Powers that you were not well I sincerely hope it was only that cold you spoke about Perhaps you will see me before you see this. The messenger is waiting for my dispatches so good bye my own darling

I am as ever your own

Jim

Compared to the Europeans, who arrived in North America wearing relatively thick-soled footwear, the Natives of the continent wore fine-soled moccasins, which not only facilitated but symbolized their sensitivities to the intricacies and messages of the land. The richly beaded moccasins seen here were made by Cree women.

"We have to wear a badge around our arms as a protection against the Sioux. Commissioner Cameron of the Boundary Survey has concluded a treaty with them and this badge is a sign the force has gone on and is now about 50 miles ahead of us, we expect to catch up to them in two or three days."

R.B. NEVITT, assistant surgeon, North West Mounted Police, 1874

of Sioux-white relations that such hospitality had been extended or accepted. Late at night, Sitting Bull crept into Irvine's tent to describe further the depredations of the cavalry – the "Long Knives," as the Sioux called them – against his people. Before leaving, he removed his fine beaded moccasins and gave them to the assistant commissioner, a sign of his profound respect and gratitude.

Unfortunately for Sitting Bull, Irvine's respectful attitude was not shared either by Commissioner Macleod or by the Canadian government, which was anxious to see the Crown's once-loyal allies out of Canada for good. "It is important that Sitting Bull and other US Indians should be induced to return to their reservations," wrote Secretary of State R.W. Scott in a message to Macleod in early summer. "But our action should be persuasive, not compulsory."

Not until August 1877, however, was Ottawa able to convince the US government, which was glad to be rid of the Sioux, to begin negotiating their return to American soil. It took Walsh even longer

to persuade Sitting Bull to participate in the negotiations.

Almost intentionally, it seemed, the Americans approached the planned negotiations with contempt for their success. For one thing, they chose as their negotiator Brigadier-General Terry, the very man who had led the reprisals against the Sioux after the massacre at Little Big Horn. For another, during the weeks leading up to the proposed conference, the US Cavalry had been relentless in chasing toward Canada groups of Nez Perce who had refused to accept a reduced reservation in Idaho. The Nez Perce were in such poor shape when they dragged themselves across the border into Canada in the early fall of 1877 that Sitting Bull took it as a sign of what would happen to the Sioux if they returned to the US.

Even so, on October 17, in the mess hall at Fort Walsh, both Terry and Sitting Bull convened for the negotiations, which were attended by a dozen or so Sioux chiefs and by Macleod, Walsh and a number of lesser NWMP officers. Newspapermen from as far away as New York and

General Ulysses S. Grant was an American hero, whose military involvements and Civil War victories are represented on this ceremonial portrait from 1885. He was elected president of the United States in 1869. But for all his achievements and power, he was perceived by Sitting Bull and the Sioux, particularly those who had fled to Canada, as just another practitioner of the relentless discrimination and injustice that the Native people had suffered in the US through much of the nineteenth century. *Clockwise from lower left*: graduation from West Point (1843); in the tower at Capultepec (1847); drilling his volunteers (1861); the Battle of Fort Donelson (1862); the Battle of Shiloh (1862); The Battle of Chattanooga (1863); appointment as commander-in-chief by Abraham Lincoln (1864); the surrender of General Robert E. Lee at Appomattox Court House (1865).

Chicago crowded the corners of the room to witness the much-anticipated meeting of the renowned Civil War general and the world's most famous Indian.

Terry and his commissioners arrived first, followed in mid-afternoon by Sitting Bull, who was wearing a wolf-skin cap, a black-and-white polka-dot shirt, and a red arm band in honour of a son who had recently died. As Sitting Bull entered the room, he glanced contemptuously at the Americans, and to emphasize his disdain offered hearty handshakes to Walsh and Macleod. Lest his contempt for the proceedings not be perceived as total, Sitting Bull brought a woman to the gathering, which was simply not done in any serious tribal or military talks.

Terry spoke first, explaining to the chiefs that President Ulysses S. Grant wanted a "lasting peace" and had promised full pardons to all Sioux who gave up their firearms and horses and went to live peaceably on their reservations. It was reported in the press that as Terry spoke, one Sioux chief, Spotted Eagle, turned several times to the press corps and winked theatrically.

Sitting Bull replied with predictable malice, recalling the US government's history of broken promises and abuse: "For sixty-four years, you have persecuted my people. You come here to tell us lies. We do not want to hear them. You can go back. Take your lies with you. I will stay with these people. The country we came from belonged to us. You took it from us. We will live here."

Macleod then spoke, telling Sitting Bull that if the Sioux stayed they would receive none of the benefits of Canadian treaty Indians, and that contrary to what the Sioux claimed about their British loyalties, the government saw them as American Indians, not Canadian. He warned Sitting Bull that the Sioux presence was putting added pressure on the dwindling buffalo population, and that when the animals were gone, the Sioux would be reduced to begging.

Eventually the meeting broke up, having achieved nothing, and the next day General Terry returned to the US, perhaps secretly satisfied that the Sioux were where his government wanted them. For the next few days, the chiefs stayed on at the fort,

THE EARLY Mounties often got their man – at least got him arrested. But they didn't always get the courtroom conviction they hoped for.

In late November 1879, nineteen-year-old Constable Marmaduke Graburn became the first member of the force to be murdered on duty. He had been with the police just six months and was stationed at Fort Walsh.

Graburn and other constables had been herding cattle. As they returned to the fort for the night, Graburn realized that he had forgotten his axe and turned back to get it.

He did not return to the fort that night. In the morning a search party, led by Jerry Potts, went to find him. The officers and scout quickly found tracks and blood, and they eventually located Graburn's body in a shallow ravine. He had been shot in the back of the head. His horse lay nearby, shot through the skull. Melting snow made the tracking of Graburn's killer impossible.

Six months passed before a pair of Blood horse thieves imprisoned at Fort Walsh admitted that they had been camped near the fort on the night of the murder. They eventually told Superintendent Lief Crozier that a fellow Blood named Star Child had committed the crime.

At the time, Star Child was away in Montana hunting, and a year passed before Potts and four Mounties were able to arrest the young warrior in a dawn raid at a Blood camp about twenty-five miles from Fort Macleod. As Star Child's friends tried to pull him away from his captors, Corporal Robert Patterson grabbed Star Child tightly by the throat, managed to get handcuffs on him and swung up into his saddle with the half-choked man under his arm. "Ride, boys!" he shouted to his colleagues, and off they went.

But their effort was wasted. It was never determined why Star Child killed Graburn. Some speculated that Graburn happened upon him as Star Child was approaching the fort in an attempt to steal cattle or horses. Whatever the truth, in October 1881, a jury of six settlers, apparently fearing Native reprisals, deliberated for twenty-four hours and returned a verdict of not guilty. Star Child, who was considered guilty even by his own people, was free to go.

This simple limestone grave marker at Fort Walsh, Saskatchewan is a reminder not just of the short dutiful life of Constable Marmaduke Graburn but of the perils of service in the early NWMP.

The numbered treaties promised the Natives support in tough times. However, by the late 1800s, help when it came was limited by ration or merchandise certificates. The one seen here, issued to Harry White Cow of the Peigan band during the winter of 1905, limits him to $5 worth of goods, to be chosen by Harry at the store of his choice, which would then be paid by the Department of Indian Affairs, via the local Indian agent.

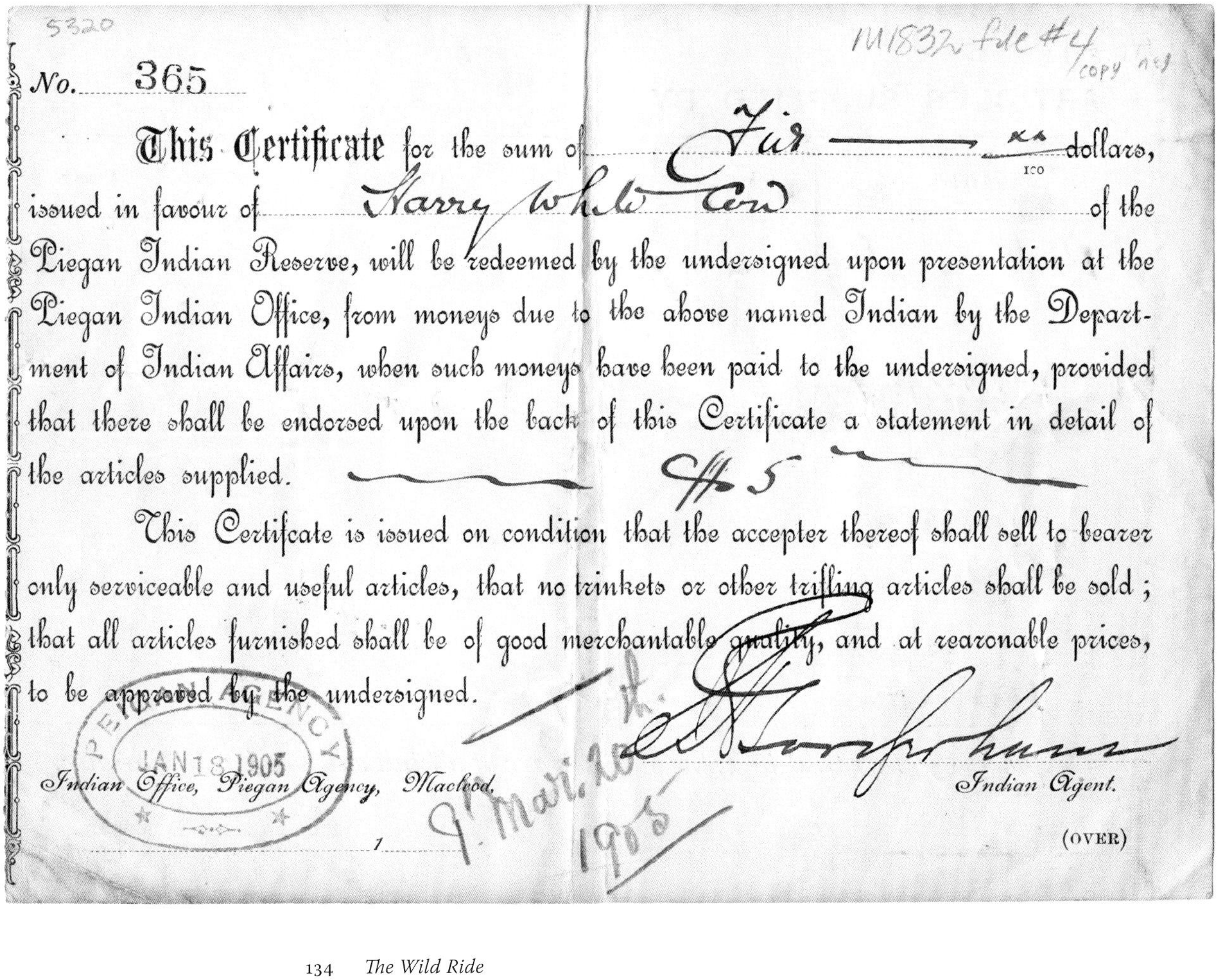

No. 365

This Certificate for the sum of Five —— xx/100 dollars, issued in favour of Harry White Cow of the Piegan Indian Reserve, will be redeemed by the undersigned upon presentation at the Piegan Indian Office, from moneys due to the above named Indian by the Department of Indian Affairs, when such moneys have been paid to the undersigned, provided that there shall be endorsed upon the back of this Certificate a statement in detail of the articles supplied. $5

This Certificate is issued on condition that the accepter thereof shall sell to bearer only serviceable and useful articles, that no trinkets or other trifling articles shall be sold; that all articles furnished shall be of good merchantable quality, and at rearonable prices, to be approved by the undersigned.

Indian Office, Piegan Agency, Macleod, 9 Mar. 1905

Indian Agent.

(OVER)

While some bands made pemmican or smoked their meat or buried it in the earth to preserve it, others sun-dried their butchered buffalo, elk or deer, which by eliminating water reduced the viability of bacteria and mould. Here, a Blood woman tends to the drying of meat on the western prairie, a less common sight as the buffalo disappeared.

where they were lavishly entertained and fed. Walsh recorded in his diary that one chief, Bear Cap, consumed pounds of rich plum pudding, overburdening his digestive system to the point where he nearly died and required emergency medical attention. By this time, Walsh's friendship with Sitting Bull was a thing of committed mutual support. Sitting Bull counted on the superintendent's advice and trust, and Walsh delighted in Sitting Bull's claim that he would not make a move without consulting him.

Meanwhile, with the Sioux in massed strength on Canadian soil, nearly two-thirds of the NWMP's total personnel, some two hundred men, were stationed in the area of Fort Walsh. Indeed, so significant had the fort become that, in 1878, it was made the headquarters of the force.

For the Sioux chiefs, the feasting that followed the conference was the last great gluttony they would enjoy for many years. The years of starvation that ensued were triggered by a light snowfall during the winter of 1877–78. The severely parched ground that resulted, and the lack of grass,

drove the dwindling herd of buffalo well south into the US. To make matters worse, American hide-hunters set grass fires behind the herds to keep them from migrating back into Canada. The northern tribes were gradually reduced to eating grass, mice and carrion – then finally their rail-thin dogs and horses.

Every police post in the north-west was besieged by starving Natives begging for food. At Fort Macleod, thousands of them were given small quantities of beef and flour every second day from the force's own supply. At Fort Calgary, Inspector Cecil Denny wrote: "It was a pitiable sight to see the parties bringing in their starving, some of them being mere skeletons. I have seen them, after I had an animal killed, rush on the carcass before the life was out of it and cut and tear off the meat, eating it raw."

A patrol from Fort Saskatchewan was approached by a group of Blackfoot who watched the police eat their meal and then leapt on the scraps, scraping and licking at the dishes and cooking pots.

The most disturbing case of starvation involved a tall, well-built Cree man

named Swift Runner who, in the spring of 1879, murdered and then ate his mother, brother, wife and five children. When questioned about the disappearance of his family and his own survival, Swift Runner claimed that he had stayed alive through the famine by boiling and eating his moose-hide teepee, while the others had died gradually of starvation. But eventually Inspector Severe Gagnon of Fort Saskatchewan found the moose-hide teepee in a tree and an array of skeletons around Swift Runner's camp. Swift Runner confessed, was tried and then hanged at the fort – the first legal execution in the North-West Territories.

At Fort Walsh alone some five thousand Sioux, Cree, Blackfoot and Bloods were begging for food. A few hundred at a time, the Sioux began drifting back across the border into the US, where they fancied their chances of survival might be better. Sitting Bull's camp was reduced to two hundred loyal followers. But still he would not return south.

Superintendent Walsh did his best to keep Sitting Bull in check, all the while

Leif Newry Fitzroy Crozier, born in Newry, Ireland, was one of the NWMP's first inspectors (1873) and for a number of years represented the force admirably in difficult relations between the Mounties and the Natives in the vicinity of Fort Walsh. As Superintendent at Fort Carlton in 1884, he attempted unsuccessfully to negotiate peace with Louis Riel and subsequently led a disastrous attack on the Metis at Duck Lake – the outcome of which blighted his career and tarnished the reputation of the Mounted Police. Crozier resigned from the force in 1886, when Prime Minister Macdonald passed him over as commissioner and appointed Lawrence Herchmer.

encouraging him to surrender to American authorities, whom he believed would deal fairly with the chief. At the same time, Walsh discouraged Sitting Bull's hopes for a reserve on Canadian soil.

Eventually, the Canadian government realized that the friendship between Walsh and the chief was actually encouraging Sitting Bull to remain in Canada, and Walsh was summarily transferred to Fort Qu'Appelle, 160 miles away. His successor, Lief Crozier, struck a harder line with the Sioux, refusing them food until they promised to return to the US.

In the spring of 1881, Sitting Bull, disconsolate and hungry, travelled to Fort Qu'Appelle to visit his friend and confidant, who it turned out was away in eastern Canada. Moving on to Wood Mountain, Sitting Bull begged for food and was told he would receive "nothing but bullets" – fired, it was implied, from a gun.

"I am cast away!" the old warrior is said to have cried out on hearing the denunciation.

With all hope vanished, Sitting Bull accepted the inevitable and, on July 21, 1881, led his pathetic band of 187 across the border, surrendering to the Americans at Fort Buford.

In the months to come, Superintendent Walsh perhaps said it best about Sitting Bull:

In my opinion he was the shrewdest and most intelligent living Indian, had the ambition of Napoleon and was brave to a fault; he was respected, as well as feared, by every Indian on the plains. In war he had no equal, in council he was superior to all. Every word said by him carried weight, was quoted and passed from camp to camp.

In Sitting Bull's absence, the Mounties turned their attention to responsibilities and tasks that had been neglected for years (their obsession with the Sioux had lasted five years). One of those tasks was the rounding up of recalcitrant groups who had refused to stay on their reserves in accordance with the treaties. And in this, the police were ruthless, refusing food to the wanderers until they were peaceably confined to their allotted lands.

A more protracted responsibility was the railway that had appeared in their midst out of the east. Its construction across the prairie was an immense step in uniting the country, but it presented a host of new challenges for the intrepid officers and constables in their now-familiar red coats.

This dramatic card, illustrating the perils faced by the early NWMP in winter, was sent by civilian W.G. McCutcheon, originally of Cornwall, Ontario, to "Miss Fawcett" in Adelaide, Australia, at some point during the early years of the Mounted Police. McCutcheon's brother Robert was a constable at Fort Walsh during the 1870s and eventually became Sheriff of Medicine Hat, Alberta. The handwriting on the front of the card says: "Was away fishing when your card came so my sister left it at a farm house a few miles from where I was and they brought it in. I have one brother in the Mounted Police so I thought I would send you one of the cards." The text on the back reads as follows: "In the great Northwest one of the duties of the Mounted Police is to patrol the country all the year round. Winter and summer the hardy constables ride from settlement to settlement, from farm to farm, gaining information, noting complaints from settlers and seeing that justice is upheld in the outlying parts – arduous and lonely duties but necessary to the building up of a law-abiding community."

Chapter Four

RAILS AND REBELLION

THE RAILWAY BROUGHT dramatic changes to the Canadian west and to the duties of the NWMP. Thousands of rail workers arrived to do the building, bringing with them labour disputes and more whisky. Towns and cities sprang up overnight and grew like Topsy with the arrival of settlers lured by the prospect of free farmland and business opportunities. Tribal lands and hunting were disrupted in ways not imagined before the era of the steel rail. Contrary to the treaties, the government attempted to push the Natives onto new reserves north of the tracks, where they were less likely to trek south into the US or to create skirmishes along the border.

In 1880, James Macleod was relieved of his duties, and Acheson Gosford Irvine, the first Canadian-born commissioner, was appointed in his place. Like Macleod, the Quebec-born Irvine had come to the force by way of the Canadian militia. Unlike MacLeod, Irvine was a slight, even delicate, man, whose red hair and beard earned him the nickname "Sorel Top."

Irvine's impeccable courtesy and democratic spirit were considered by some to be too patrician for the job of leading the sometimes unruly force in their rough-and-tumble duties.

But Irvine was a practical man, too, and within months of his appointment he successfully petitioned Ottawa to expand the force from three hundred to five hundred men. His rationale was that the Mounties had 375,000 square miles to patrol, an area bigger than France. They also had a proliferating number of farmers and townsfolk to control, as well as 27,000 Native people, many of whom were disgruntled, even vengeful, after losing their land and the buffalo.

Some bands were starving – were in fact begging the Mounties for food. This was in part because they had not taken to agriculture, as the government had hoped. "We are hunters, not farmers," Chief Crowfoot protested to the NWMP commissioner in 1883. Even in areas where small groups of Natives were enjoying modest success with their endeavours on the land, their attitudes were hardly

Below: A pair of Sarcees, looking uncannily like European settlers in their jackets and broad-brimmed hats, plow a watery field during the 1890s.

Right: With the railway moving west into traditional Native territory, the government of Canada was determined to confine the tribes to reserves and turn the one-time hunters into farmers. Here, two Blackfoot men, Frank Tried to Flay and George Left Hand, sow seed by hand.

"We had a great row about the bread a few days ago. It was cut into slices and put upon the table in plates and each one helped himself, well the natural consequence was that some got more than others, a pound of bread a day divided into three meals is not a great deal to men with prairie appetites. The early birds in this got all the worms, and those who were detained for any reason usually got none."

R.B. NEVITT, assistant surgeon, North West Mounted Police, 1874

those of the self-disciplined tiller of the soil. When wondering Indians raided a well-tended patch of turnips and potatoes on a reserve near Battleford in 1884, the reserve residents, rather than fighting the invaders, joined gaily in the "harvest," pulling up the crops and engaging in a kind of food fight, a vegetable melee, before retiring to their encampment for a feast.

THE COMING of the railway made it easier for recruits to reach the NWMP forts across the west. Unfortunately, the conditions when they got there were little improved over what they had been in the earliest days of the force. During the winter of 1881, meals at Fort Walsh included the usual green-tinged meat and bread made of flour infested with bugs and mouse dirt. At Fort Macleod, the meals got so bad that the men were forced to fend for themselves by buying supplies from the local traders.

In 1882, with the Sioux threat ended, the headquarters of the force were shifted yet again, this time to Regina, alongside the seat of the territorial government.

However, buildings at the new post – an assortment of prefabricated shacks from the US – were so lightly constructed that wash water froze solid in basins on winter nights, just as it had earlier in the flimsy barracks of Fort Macleod and Swan River. Clerks worked through the day in buffalo robes and had to thaw their ink before they could put pen to paper. The surrounding grounds were described by recruit John Donkin as "an endless mire of foot-deep mud."

Owing to shortages of riding tack, recruits at the new headquarters were forced to learn horsemanship without the benefit of stirrups, leading to rashes so severe that the men's britches were commonly soaked with blood by the end of their daily drills. The food at the new post included breakfasts of what the men called "mystery," a dish concocted largely of lumpy oats and the leftovers from the previous day's equally appalling cuisine.

At several smaller posts, the men lived through the winter in tents or, in a few cases, abandoned sod huts. Because of the lack of space – and perhaps for warmth – they often slept three or four to a bed.

Given these conditions, it was not surprising that alcohol continued to be a problem among the constables and officers. On Christmas Day 1882, at Fort Walsh, Acting Sergeant Alex Bethune and Constable Charles Scott broke into the fort's medicine locker, liberated nine gallons of whisky and brandy, and proceeded to get the entire command, plus a number of private citizens, roaring drunk.

Winter boredom at the forts could be excruciating. At the Souris River detachment in 1884, a recruit named Algernon Dyre wrote home to his brother in Manotick, Ontario, begging him to send the family dictionary so that the men would have something – anything – to read.

For some, the life was unbearable. Twenty-seven men left the force in 1883 because of sickness, either real or contrived. A bugler at Battleford gained his discharge when he complained that blowing his trumpet strained his eyes. Another constable was given his freedom when he claimed that a mysterious pain in his shoulder prevented him from shooting straight, and that he was afraid for his

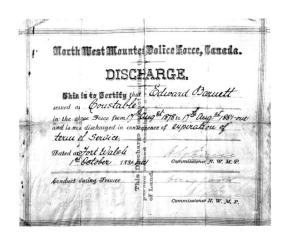

While some members of the NWMP deserted the force or were thrown out for misbehaviour, many completed three-year contracts and, in appreciation, were given land by the government of Canada. Constable Edward Barnett, whose discharge certificate is seen here, completed his contract in 1881.

fellow policemen when he had a gun in his hands.

Regular desertions also occurred. In 1883, twenty-five constables deserted the force outright, and during a single month in 1884, Fort Macleod alone lost eleven men.

One of the problems in maintaining order was that the men's jobs and responsibilities were so ill-defined. Commissioner Irvine was aware of the deficiency, and when Inspector Richard Deane joined the Mounties in the summer of 1883, his immediate assignment was to investigate the lack of standardized procedures and draft a list of standing orders that would apply to every rank at every level of the force.

Deane would eventually report that one of the constables he talked to had been assigned to ride the trains, which he had been doing for a year with no idea whatsoever of any specific duties. The constable, as it turned out, had spent most of the year acquiring land titles from Metis travellers, each for just enough money to cover the cost of a bottle of liquor. The constable had not filed a single written report on his activities. Operating procedures were so

loose that many among the ranks simply kept the fines they imposed, or split them with the post administration. Confiscated liquor became the life of the force's parties.

THE CONSTRUCTION of the transcontinental railway had been talked about for ten years. Indeed, British Columbia had joined Confederation in 1871 on the understanding that a railway would link the new province to eastern Canada within a decade. Had the government of Sir John A. Macdonald maintained power throughout the intervening years, the line would probably have been built sooner. But once Parliament and the Canadian Pacific Railway (CPR) committed to construction in February 1879, the vast and ambitious engineering project moved forward at breakneck speed.

With a $25-million subsidy, the CPR began work that spring. On the west coast, some twenty-two thousand men, many of them brought from China, began dynamiting their way east through the mountains. Passage through the mountains would ultimately require construction of

IN 1879, the government of Canada started construction on the western section of the CPR. A New York entrepreneur, Andrew Onderdonk, was awarded the contract to build the railway through the mountainous terrain from Port Moody on the Pacific Ocean to Eagle Pass near Revelstoke.

Even before railway construction began, a number of Chinese workers had migrated north from California, and the residents of British Columbia were afraid that these Chinese would take their jobs. As anti-Chinese feeling grew, Onderdonk assured the community that he would hire North Americans first. But when many of the Caucasian workers proved to be unreliable, Onderdonk proceeded to hire Chinese labourers, recruited from both San Francisco and Portland, and later from Hong Kong.

The wages for Chinese workers were $1.00 a day, from which they had to purchase their own camping and cooking gear. In contrast, Caucasian labourers were paid up to $2.50 a day and did not have to pay for their gear.

Many Chinese workers died from the exhaustion of working dawn to dusk and walking as much as thirty miles a day back and forth between the job site and the work camp. Some perished in rock explosions or were buried in collapsed tunnels. Many others drowned due to the collapse of unfinished bridges. The Canadian winter was a trauma unto itself for workers from a largely temperate climate. Many more died from scurvy and malnutrition. Chinese workers were routinely dismissed and rehired depending on weather and the whims of the contractor.

When the last spike was driven in November 1885, not a single Chinese worker was invited to attend this historic ceremony. Instead, most of them were simply let go. Some went back to China while others found work in industries such as forestry, food processing and mining. Others founded restaurants or laundries. Many moved to the eastern provinces.

During the years after the completion of the railway, a number of BC newspapers, politicians and labour groups pressured the government of Canada to exclude the Chinese entirely from Canadian life. In response, the federal government enacted the Chinese Immigration Act, imposing a "head tax" of $50 on all Chinese entering Canada. At first, the regulation proved effective, but only for five years. By 1890, the number of immigrants began increasing. In 1900, fearing an "oriental invasion," the government raised the head tax to $100, and in 1904 to $500 (the equivalent today of $8,000).

Today, the Chinese are an important and respected part of the culture of the country. But it was only through the persistence of Chinese-Canadians and their forward-thinking supporters that attitudes were gradually reversed, bigoted laws revoked, and the Chinese were able to their rightful place as Canadian citizens and nation builders.

James Weston's cartoon from April 1879 depicts BC Member of Parliament Amor de Cosmos forcing a "Heathe Chinee" back where he came from. Canadian bigotry of the day was based on fear the Chinese would take jobs that might otherwise go to "honest" Canadians and the fact that Chinese men didn't look, sound or behave like Canadian men. As de Cosmos explains to the man in his grip, "You won't drink whiskey, and talk politics and vote like us."

Below: As rail was laid through the mountains of British Columbia, the CPR built heavy-timbered sheds, sometimes half a mile in length, to protect the track in areas where it was vulnerable to snow or landslides.

Right: A temporary trestle built of unfinished timber spans the Pic River east of Heron Bay in northwestern Ontario. Such structures were constructed to make a line operational in the shortest possible time and were usually replaced later by structures of finished timber or steel. This particular span, built in 1885, was more than eighty feet high and some six hundred feet long.

The first railway train in Winnipeg arrived on October 9, 1877 – by water! The locomotive, named the *Countess of Dufferin* and belonging to railway contractor Joseph Whitehead, was shipped down the Red River from Fisher's Landing, Minnesota, along with six flatcars and a caboose, aboard the barge SS *Selkirk*. Trains from the east would not arrive until the line was completed in 1885, but the *Countess* was in use by 1881 in the construction of the rail line across the prairie.

six hundred bridges and trestles, as well as twenty-seven tunnels through solid rock. To prevent floods from washing away the track, every inch that was laid had to be constructed on cribs of buried stone. Snowdrifts as deep as forty feet, as well as frequent avalanches, obliged the construction of heavy wooden snowsheds over much of the track through the Selkirk mountain range. At times, progress was as slow as six feet a day. On average, at least two men died for every mile of progress. As one writer put it, "Dynamite claimed many of them in a blast of red mist." Some were crushed by falling or exploded rock; others fell from trestles or drowned in flood-swollen rivers.

In the east, at the other end of the line, more than seven thousand men moved the track west from Lake Superior, working at such a phenomenal pace that by the end of 1882 some six hundred miles of railway existed between the Lakehead and what is now Colley, Saskatchewan. Another year took construction to Calgary.

To keep the railway from being buried in drifted snow, the tracks across the prairie were laid on four-foot-high embankments flanked by twenty-foot-wide ditches. This ambitious project was the making of dozens of prairie towns – and the remaking of others. Within months after the arrival of the railway, Calgary, for example, expanded from an isolated fort into a lively little city with banks, churches and schools – and, of course, brothels and saloons.

In areas perceived to be ideal townsites along the railway's planned path, squatters put up tents and waited to see precisely where the track was going to run. When it arrived, they built permanent buildings alongside it.

But just as some towns were created by the railway, others were doomed by its arrival. Battleford, for example, was bypassed well to the south, resulting in a shift of the territorial capital to the rail-serviced site of an old tribal hunting camp named Pile of Bones, soon after redubbed Regina.

DESPITE THEIR ENFORCED move onto reserves, the Natives still hunted widely, and objected with vehemence to the

The great Cree chief Piapot resisted not only the building of the railway but the Canadian government's attempts to supress Native belief systems. Years after the creation of the reserves during the 1880s, Piapot's people continued to hold an annual Sun Dance, which the government had declared an unlawful act. Piapot was ousted as chief by government officials when he would not use his authority to stop these ceremonies. Only in 1901, when Piapot was eighty-five, did the government belatedly recognize his authority as chief.

railway passing through territory, such as the Cypress Hills, where by treaty they had been granted freedom to hunt. Had the local Cree and Assiniboine not been destitute, they would undoubtedly have mounted a more vigorous campaign against the coming of the trains and the presence of the NWMP constables who protected the line. It is indicative of the control the police had over the hungry Natives that just one constable, Daniel "Peach" Davis (so named for his love of canned fruit), was put in charge of escorting a thousand or more Assiniboine some 250 miles from Fort Walsh to their new reserve well north of the railway. Davis succeeded in the long march by moving the provision wagons a few miles ahead of the procession so that his charges would be persuaded to keep moving.

Despite such acquiescence, the Cree chief Piapot decided in 1882 to make at least a symbolic gesture of defiance by uprooting the CPR's survey stakes for forty miles across the flatlands west of Moose Jaw. A few months later, he pitched his entire camp, some sixty occupied lodges, in the path of a rail construction crew at Maple Lake. A young NWMP constable bearing the rather apt name of Billy Wilde was sent with another constable to move Piapot along. With great self-confidence, Wilde rode into the Cree camp and, surrounded by warriors, took out his watch and told the recalcitrant chief that he had exactly fifteen minutes to get his show on the road. Immediately, the warriors began to insult and jostle Wilde and his fellow constable, who for the next quarter hour sat unperturbed on their horses. Eventually, Wilde glanced at his watch and called cheerfully that time was up. Having dismounted, he walked straight up to Piapot's lodge and yanked out the centre pole, collapsing the decorated buffalo skins on the startled women inside.

As the warriors watched, dumbfounded, the two Mounties strode through the camp, collapsing every lodge. Respecting courage above all other traits, the Cree were so impressed by the constables' appearance of fearlessness and invincibility that they yielded without protest, and Piapot ordered his people to break camp and move on.

Below: A lone armed Mountie guards the end of the rail line as construction advances west toward the Rockies.

Right: The pillbox hat was a distinctive part of the early NWMP uniform but was worn chiefly for ceremonial or dress purposes, as it provided neither comfort nor warmth nor protection from sun or rain. As seen below, the pillbox was at least occasionally worn on duty.

Cree chief Poundmaker, or *Pitikwahanapiwiyin*, emerged as a political leader during the tumultuous years surrounding the signing of Treaties Six and Seven and the influx of settlers into present-day Saskatchewan. He was recognized as a skilled orator and leader by both Native and non-Native communities and, in July 1881, acted as a guide and interpreter during Governor General Lord Lorne's trip from Battleford to Calgary. This portrait was taken in 1885 at Stoney Mountain Penitentiary after he was tried for treason for supporting Riel during the North-West Rebellion.

THE FIRST RENOWNED passenger on the western portion of the CPR was Canada's governor general, John Campbell, the Marquess of Lorne, who in 1881 took the train to the end of the line at Portage la Prairie. He then travelled by steamer up the Assiniboine River to Fort Ellice, where he was received by the fort's twenty-strong NWMP detachment. From that point west, the detachment became the governor general's official escort. At Battleford, the party was joined by Chief Poundmaker, a striking-looking young leader, who would accompany Lord Lorne to Calgary.

Poundmaker was a model of what the proud Native could be – courageous, outgoing and handsome. However, if the governor general expected the chief to be a skilled hunter in the Native tradition, his expectations went unmet. At one point, Poundmaker tried and failed twice to shoot down a duck from a good-sized flock at close range. And when he participated in a hunt for buffalo – the last buffalo hunt on record – he was again unable to bring down an animal.

At Blackfoot Crossing, several thousand Blackfoot, led by Chief Crowfoot, came out to entertain the governor general with displays of dancing and horsemanship. During a grand council afterward, one of the Blackfoot chiefs, Loud Voice, harangued His Excellency at great length. Having completed his tirade, Loud Voice shook the governor general's hand and sat down. At once, all eyes turned to the translator, Jerry Potts, for a full articulation of this obviously significant address. Potts fidgeted for a few seconds, eventually found his voice, and is reported to have said softly, "He wants grub." And that was all.

Lord Lorne's journey ended at Fort Shaw, Montana, where he was greeted by US soldiers and their wives, one of whom wrote admiringly in her diary of "the gorgeously dressed Mounties with their jaunty side-tilted caps." However, she was less impressed by the detachment's hard-driven horses, which she called "wretched little beasts, underfed and clearly overworked."

THE EXPANSION of the force in 1882 couldn't have come at a better time, given the challenges that then faced the Mounties, including general responsibility for maintaining control along the tracks. On a typical day, this could mean anything from putting out a fire started by live coals from the engine, to arresting a con man who had stolen money from fellow travellers, to intercepting a shipment of alcohol being smuggled from the east.

At times, the sheer number of arriving passengers threatened to overwhelm the beleaguered force. When the police had come west ten years earlier, settlers numbered in the hundreds. Now, some thirty-five thousand new arrivals required everything from arbitration in land disputes, to life-saving health care, to protection from horse and cattle thieves.

The alcohol prohibition that existed during the 1870s became increasingly difficult to sustain. The smuggling of liquor was both rampant and ingenious in its variety of methods. Contraband liquor entered the territory in containers that ranged from hollowed-out Bibles to upholstered furniture to false-bottomed molasses and sugar barrels. On one

Below: Thirty-eight-year-old British painter and print-maker Sidney Prior Hall accompanied Canada's governor general, the Marquess of Lorne, on his western journey in 1881. This pastel sketch, based on a pencil drawing Hall did during the trip, became the basis for his famous painting "Pow-wow at Blackfoot Crossing," which depicted Chief Crowfoot addressing the Marquess and his entourage.

Right: With his appointment as governor general in 1878, the Marquess of Lorne brought royalty to Rideau Hall for the first time, in the person of his wife, Princess Louise, the fourth daughter of Queen Victoria. The Marquess was a poet, an essayist and a significant patron of the arts in Canada. His marriage to Princess Louise in 1871 made him the first commoner in 350 years to marry a member of the British royal family.

Below: Anxious to populate the prairie, as well as to provide the railway with people to carry and to service (manufactured goods west, agricultural products east), the CPR and the Canadian government colluded through the early 1900s to see that colonists got easy passage into the country and workable farms once they reached the west. Here, a party of US farmers from Colorado arrives at Bassano, Alberta.

Right: While spartan, the colonist sleeping cars introduced by the CPR in 1884 were a decided improvement over ordinary day coaches for transporting immigrants to the west. Life for the settlers often got considerably less comfortable upon arrival.

Early NWMP detachments in British Columbia, such as this one at Beavermouth, in 1885, had the unenviable task of policing the wildly drunken little settlements that grew up along the advancing CPR route during the mid-1880s. Left to right, sitting and standing are: Sergeant Fury, Sergeant Cudlin, Constable Purchase, Constable Racey, Inspector Sam Steele, Constable Leslie, Sergeant Fane, Constable Kerr, Constable Pennefather. Left to right, lying: Constable Flynn, Constable Fleming.

occasion a coffin full of liquor was taken from a train and paraded past an honour guard of Mounties, who stood with heads bowed. On another the police opened two barrels of oatmeal destined for the Reverend Leo Gaetz of Calgary, discovering in the process that each contained ten gallons of whisky.

In 1883, an editorialist for the Regina *Leader* complained with characteristic racism that prohibition was "never intended for civilization but for the suppression of nefarious traffic amongst the Indians." Commissioner Irvine pointed out in a report to Ottawa that "the suppression of alcohol traffic is the most disagreeable duty the police are called upon to perform." Constable John Donkin noted in his diary that "any officer who persistently prosecutes for this offence is looked upon with contempt." If for no other reason, the police wanted an end to prohibition so that they could more easily obtain liquor for themselves.

As more settlers arrived and the non-Native population grew, relations between the police and the Natives deteriorated. Not only were the latter confined in their hunting and living arrangements, they were under pressure to abandon the spiritual beliefs that had sustained them for generations. Their tribal dances and initiation rites, while not exactly prohibited, were discouraged. Meanwhile, American Indians, in greater numbers than ever, were crossing the border and stealing horses – sometimes from the police themselves. But there were too few Mounties in the area of Fort Walsh to do anything about it.

Across the prairie, starvation continued to plague the Natives. It was surely one of the Conservative government's less thoughtful acts to cut back resources to the Indian Department in 1883. The result was significantly reduced rations for the tribes and fewer agents to look after their proliferating needs.

On the rail line itself, the police stationed two or three constables at each construction camp to keep crime and drunkenness to a minimum. As the railheads from east and west grew ever closer together in the Rocky Mountains, and people poured into the area, a mobile twenty-five-man

OF COURSE IT HURTS!

As early as the late 1800s, westerners shipping agricultural products east were disconcerted by the way the CPR favoured eastern manufacturers, who were given reduced rates to move finished goods west. This cartoon, which appeared in the Regina Leader *in 1912, criticizes the relationship between eastern industrialists and the administration of the railway.*

detachment under Inspector Sam Steele was established to assist smaller detachments in the rough camps and boom towns of British Columbia. The group's work was aided somewhat by a law prohibiting the sale of liquor in a twenty-mile-wide zone that ran the length of the railway. The law's shortcoming was that it did not prohibit the drinking of liquor in the zone.

As winter descended in late 1884, Steele set up his headquarters high in the Rockies at a little shantytown called Beaver River, west of Kicking Horse Pass. The approach of the construction gangs from both east and west had been the making of this settlement of rickety boarding houses and all-night saloons. Located just outside the railway's prohibition zone, the shantytown was a non-stop ruckus of partying, prostitution and petty crime. According to Sam Steele, "The people of Beaver River and places like it lived by preying upon the navvies who appeared among them on pay day and got drunk."

The rail workers in the area were both restless and exhausted by this point in their commitment to the project. The

work, which went on seven days a week, was excruciatingly difficult and dangerous. And the amenities were few. As at the NWMP forts, the food was an iniquitous imposition of half-rotten potatoes, rancid meat and weak tea. Blizzards were frequent. Clothing was inadequate. Many of the men worked drunk.

To top off the indignities and hardships, work gangs in the area were not paid regularly, sometimes not for weeks. Nevertheless, serious trouble was avoided until March 1885, when a delegation of labourers came to Steele to protest their situation, threatening a mass strike if overdue wages were not paid immediately. Steele, fearing a strike could turn into a riot, begged the men to be patient. But in private he notified Ottawa, informing the government that he feared the worst.

As the unrest escalated, Steele happened to take ill with a fever and could not get out of bed. When twelve hundred navvies walked away from their jobs in protest on April 1, the superintendent warned their representatives against the violence they had threatened. While some of them

Given the toboggan on the roof and the skewed angles of everything from the chimneys and telegraph pole to the logs and roof line, this early telegraph station at Humboldt, Saskatchewan, might have passed for a whisky trader's shack. Governor General Lord Lorne's personal body guard, Major Frederick Denison of the Canadian Militia (centre, seated), relaxes in the heat during Lord Lorne's tour of the west in 1881.

The carousing was fierce in British Columbia's mountain camps and villages as track was laid through the Rockies and Coastal Range during the mid-1880s. This impressively constructed log cabin – the Edd and Joe Q.T. Saloon – was a partying base for men and women alike in the working settlement of Donald, BC.

The standard-issue Winchester 1876 carbine was used by the NWMP from 1878 until 1914. Made in the US, the carbine was famous for its versatility and was produced in such quantities that it eventually became an all but ubiquitous sight on the prairie and plains and was nicknamed "the gun that won the west."

were persuaded to return to work, the others, armed and egged on by mischief-makers in the shantytown, headed out along the tracks to where they hoped to disrupt and intimidate the teamsters and track-laying crews who had returned to their jobs or who had never left. The strikers managed to stop a trainload of workers who were headed for the railhead. However, James Ross, the man in charge of construction, boarded the engine himself, ordered full steam ahead and drove through the mob as bullets bounced off the cab.

Steele immediately sent eight of the twenty-five men at his disposal to protect those who had remained on the job. The others were on duty elsewhere. The constables were led by Steele's assistant, a tenacious little sergeant named Billy Fury, who guided his men through the surrounding wilderness to a narrow pass along the tracks. There they hoped to block the strikers from getting to the railhead and carrying out their plans.

Eventually, the strikers advanced on the tiny contingent, firing their guns into the air and screaming threats. Fury hollered back that the strikers should turn around or he would shoot them in their tracks. After much milling and confusion among the strikers, and continued threats from Billy Fury, the chastened and intimidated strikers turned and walked back to Beaver River, allowing the rail builders to finish their day's work.

Later the same day, one of the constables, a young man named Kerr, spotted someone in the settlement attempting to incite the strikers to violence. In attempting to arrest the provocateur, Kerr was roughed up by someone in the crowd. On hearing news of the altercation, Steele sent Fury and a pair of constables to make an arrest. Steele described in his memoirs what happened next:

After a long interval, Fury returned with his jacket torn, his face bloodied, saying as he entered, "They took the prisoner from us, Sir." I replied, "That's too bad. Take your revolvers and shoot anyone who interferes with the arrest!" The local magistrate, George Johnston, who had been visiting me, went to the window and watched the party cross the bridge which connected our barracks with the town.

Within minutes, Steele and Johnston heard a shot and assumed the accused had either been arrested or killed. Then the pair saw two constables dragging the prisoner toward the bridge, pursued by a local prostitute who was shrieking at them in protest. Despite being barely able to walk, Steele rose from his bed and headed out the door, ordering Johnston to fetch the house copy of the *Riot Act* and join him at the scene of the action.

"Seizing the Winchester rifle from the constable on guard at the gaol," wrote Steele, "I ran to the bridge, and as the crowd was on the point of making a rush onto it, I covered them with the rifle and called upon them to halt or I would fire."

By this time, the prisoner had been knocked unconscious by one of the constables. The strikers had fire in their eyes and in some cases firewater on their breath. Johnston arrived quickly, brandishing the *Riot Act.*

"Our Sovereign Lord the King chargeth and commandeth all persons, being assembled, immediately to disperse themselves, and peaceably depart to their habitations, or to their lawful business, upon the pains contained in the Act made in the first year of King George the First for preventing tumults and riotous assemblies."

Riot Act proclamation, 1715

A shortcoming of the standard-issue one-size-fits-all handcuffs was that men and women with tiny hands were occasionally able to slip them off. This pair of forged steel cuffs was stolen from an NWMP constable in the Cypress Hills near Fort Walsh during the mid-1880s. They were later recovered from a prisoner's clothing while he was being escorted to the guard room at the nearby Medicine Lodge posting.

Below: While the iconic photo of the driving of the last Canadian Pacific Railway spike features the white-bearded railway executive Donald A. Smith wielding the sledgehammer, the less familiar photo below shows an unnamed CPR employee, perhaps an engineer or surveyor, doing the ceremonial pounding near Donald, BC, on November 7, 1885.

Two NWMP officers were present at the occasion, one of them visible directly above the man holding the tie in place.

Right: Donald A. Smith (ultimately Lord Strathcona) was a Hudson's Bay Company trader who, in 1874, became the company's chief commissioner and, in 1889, its governor. He was also a politician, financier and railway builder who saw tremendous value in a national railway in the development of the Dominion of Canada. Of Scottish origin, Smith was part of the original CPR syndicate, and eventually became a major shareholder in the company and, in 1883, a CPR director. He was never appointed CPR president, as he'd anticipated, but he is immortalized in the history of both the company and the country by the famous photo of him driving the last spike in the transcontinental railway, at Craigellachie, BC, on November 7, 1885, just nine days before the hanging of Riel in Regina.

For a brief period during the mid and late 1880s, new trains and historic Red River carts could both be seen crossing the prairie laden with goods. But the trains gradually wiped out any need for the Metis conveyances, seen here in Calgary in 1888 laden with $75,000 worth of furs.

"Listen to this," cried Steele to the crowd, "and keep your hands off your guns!" He then ordered Johnston to read the part of the act that instructed groups "unlawfully, riotously, and tumultuously assembled" to disperse. To underscore the magistrate's warning, eight Mounties cocked their loaded rifles. Steele, in weakening voice, told the crowd, "If I find more than twelve of you standing together or in any large group I will open fire upon you and mow you down! Now disperse at once and behave yourselves!"

"By the next day," Steele wrote in his report to the commissioner, "the area was as quiet as a country village on a Sunday morning at dawn."

Just days later, the overdue wages arrived, and, thanks to Inspector Steele, the building of the line through the Rockies entered its last laborious phase under a modest though peaceable truce.

SIX MONTHS LATER, the converging lines were united high in the mountains of British Columbia. Already, William Van Horne, the general manager of the CPR,

had written to Commissioner Irvine and expressed his gratitude for the role the Mounties had played in bringing the railway into being. "Without the existence of the officers and men of the splendid force under your command it would have been impossible to have accomplished so much as we did. On no great work within my knowledge where so many have been employed has such perfect order prevailed."

On November 7, 1885, Van Horne and other officials stood with dozens of labourers and civilians at Craigellachie, where Smith, the eldest of the railroad's directors, drove the final spike into the last of nearly a million ties laid across the country. A silence is said to have descended on the crowd as the hammering stopped. "It seemed as if this last symbolic performance had worked a spell on all present," recalled Sir Sandford Fleming, another of the railway's directors.

Then a cheer broke out, and the crowd demanded a speech from Van Horne who, after years of guiding the project, could tell his audience only that he believed the work had been done "well in every way" and

was a credit to the great land it had united.

WHILE THE WORK may have been a credit to the land, the transcontinental railway was by no means universally appreciated. A thousand miles to the east, hundreds of Metis were as disturbed by the advances of civilization as Van Horne was pleased. As the frontier moved forward, many Metis had moved west ahead of the tide, settling along the north and south branches of the Saskatchewan River. But with the coming of the railway, they were again under pressure, this time from land speculators and homesteaders who were arriving by the thousands. To make matters worse, the railway was rapidly eliminating their lucrative freight-carrying operations.

As far as the Canadian government was concerned, the Metis had no more right to their fields, which they considered an ancestral entitlement, than did any settler arriving by train to establish a farmstead. Eventually, Ottawa agreed in theory that the Metis indeed had a natural right to the land that they had improved for generations.

Gabriel Dumont was in many ways the archetype of the nineteenth-century Metis male: a superior hunter and scout, as tough a soldier as existed on the prairies, and a believer in the spirit and destiny of his people. He was also a legendary gambler and drinker. Dumont is seen here at Fort Assiniboine in 1885, prior to joining the Buffalo Bill's Wild West Show, where he was promoted quite accurately as a crack marksman and fearless rebel leader.

This albumen portrait of Louis Riel was probably taken as he travelled to Keeseville, New York, in early 1878, following his release from the asylum in Beauport, Quebec. The photograph is in the *cartes-de-visite* format, and is one of very few signed photos of the Metis visionary.

However, the government was slow to survey the lands in question, and slower still to issue title. When the surveyors did apply themselves to Metis land, they chopped it up into squares with no water access, rather than leaving it in the water-accessible strips that the Metis preferred.

Time and again the Metis petitioned Ottawa for fair surveys and prompt title – and for a voice in their own affairs. By 1884, rancour among the Metis had reached such a pitch that, in utter frustration, they turned to the man who had so courageously represented their cause in the past, the exiled Louis Riel.

Since his banishment from Canada fifteen years earlier, Riel, now forty years old, had wandered the US plains, increasingly given to mystic visions and opinionated diatribes. He had become a US citizen, had married a Metis woman named Marguerite Monet, and in 1884 was teaching Indian children in a mission school at Judith Basin, Montana.

Riel had long believed privately that he was God's chosen instrument for the deliverance of the Metis. He claimed once to have been visited by a heavenly spectre that had wakened him in the night and intoned the words, "Rise up, Louis David Riel! You have a mission to fulfill."

So he could hardly have been surprised on Sunday, June 4, 1884, when he was called from a church service to meet four horsemen who had come from afar with a request that he take up the cause of his people. The leader of the visitors was a forty-seven-year-old legend named Gabriel Dumont, whose admirers called him "the prince of the prairies." He was a horseman, sharpshooter and long-time leader of the Metis buffalo hunt. Sam Steele would eventually write of Dumont, "One could travel the plains from one end to the other and never hear an unkind word said of him. He would kill bison by the score and give them to those who were either unable to kill or had no buffalo…When in trouble the cry of all was for Gabriel."

But Dumont had no gift for oratory or political leadership and did not speak English or even French with any great skill. That is why he and his companions had ridden seven hundred miles from the

The Metis flag is Canada's oldest indigenously created flag, having appeared first at about the time of the Battle of Seven Oaks in 1816. The red background is associated with Metis who worked with the Hudson's Bay Company, while the blue, the official flag of the Metis National Assembly, hearkens to those who worked with the North West Company of fur traders. The infinity sign is said to represent the faith, harboured by the culture, that it will live forever. Alternatively, it is said to be two circles representing the founding cultures of the Metis: Native North American and European (primarily French). The red flag is now the provincial ensign of the Metis Nation of Alberta.

Saskatchewan River Valley to enlist the man who could do what Dumont could not.

Assured that both French- and English-speaking Metis, as well as Indians, would rally to his side, Riel packed his wife, two children and their minimal possessions on a Red River cart and, accompanied by Dumont and friends, embarked immediately for the north.

In early July, after nearly a month on the trail, the party of eight arrived to a great celebration in Batoche, the major Metis settlement on the South Saskatchewan River. There, over the next few months, Riel spent his time addressing meetings, urging his brethren to defend their traditions and petitioning Ottawa for proper rights for his people. Among his demands were appropriate surveys and title to farmland, representation in the Dominion Parliament and a new railway linking the Saskatchewan River Valley to ports on Hudson Bay.

By February, however, Riel, having had no satisfactory response, became convinced that further petitioning was useless. As a result, on March 5, he and

Dumont announced that the Metis were "going to take up arms for the glory of God, the honour of religion and for the salvation of our souls."

Riel was not above a bit of chicanery in rallying his forces. On March 15, realizing that a partial eclipse of the sun was to take place, he told a meeting of hunters and settlers that God would now let them know he was behind their endeavours by drawing his hand over the face of the sun. On cue, the day darkened.

A few days later, Riel repeated the bold move he had made at Red River years earlier and declared himself head of the provisional government of Saskatchewan. Immediately, Dumont began organizing an army of two hundred tough Metis into squadrons of cavalry. The Cree, led by Poundmaker and Big Bear, expressed their support for the revolt. Chief Crowfoot, however, refused to participate, declaring once again his allegiance to the White Mother and her mounted forces.

Intent on impressing Ottawa, the guerrillas went to work, cutting the telegraph line at Batoche, seizing government stores

Chief Poundmaker with his fourth wife outside their teepee during their last weeks together, in 1885, in what is now central Saskatchewan. Poundmaker would shortly go to prison for his role in the 1885 rebellion and would die in Alberta upon his release in 1886, in the care of his stepfather, Chief Crowfoot.

THE GREAT Cree chief Poundmaker inherited his unusual name from his grandfather who, it is said, was able to coax buffalo into a pound or corral with his sweet high-pitched singing. Born in 1842 in what is now central Saskatchewan, Poundmaker saw many changes during his short life – the disappearance of the buffalo, the coming of the railway, the diminishment of his people from proud hunters to impoverished reserve dwellers. Through it all, however, the legendarily handsome chief maintained his dignity, as well as his sense of fair play.

Poundmaker came to prominence in 1873 when, at age thirty-one, he was adopted by Chief Crowfoot of the Blackfoot Confederacy. The move cemented ties between the Blackfoot and Cree and ended the tribes' quarrelling over the right to hunt the few remaining buffalo.

As a negotiator on Treaty Six, Poundmaker first resisted then accepted the treaty, but eventually complained bitterly that the government did not keep its promise of support for his people.

While the history books suggest that Poundmaker and his warriors looted Battleford during the North-West Rebellion as the people of the town sheltered in the nearby NWMP fort, there are also reports that the looting was done earlier by non-Natives or by Stoneys, and that Poundmaker tried to stop them.

A few weeks later, 332 Canadian troops attacked Poundmaker's camp near Cut Knife Hill. When the Cree opened fire, forcing the soldiers to retreat, Poundmaker, who had not personally been involved, prevented his warriors from pursuing the troops, thus saving many lives.

Nevertheless, Poundmaker was eventually tried for treason for his nominal support of Riel during the rebellion, and was sentenced to three years in Stoney Mountain Penitentiary.

At his trial he said, "Everything that is bad has been laid against me this summer. But there is nothing of it true...Had I wanted war, I would not be here now...You did not catch me. I gave myself up. You have got me because I wanted justice."

Poundmaker's one request in prison, that the guards not cut his hair, was respected because of Crowfoot's intervention. But the cold, damp conditions devastated his health. When after seven months he was released, he travelled to visit Crowfoot in Alberta, where he died of a lung hemorrhage at the age of forty-four.

He was buried at Blackfoot Crossing, but his remains were exhumed in 1967 and reburied at Cut Knife Hill on the Poundmaker reserve, about 25 miles west of Battleford, Saskatchewan. Such are the reversals of time and perspective that Poundmaker is now rightly honoured for the service and leadership he gave his people through one of the darkest periods in Cree history.

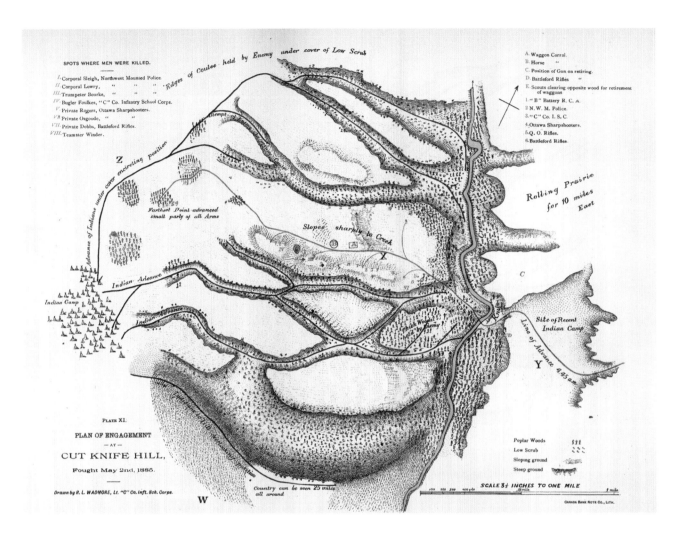

A. Waggon Corral.
B. Horse
C. Position of Gun on retiring.
D. Battleford Rifles "
E. Scouts clearing opposite wood for retirement of waggons
1. "B" Battery R.C.A.
2. N.W.M. Police.
3. "C" Co. I.S.C.
4. Ottawa Sharpshooters.
5. Q.O. Rifles.
6. Battleford Rifles.

Rolling Prairie
for 10 miles
East

PLATE XI.

PLAN OF ENGAGEMENT
— AT —
CUT KNIFE HILL,
Fought May 2nd, 1885.

Drawn by R. L. WADMORE, Lt. "C" Co. Infy. Sch. Corps.

Poplar Woods
Low Scrub
Sloping ground
Steep ground

SCALE 3¼ INCHES TO ONE MILE

CANADA BANK NOTE CO., LITH.

The Battle of Cut Knife Hill on May 2, 1885, was the second last major engagement of the North-West Rebellion. During the weeks leading up to it, at nearby Battleford, hundreds of townspeople had been trapped in the local fort, under siege by Chief Poundmaker and his Cree warriors, who supported Riel and the Metis. Seeking revenge on behalf of the town, which had been sacked, Colonel William Otter, with 250 fifty soldiers and volunteers, plus 75 Mounties, advanced on Poundmaker's camp at Cut Knife Hill. As in previous battles, the result was disastrous for the Canadians, who fired away at the teepees of Poundmaker and his warriors while the Natives, who knew the territory, circled around behind on snowshoes and, despite their inferior weapons, held Otter and his men under fire for hours, ultimately killing eight and injuring dozens.

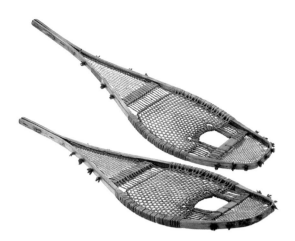

It was snowshoes such as these – an invention of the Natives and in use since 4,000 BC in a variety of forms – that gave Poundmaker and his warriors a logistical advantage at the Battle of Cut Knife Hill.

and taking several government employees hostage, including the local Indian agent.

Superintendent Lief Crozier, late of Fort Walsh and now in charge of the detachment at Fort Carlton, near Batoche, sent a frantic report to his superiors that a rebellion was about to begin. The news prompted Commissioner Irvine to march north from Regina with a force of ninety men and sixty-six horses. The two-hundred-mile trek through fierce blizzards took them seven days, during which the men suffered daily frostbite and snowblindness.

Before Irvine arrived, however, the impetuous Crozier decided to engage the enemy himself. The confrontation took place at Duck Lake, east of Fort Carlton, where Dumont had established camp and seized supplies at a hastily abandoned trading post.

Crozier had with him fifty-five Mounties and several dozen poorly armed volunteers from Prince Albert. However, as the column approached Duck Lake, hauling its twenty sleighs and a seven-pound cannon, the Mounties realized with alarm that they were slowly being surrounded by

Metis who were padding silently through the woods on snowshoes. Crozier quickly ordered his troops to pile their sleighs into a kind of barricade and, with his interpreter, John Mckay, advanced to parlay with Gabriel Dumont, whose brother Isidore had raised a white flag of truce.

But Crozier soon discerned that Dumont and his men were simply playing for time as they moved more men into position. Without further negotiation, Crozier turned to his troops and ordered them to commence shooting. Isidore Dumont was the first casualty, falling dead in the snow.

Crozier then realized that many of the "men" he had seen on the horizon were just decoys planted by the Metis and that the real guerrillas lay concealed in the woods and in the former trading post, which now blazed with gunfire.

Suddenly, 150 additional Metis poured over a nearby hill. Riel himself appeared among them on horseback, brandishing an immense crucifix he had taken from the little Catholic church at Duck Lake. Crozier's men fired at him, and when their shots missed, he hollered at the Metis to

fight on, inspiring them to a rout of the now-demoralized Mounties.

In the end, five rebels lay dead, as compared with ten Mounties and volunteers. As Crozier and his forces retreated, Gabriel Dumont shouted to the rebels to complete the job, to annihilate the fleeing forces. But Riel quickly countermanded the order, commanding the Metis instead to gather the bodies of the enemy and to put them in the trading post. Later that afternoon, he sent word to Crozier that anyone coming to claim the bodies would not be harmed, and followed up by ordering his men to help the Mounties load the dead onto wagons.

Crozier had barely returned to Fort Carlton when Irvine and his men staggered in from the south. But with his men weary from travel, Irvine wisely decided not to extend the day's battle or even to attempt to defend Fort Carlton, which was lightly built and provided no real protection against any sustained assault.

Instead, Irvine marched his forces to nearby Prince Albert, a major settlement, where they could more easily obtain

The ferry across the North Saskatchewan River at Fort Carlton, Saskatchewan, near Batoche, had never seen the traffic it experienced during the days leading up to and following the North-West Rebellion.

Here, in May 1885, some of the thousands of men who came into the area to oppose Riel and the Metis make the crossing with their horses.

supplies and would be less isolated under attack. Dumont, whose scouts reported every move the Mounties made, wanted to ambush Irvine's forces while they were on the move. But again Riel restrained them, perhaps unsure now of the ultimate wisdom of his undertaking.

Within days, Irvine's men had erected a stockade around Prince Albert's Presbyterian church and manse and, with most of the town's population of sixteen hundred, had moved inside.

Meanwhile, news of the rebels' startling activities had reached the east, inspiring public outrage and a thirst for revenge.

At Batoche, Riel was busily firing off messages to the leaders of local tribes – in particular to Poundmaker and Big Bear – encouraging them to join actively in his campaign. A day or so later, Poundmaker and two hundred warriors in face paint advanced on Battleford, a hundred miles west of Batoche. Fearing the worst, more than five hundred citizens quickly took refuge, along with forty-two resident Mounties, in the fortified NWMP barracks outside town.

Upon arriving, Poundmaker and his warriors approached the fort to demand food, clothing and ammunition. Battleford's Indian agent immediately telegraphed his superiors, requesting authority to issue food to the hungry Natives. In the ensuing delay, Poundmaker and his men turned their attention to the town itself, plundering the vacated Hudson's Bay post and slaughtering livestock before burning several houses and murdering a settler who had not taken refuge at the barracks.

For three weeks, Poundmaker laid siege to the NWMP fort and, finally, having grown weary of the tactic, ordered his warriors back to their encampment in the woods.

Meanwhile, at Frog Lake, Big Bear and a hungry contingent of armed followers invaded a Catholic church during a Sunday service, terrorizing the worshippers and taking thirteen prisoners. The local Indian agent, Thomas Quinn, bravely objected to the assault and was shot dead, point blank, by a notoriously violent warrior named Wandering Spirit. As the prisoners were herded out of the church, the Cree opened fire, killing nine men in all, including the

priest, Father François Fafard. As a final act of aggression, the Natives took several female hostages and disappeared in the direction of their camp.

The prime minister responded with anger, hastily mobilizing some eight thousand troops throughout the country and arranging to move them to the north-west on the newly created railway. Seeing his opportunity to pry money out of the government and complete gaps in the railway across the north shore of Lake Superior, William Van Horne, the general manager of the CPR, promised to get the troops out west within eleven days if Ottawa would finance the remaining construction of the railway.

Sir John A. Macdonald acceded, and Van Horne did what he had promised and began moving soldiers. Where there was no track, he transported the men on open sleighs, over perilous ground and in temperatures as low as −50°F, or marched them across the ice of Lake Superior. Otherwise, they rode on open flatcars, often so dazed and drained by the cold that when they arrived at areas where there was no

Bishop's North-West War Map (10 cents) was one of the more sensational souvenirs offered for sale to a fascinated, gullible and patriotic public during the North-West Rebellion. All of the map's pictorial elements were copied from government publications, or in the case of the map, from a brochure published by the Canadian Pacific Railway. However, with the exception of the portrait of Louis Riel, none of the scenes had any obvious connection to the Metis or their cause in the Canadian west. The scalping scene in particular seems to have been thrown in to appeal to thrill-hungry buyers – just as the inclusion of bits of Montana and Dakota on the map were probably included to appeal to US buyers.

BISHOP'S
NORTH-WEST WAR MAP.

THE QU'APPELLE VALLEY

SIR JOHN A. MACDONALD

MEDICINE HAT

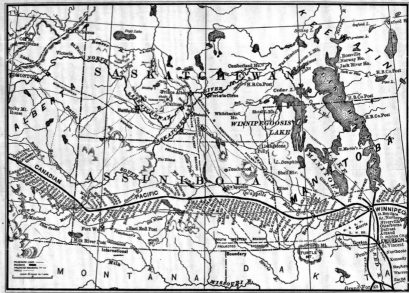

KOOTLASHOOWRAN

MAJ.-GEN. MIDDLETON

LOUIS RIEL

NE-BAIF-A-SHAW

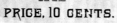

PRICE, 10 CENTS.

PUBLISHED BY THE GEORGE BISHOP ENG. & CO.,
MONTREAL.

Below: Members of 10th Battalion, Royal Grenadiers, Toronto, are shown here on ox-drawn wagons en route to put down the North-West Rebellion. The man standing on the second wagon appears to be serenading the rest with his fiddle.

Right: Reconnaissance men – scouts – were as important to the efforts of both sides in the North-West Rebellion as soldiers. Their presence and ingenuity made it possible for a force to surprise and outmaneuver an enemy, as Riel and Dumont showed on various occasions. The "government" scouting party pictured at right at Maple Creek, Saskatchewan, includes a number of non-military men, as well as NWMP sergeant Thomas Mc-Ginnis, third from right.

track, they had no strength even to eat the food or drink the hot coffee that Van Horne had provided for them by the tons.

In spite of the hardships, units coming from both east and west reached their staging point along the railway west of Winnipeg by mid-April. From that point the plan was to send the main force, under Major-General Frederick Middleton, the overall commander, marched north from Fort Qu'Appelle toward Batoche. A second force, under Colonel William Otter, would march north along a more westerly route from Swift Current. A third battalion, under Major-General Thomas Strange, would march north from Calgary to Edmonton, then east into the heart of Metis country.

Middleton was an old-school strategist who had helped put down the Maoris in New Zealand and the Sepoys in India. But he knew little of the wooded territory of what is now north-central Saskatchewan. Mainly, he failed to realize that long marches in the open left his troops vulnerable to the guerrilla tactics of the more mobile Cree and Metis.

Allowing time out for drill, Middleton took three weeks to march his force of eight hundred men in two columns to within twenty miles of Batoche. He had left most of his cavalry behind to guard supply depots and protect the railway and had thus forfeited much of his capability to manoeuvre quickly. And this would cost him.

On the morning of April 24, as Middleton and his troops slogged the final miles toward Batoche, Gabriel Dumont concealed a force of 130 Metis in a small ravine along Fish Creek, a few miles from Middleton's starting point that day. Dumont's plan was to catch Middleton's men as they came over a nearby hill silhouetted against the sky. Middleton's scouts, who were constantly on reconnaissance ahead of the main column, sussed out the plan and reported on it to the general. But instead of altering strategy, Middleton pressed forward, and was eventually greeted by sheets of gunfire from the rebels. In response, the Canadian troops quickly moved two pieces of heavy artillery into position, but the bulky ordnance

Militia men trained at Fort Qu'Appelle are seen here at Qu'Appelle Lake during the spring of 1885, on their way north to Batoche under General Middleton to fight Riel and his rebel forces.

General Middleton, shown here with his wounded aides on the approach to Batoche, was deeply distressed, indeed cowed, by the resilience and shrewd battle tactics of Riel, Dumont and the Metis.

proved too imprecise to put shells into the creek ravine where the Metis lay hidden.

The troops twice attempted bayonet charges and twice were turned back by the relentlessness of the Metis fire. By day's end, the rebels, who were outnumbered five to one, had lost six men (two dead, four injured), while Canadian casualties numbered more than fifty.

Middleton, shaken by his losses and by the resilience of the Metis, simply hunkered down at his encampment near Batoche and attempted to regroup.

One hundred miles away, at Battleford, Colonel Otter had arrived from Swift Current with 534 men. After a 3-day rest, some 250 of the new arrivals, plus 75 Mounties, set out to confront Poundmaker and his warriors at their camp at Cut Knife Hill. Again, however, the Cree were too wily to allow themselves to be bested by cumbersome cannons and Gatling guns. While Otter and his men pounded away at the tribes' teepees, Poundmaker and his warriors slipped off into the bush on their snowshoes, circled around and came up quietly behind their attackers.

Although many were only armed with bows and arrows, and old rifles, the Natives kept Otter and his men pinned down for seven hours, costing the Canadian forces another eight dead and some fifteen seriously wounded.

THE DAY CAME AT LAST, in early May, when Middleton was ready to do the job he had come to do – to take back Batoche and to eliminate Riel and his followers. For once, his strategy broke radically with tradition. His plan was to send the *Northcote*, an old flat-bottomed sternwheeler, into Batoche along the South Saskatchewan River and to pound Riel's headquarters with a seven-pound cannon and Gatling gun mounted on its deck. Thirty-five troopers with rifles would provide light armament. Under cover of this diversion, Middleton's main force would advance into town, move artillery into position, and overwhelm Dumont with sheer firepower.

But the strategy went awry when the rebels, who had discovered the plan for the water raid in advance and had rigged a trap for the *Northcote*, dropped an overhead

ferry cable into the water behind the vessel as it steamed into town, thus preventing its retreat. Another overhead cable was supposed to come down in front of the boat, trapping it, so that the rebels could bombard and sink it. However, the second cable fell directly onto the *Northcote*'s prow, sheering off its smokestack, mast and loading spars. A fire quickly broke out on deck, and as the Canadian soldiers formed a bucket brigade, the Metis splintered the old boat's hull with round after round of rifle fire, coming close to demolishing it as the pilot forged ahead around a bend and disappeared from sight.

Middleton's ground force enjoyed no better success, again falling prey to Dumont's irregulars, who were hidden in an elaborate network of camouflage pits and trenches as the Canadian soldiers approached. When Middleton's soldiers attempted to outflank Dumont's men, the rebels stealthily ignited great piles of underbrush in their path, blinding them with smoke. In the chaos, it was all the Canadians could do to fire aimlessly into the smoky haze, hoping to discourage a Metis counterattack.

This detailed plan for Middleton's attack on Batoche also serves as a historical record of the battle. Places where members of the field force were cut down are shown: "Phillips Shot," "Moor Shot," "Fitch Shot." The plan also lists the names of all government troops and militia engaged, marks gun placements, and identifies the "house in which prisoners were confined."

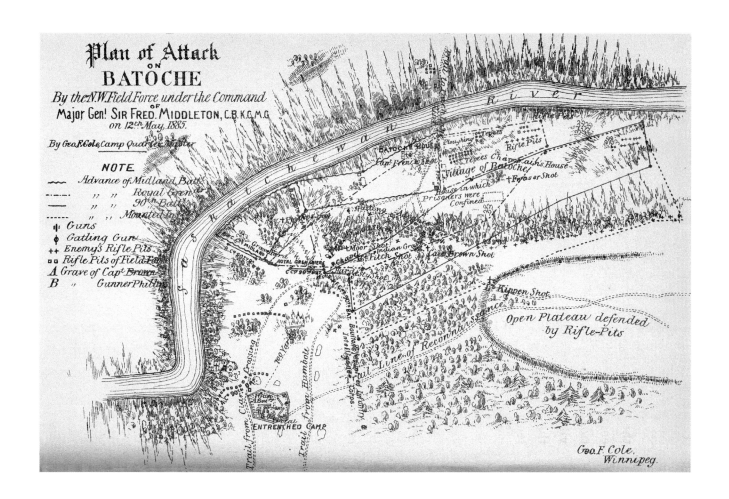

This note, written by General Middleton to Big Bear on June 2, 1885, was transported to the chief by Middleton's scouts. Casually signed "Fred Middleton," the note's contents, while respectful, even appreciative in parts, are by no means amicable: "I have utterly defeated Riel, at Batoche, with great loss and have made prisoners of Riel, Poundmaker, and his principal chiefs, also the two murderers of Payne, and Fremont…I expect you will come in with all your prisoners, your principal chiefs, and give up the men who have committed murders at Frog Lake. I am glad to hear that you have treated [your prisoners] fairly well. If you do not, I shall pursue & destroy you, and your band, or drive you into the woods to starve."

Camp North of Indian Camp
rifle-pits

June 2nd 1885

Big Bear:
I have utterly defeated Riel, at Batoche with great loss, and have made Prisoners of Riel, Poundmaker, and his principal chiefs, also the two murderers of Payne, and Fremont, and I expect that you will come in with all your prisoners, your principal chiefs, and give up the men, who have committed murders at Frog Lake, and I am glad to hear that you have treated them fairly well. If you do not, I shall pursue & destroy you, and your band, or drive you into the woods to starve.

Fred Middleton
M. General

At dusk, with nothing accomplished, Middleton and his men retreated to the shelter of their transport wagons outside town. No fires were permitted. However, at midnight Dumont sent a flare out over the encampment, which exploded with a terrifying boom, spooking both horses and soldiers and permitting the Metis to pour rifle fire into the now visible shelter.

The next morning, with the battle at a stalemate, Riel appeared among the rebels, praying with them for courage and justice, and exhorting them on to victory.

And so things stood for two days as Middleton's officers begged him to order a bayonet attack, to send all nine hundred of the men at his disposal in a mass assault against the two hundred-odd buffalo hunters who continued to occupy their foxholes on the fringes of Batoche. But Middleton had twice been exposed to Dumont's cunning strategies and was determined to wait for what he hoped would be an ill-considered move on the part of his enemy.

Then, at about noon on the fourth day, as Middleton was eating lunch, one of his colonels, A.T. Williams, took things into

his own hands and charged the rebels with his Midland Battalion, accompanied by the 90th Winnipeg Rifles and the Royal Grenadiers of Toronto. Infuriated by this gross insubordination, Middleton screamed at his bugler to sound a recall. But it was too late – Williams refused to halt. Middleton and his battalion were forced to join the charge.

Dumont's problem at this point was not merely that he was vastly outnumbered but that his men had run out of ammunition. The night before they had crept out in the dark, scouring the fields on their hands and knees for spent slugs to load into what muskets they possessed. Without bullets, their rifles were useless to them. Reduced to firing rusty nails and pebbles, the Metis were at last forced to concede their first line of trenches to the enemy – then their second and third lines, until they were obliged to take shelter in the ruined buildings of the town and among the trees along the banks of the South Saskatchewan.

By evening the battle was over. Metis women and children, who had taken shelter in basements and riverbank caves,

emerged into the streets. Their men appeared one or two at a time, now without guns, and surrendered. While the day's casualties were not heavy, the Metis had lost sixteen warriors in all. Many more were wounded. Middleton had lost no one that day, and his troops celebrated openly amidst the ruins of Batoche. Predictably enough, Dumont himself refused to surrender. Over the next few days he evaded the patrols sent out to capture him, and eventually turned up in Montana. His shooting and riding skills were such that he later became a star in Buffalo Bill Cody's Wild West show, where he appeared alongside Chief Sitting Bull.

Riel hid out for three days in the woods near Batoche, then gave himself up to a pair of NWMP scouts, volunteering his .22 calibre revolver as he was arrested. Lacking a coat, and shivering from cold, he was presented a few hours later to General Middleton, who immediately offered him his military greatcoat.

Asked by Middleton how he had even dreamed of defeating the Canadian army, Riel responded that he had no such

dream, that he had merely wanted to "make a last desperate stand," hoping to convince the government "to deal fairly with the people of the territories and their long-neglected rights."

After a week in captivity at Batoche, Riel was taken by steamer to Saskatoon and then in a wagon caravan and by special train to Regina, where he awaited trial in the NWMP guardhouse.

In the days that followed, General Middleton led a triumphal march to Prince Albert, where he relieved Commissioner Irvine, who had remained with his Mounties and the townsfolk in the stockade they had built around the Presbyterian church. Irvine would eventually be criticized by Ottawa for not having joined in the fight against Riel and Dumont – or for that matter against Poundmaker and Big Bear. Middleton referred to the absentee commissioner and his forces as "gophers" – animals that, at the first sign of danger, retreat into their holes.

Irvine responded vehemently that he had received no order from Ottawa to join Middleton, who he knew could have used

Soldiers from the Winnipeg field battery shown resting as they escort Louis Riel from Swift Current to Regina in a coach especially furnished and reinforced for the purpose, on May 22 or 23, 1885.

Below: The common grave of sixteen Metis who died during the North-West Rebellion and were buried on the open prairie where they had once hunted buffalo. St. Antoine de Padoue church and rectory are visible in the background.

Right: Dead Canadian soldiers lie on the field after the Battle of Fish Creek, in what is now central Saskatchewan. A soldier is seen sewing one of the corpses into a shourd.

his help, but that otherwise his work at Prince Albert had been "as important to the overall cause as it had been successful."

Dressed in his white helmet and tweed shooting clothes, Middleton then moved on to Battleford, where he received the unconditional surrender of Poundmaker and his warriors.

As Middleton had been attacking Batoche, General Thomas Strange, newly arrived from Edmonton after a 250-mile march, had advanced on Big Bear and his warriors at Fort Pitt to avenge the massacre in the church at Frog Lake. On May 26, Strange and his force of five hundred (including twenty-five Mounties under the command of Sam Steele) met Big Bear's two hundred warriors at Frenchman's Butte. However, with an inexperienced army, and his awareness of the Cree's craftiness and mobility, Strange quickly withdrew from battle, wary of "committing Custer," as he put it.

A week would pass before Strange was joined by Middleton with an additional two hundred troops. But by this time, Big Bear had prudently decided

to retreat into the all but impenetrable northern wilderness. Nevertheless, a few days later, Steele and his small contingent of Mounties caught up with the chief and his men at Loon Lake. In a brief but fierce exchange of gunfire, several Cree were killed, and Big Bear escaped further into the wilds.

On June 18, the Cree unexpectedly released the last of their prisoners from Fort Pitt and sent a message to the Mounties pleading that "the Great Mother, the Queen, stop the government soldiers from shooting at us."

Over the next couple of days, Big Bear's warriors stumbled into Fort Pitt, half starved, to give themselves up. Big Bear himself made an astonishing one-hundred-mile trek to Fort Carlton where, on July 2, he surrendered and was immediately taken to the police barracks at Prince Albert. One of his escorts, Constable John Donkin, described him as being "in a pitiable condition of filth and hunger." At Prince Albert, according to Donkin, "the great chief was given a good scrubbing in a tub, his horror of the cleansing process

Cree chief Big Bear, seen here in leg shackles, was sentenced to three years in Stony Mountain Penitentiary for his part in the North-West Rebellion. Among other prison jobs, Big Bear tended the pigs and the warden's private zoo, which included both bears and buffalo. The proud chief is said to have felt particularly close to the bears, his namesakes, which he believed had given him supernatural powers as a boy.

appearing both pathetic and comic. His breech-clout had done duty for a decade and was as black as the ace of spades which, by the way, it rather resembled."

FOR THE GALLANT if perhaps reckless Riel, Regina was the end of the line. On July 28, 1885, the messiah of the Metis was marched to the prisoner's dock in a make-shift courtroom, where he would face a part-time territorial judge and a jury of six non-Native settlers.

The courtroom was hot and crowded. A dozen or more newspapermen had been given a table to one side, while an-other section had been given over to "the ladies," whose numbers included the wife of Major-General Middleton, attired in a bonnet and Sunday finery. Four red-coated Mounties flanked Riel, who for the occasion was attired in a black frock coat and black ribbon tie.

To the charge of high treason, the ulti-mate crime against the Crown, Riel rose and responded firmly, "I have the honour to answer the court, I am not guilty."

For Riel's four lawyers, it was all but impossible to show that he had not led a rebellion against the government. Instead, to save his life, they hoped to convince the jury that he was not guilty because of insanity. A pair of doctors testified that he was "a victim of megalomania, the mania of ambition."

Riel himself preferred condemnation and the noose to what he described as "the stain of insanity." On several occasions, he interrupted proceedings to protest the effort to prove him insane, insisting that he would never "consent to the animal life of an asylum."

When on the fourth day he rose to speak on his own behalf, the courtroom fell silent. In an impassioned voice he painted a de-spairing picture of what he discovered when he returned from Montana: "I found the Indians starving. The half-breeds were subsisting on the rotten pork of the Hud-son's Bay Company. This was the condition, this was the pride, of responsible Govern-ment!" He explained how he decided to "assist all classes, irrespective of creed, colour or nationality"...to relieve the state of affairs that he had found.

IN THE 1890S, food was scarce and life bleak on the One Arrow reserve in what is now north-central Saskatchewan. On October 22, 1895, a twenty-year-old Cree warrior named Almighty Voice, known as *Kah-kee-say-mane-too-wayo* (Voice of the Great Spirit) by the Natives, slaughtered a stray cow for the meat, a seemingly insignificant act that led to the longest police manhunt in Saskatchewan history.

NWMP accounts say the cow belonged to the government. Those on the reserve claimed it belonged to Almighty Voice, who simply didn't have a permit from the Indian agent to kill it.

Either way the killing of the cow was considered a crime, and Almighty Voice was arrested and locked up in the Duck Lake jail. Fearing for his life, Almighty Voice escaped and swam across the icy Saskatchewan River to his reserve.

According to police accounts, NWMP Sergeant Colin Colebrook caught up with the fugitive after a few days and attempted to make a peaceable arrest. Other accounts say the policeman fired at the young man and missed, and that Almighty Voice, a crack shot, turned and fired back, putting a slug into the policeman's chest.

Whatever the truth, Colebrook died instantly and for the next nineteen months, Almighty Voice eluded an ever-intensifying NWMP manhunt. According to the inhabit-

ants of One Arrow, the warrior spent most of that time on his home reserve, protected by his people, often hiding in a crawl space beneath his house.

In May 1897, as policemen visited the One Arrow reserve to investigate a cattle theft, they spotted a trio of young men, one of whom was Almighty Voice. An officer went closer to investigate and was shot through the arm.

The next day, reinforcements, including a number of civilians, returned to the spot and caught sight of the same men hiding in the undergrowth. When three officers went to investigate, they were fired on, and two of them were wounded.

Efforts were made to flush the men out by setting fire to the trees and undergrowth. When that failed, the posse decided to rush the bluff, with disastrous results. Two Mounties and a civilian postmaster were shot dead and another man wounded.

At dusk, in an effort to keep the men from escaping in the night, some ninety officers and a group of local civilians surrounded the hill.

The next day, police brought in seven- and nine-pound cannons and shelled the bluff. The entire population of One Arrow watched powerlessly from a nearby hillside. Among them was the mother of Almighty Voice, Spotted Calf, whose voice could be heard above the gunfire, singing the Cree death song.

By late afternoon, Almighty

Voice and his companions had fallen silent forever – a dire conclusion to a standoff often said to be the last battle between non-Natives and Natives in all of North America. While police say they killed the young warrior, the people of One Arrow claim he was only injured by the cannon fire and that, tired of being hunted, he took his own life.

Either way, the Mounties got their man, and the story of Almighty Voice, the last chapter of which was enacted just a few miles from Batoche, has become one of the legends of the early years of the North West Mounted Police.

This studio portrait, entitled "Almighty Voice, Cree, Duck Lake area, Saskatchewan" was taken two or three years before the exotic-looking young man with the intricately braided hair ran afoul of the NWMP at the age of twenty, in 1895.

THOMSON & WILLIAMS,
UNDERTAKERS.

Winnipeg, *Dec. 7th* 188__

Section
Plot *At St Boniface*
Name of deceased *Louis Riel*
Cause of Death *Hung & Released*
Where Born *St Boniface*
Where Died *Hung at Regina*
Date of Death
Religion *RC*
Married ~~28 yrs~~ Single
Name of Attending Physician
Charges

It was not until December 7, 1885, twenty-one days after Riel was hanged in Regina, that a formal death certificate was issued for him, in St. Boniface, Manitoba. Meanwhile, his poorly embalmed body had run a rather adventurous course. Three days after the hanging it had been entrusted to Pascal Bonneau, a Regina Metis, who buried it for more than two weeks beneath the floor of a Regina Catholic chapel. There, with his brother, he kept watch over it around the clock to prevent it being stolen or savaged by Riel's Protestant enemies. In early December, Bonneau was notified secretly by Governor Dewdney that a rail car was waiting at the city limits to transport the body to Manitoba. Under cover of a dense blizzard, Bonneau dug up the corpse, transported it to the train and accompanied it to St. Boniface, where he handed it over to Riel's family. Note the misspelling of, Riel, on the document.

Toward the close of his hour-long address to the court, Riel said quietly, "In the end, I acted reasonably and in self-defence, while the Government, my aggressor, cannot but have acted madly and wrong; and if high treason there is, it must be on the Government's side, not on my part. I say humbly through the grace of God, I believe I am the prophet of the new world."

The courtroom listened with fascination and no small measure of sympathy. Women cried openly throughout Riel's impassioned self-defence.

On the fifth day, the jury retired to deliberate. As they did so, Riel fell to his knees, praying in French in a soft monotone until the jury returned an hour and twenty minutes later.

"We find the defendant guilty," the foreman announced solemnly, before asking that the court show clemency in sentencing the Metis leader.

But there would be no clemency. After several rejected appeals to higher courts, and a number of stays of execution, Riel was escorted from his cell on the morning of November 16 to the prison courtyard where a gallows had been erected. With a pair of priests at his side, Riel repeated the Lord's Prayer as a white hood was secured over his head and the noose placed around his neck. At the words "lead us not into temptation, but deliver us…" the trap opened beneath him, and Louis Riel plunged nine feet to his death. His body was laid in a rough pine box and taken east on a CPR train to Winnipeg, where he was buried in a tree-sheltered grave in the yard of St. Boniface Cathedral.

And so ended a dramatic chapter in the history of the Canadian west – one shaped by the complex relations between the country's indigenous peoples and the Europeans who had arrived to make the country their own.

New chapters would be shaped by Riel's struggles and philosophy, and his story would not be forgotten. In fact, the complex relations that he epitomized would be the subtext of the country's history for more than a century to come.

From their beginnings, the Mounties were a symbol of adventure and masculinity. Their activities in uniform became a favourite motif of filmmakers and storytellers, as evidenced by the July 1945 edition of *Mon Magazine Policier* and the July 1941 edition of *Yarns: Canada's All-Story Magazine.*

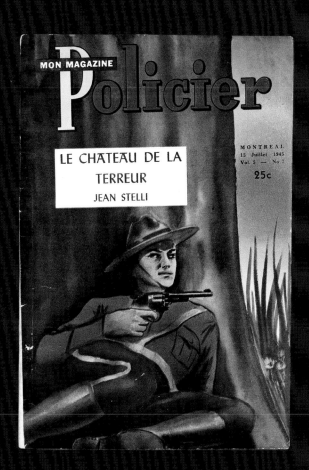

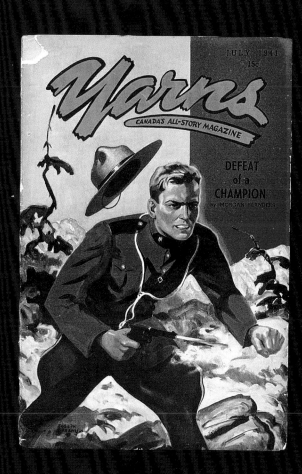

Chapter Five

THE MOST EXTRAORDINARY TREASURE HUNT IN HISTORY

F OR HIS RELUCTANCE TO participate in putting down Riel's rebellion, Commissioner A.G. Irvine was relieved of his duties in March 1886. While it was assumed that Sir John A. Macdonald would appoint a veteran of the force to replace Irvine – perhaps Sam Steele or Arthur Griesbach – he turned instead to Lawrence Herchmer of Kingston, Ontario, the relatively unknown scion of a United Empire Loyalist family. The new commissioner's family was, in fact, so loyal to the Empire that Herchmer's mother had, at her husband's urging, crossed the Atlantic thirteen times to give birth so that her children would be true citizens of the old country. At various times Herchmer had been an officer of the US – Canada Border Commission, a Winnipeg brewery owner and a Manitoba Indian agent.

Stubborn, opinionated and dedicated, Herchmer was determined to bring stability and order to a force that had suffered laxness, desertions and unparalleled drunkenness under its previous administration. To that end, his first act as commissioner

was to appoint his like-minded brother William Herchmer ("Colonel Billy") as assistant commissioner and to introduce higher standards for admission to the force. In the wake of the North-West Rebellion, the N W M P had been quickly expanded to one thousand men, including many recruits of questionable background and constitution. Herchmer dismissed drunkards and deadbeats, improved living conditions and raised pay. He also created a pension plan to induce good men to stay in the force. Some of those barely up to the improved standards were reassigned as "special constables," employed as cooks, dog drivers and construction labourers.

To prevent the stockpiling of alcohol in various posts, Herchmer ordered the cellars in all barracks nailed shut. Officers caught drunk, even once, were given the choice of dismissal or resignation. But drinking was harder to eradicate than the new boss had imagined. Even four years later, at Fort Macleod, there were twelve instances of what Sam Steele referred to as "extreme drunkenness," several of

Lawrence W. Herchmer was appointed commissioner of the NWMP in 1886 and, more than anyone, transformed the Mounties from a chaotic and demoralized patchwork into a modern and disciplined institution.

One of his great challenges was that, toward the end of the nineteenth century, he was caught between a government that wanted to spend less on policing and a public that wanted more and better police services. He also suffered an intense, contrived dunning from the Regina *Leader* whose editor, Nicholas Davin,

he had once arrested for wandering drunk and half naked through an Ottawa-bound train. But a government inquiry acquitted Herchmer of all the misconduct charges against him trumped up by the newspaper.

which led to dismissals. And in 1891, at Maple Creek, the bugler was given three months of hard labour and fined $10 for falling over drunk while attempting to play the last post.

Herchmer himself was far from restrained in his consumption of alcohol. In one sixteen-month period beginning in January 1887, he received at headquarters 22 gallons of whisky, 9 gallons of wine, and 316 gallons of beer. One of his lieutenants, Superintendent Richard Deane, with whom Herchmer often fought, received a preposterous 56 gallons of whisky, plus 5 of gin – nearly a fifth or twenty-sixer for every day of the period in question.

In the wake of the unpopular new discipline, good men as well as laggards were lost to the force through desertion. During one month in 1888 at Fort Macleod, twenty-four men headed south across the border, fed up with the rigorous drill standards imposed by Sam Steele.

The application of the new disciplinary standards could be petty in the extreme. Fred Bagley, the famed boy bugler, who had risen to the rank of staff-sergeant,

was demoted to sergeant by Herchmer for neglecting to insist that company musicians belonging to the Church of England attend choir practice. The fact that Herchmer was a member of the Church of England and Bagley a Catholic was suspected to have been at the root of the demotion.

On the positive side, Herchmer improved living and recreation conditions. Among other things, he built a meticulously regulated drinking canteen at headquarters in Regina, where a pint of low-alcohol beer could be purchased for a nickel, and made money available for sports, drama clubs and social events. He created a billiards room, bought band instruments and books, and constructed a bowling alley from the profits of the canteen. In 1891, the fort in Calgary became the first NWMP post to get electric lights.

IF THE FORCE NEEDED a rallying point around which to shape its new image, it got one in August 1896, when San Francisco prospector George Carmack, his wife Kate and brother-in-law Skookum Jim Mason

Left: Chilkoot Jack, a member of the coastal Tinglit tribe in Alaska, is said to have guided the first white prospectors along the Chilkoot Trail over the mountains into the Yukon in approximately 1880. He is seen here in ceremonial dress in front of a store in Dyea, Alaska in 1899.

Below: "Skookum" Jim Mason was a legendary guide and prospector in the Yukon. During the early 1890s, he befriended George Carmack, and introduced Carmack to his sister Kate, who would eventually become Carmack's wife. All three were involved in the discovery of gold in Rabbit Creek (quickly renamed Bonanza Creek) in August 1896. Mason, who was of the Tagish tribe, is seen here with his wife and daughter. He is a member of the Canadian Mining Hall of Fame.

In the summer of 1897, a ship arrived in Seattle carrying more than two tons of gold from the area around Dawson City in the Canadian Yukon. During the next two years, more than 100,000 hopeful people, most of them Americans, would seek their fortune in the Klondike. To get there, a few hardy souls headed north overland from what is now northern Alberta, but most took water routes, either by ship to Skagway and Dyea in southern Alaska, then inland over the Chilkoot Pass, or up and around Alaska into the Bering Sea and from there up the Yukon River to Dawson City. The accompanying map, produced by the Alaska Exploration Company – an outfit that made a fortune selling passage and freight transport, often to naive treasure hunters – marks the latter route from San Francisco to the Bering Sea and upriver to the Yukon. Note on the right side of the map the list of nine reasons why a prospector might better leave for the Klondike from San Francisco than from anywhere else.

unearthed such an abundance of gold at Bonanza Creek in the central Yukon that within a year the entire world was riveted by fantasies of the exorbitant and available wealth. Carmack, who had been steered to the gold by another prospector, Robert Henderson, described the gold lying "like cheese in a sandwich," between slabs of bedrock. Immediately, he hustled down the Yukon River to the settlement at Forty Mile, where his display of nuggets emptied the saloons of men determined to find gold of their own. The next day Carmack crossed the river to Fort Constantine, a recently erected conclave of buildings that housed the northernmost contingent of Mounties, and for $15 registered his claim with Inspector Charles Constantine.

As it turned out, the solid and placer gold in the streams and rock along the Klondike River was so abundant – the news of it so wide-ranging and glittering – that as far as anyone on the outside could imagine, the newly found lucre could be scooped up by anyone with the gumption to go and get it.

And go they did, by the thousands, creating chaos in the Klondike and, with

it, such a demand for Mounties that between the summer of 1896 and early 1898 the Yukon division expanded from a handful of men at Fort Constantine to a contingent of 285 officers and constables. Determined to keep order and to establish a strong Canadian presence along the border with Alaska, Canada's governor general, the Earl of Aberdeen, declared the Yukon a judicial district and in 1897 appointed James Walsh, the former NWMP superintendent, the first commissioner of the territory.

For the fifty-four-year-old Walsh, who was now retired and living in Brockville, Ontario, the appointment began inauspiciously. He left Ottawa for the Yukon in early autumn, arriving after freeze-up, unable until spring to proceed north to Dawson City, the centre of the gold rush, at the confluence of the Yukon and Klondike rivers. Instead, he spent a lonely and debilitating winter in an inadequate log building, in the dark and cold, along the banks of the Yukon River, north of Bennett Lake.

For most of the roughly forty thousand men and women who ventured into the

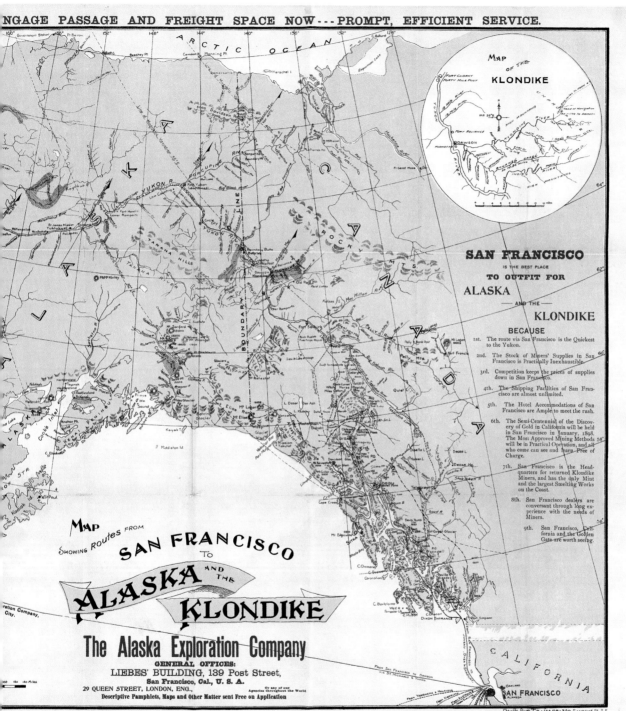

SAN FRANCISCO

IS THE BEST PLACE

TO OUTFIT FOR

ALASKA

AND THE

KLONDIKE

BECAUSE

1st.   The route via San Francisco is the Quickest to the Yukon.

2nd.   The Stock of Miners' Supplies in San Francisco is Practically Inexhaustible.

3rd.   Competition keeps the prices of supplies down in San Francisco.

4th.   The Shipping Facilities of San Francisco are almost unlimited.

5th.   The Hotel Accommodations of San Francisco are Ample to meet the rush.

6th.   The Semi-Centennial of the Discovery of Gold in California will be held in San Francisco in January, 1898. The Most Approved Mining Methods will be in Practical Operation, and all who come can see and learn. Free of Charge.

7th.   San Francisco is the Headquarters for returned Klondike Miners, and has the only Mint and the largest Smelting Works on the Coast.

8th.   San Francisco dealers are conversant through long experience with the needs of Miners.

9th.   San Francisco, California and the Golden Gate are worth seeing.

MAP

SHOWING ROUTES FROM

SAN FRANCISCO

TO

ALASKA AND THE

KLONDIKE

The Alaska Exploration Company

GENERAL OFFICES:

LIEBES' BUILDING, 139 Post Street,

San Francisco, Cal., U. S. A.

29 QUEEN STREET, LONDON, ENG.,   Or any of our Agencies throughout the World

Descriptive Pamphlets, Maps and Other Matter sent Free on Application

wson City and Points on the Yukon River via St. Michael---We take your Baggage and Freight with you.

THE MOST EXTRAORDINARY TREASURE HUNT IN HISTORY   187

The Klondike gold rush spawned a thriving support industry in cities such as Victoria, Portland and San Francisco. Everything a man or woman needed (or thought they needed) to get to the goldfields and succeed could be bought in advance, often at an exorbitant price: tools, food, clothing, transportation, survival advice. The transportation guide at left advertised steamer transportation from San Francisco, simultaneously suggesting the excitement, glamour and riches that would undoubtedly accrue to any adventurer willing to make the trip.

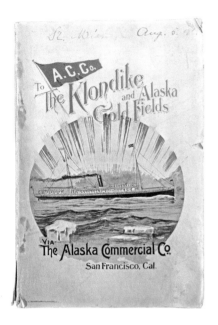

Yukon seeking their fortune, conditions were no better than they were for Walsh. In some cases, they were far worse. Many of those transfixed by thoughts of gold travelled by steamer from San Francisco and Seattle, landing at Skagway or nearby Dyea, on the rugged west coast of Alaska. From there they packed inland on foot over the mountains to Bennett Lake and boated down the Yukon River into the expectant delirium and squalor of the newly built Dawson City, the notoriously dubbed "Paris of the North."

To say that the journey was difficult is an understatement of breathtaking proportions. The boats carrying the gold seekers up the coast were crowded, smelly and poorly provisioned. Starving horses competed for space with human beings, some of whom were said to be half dead with seasickness by the time they disembarked. In many cases, the vessels were barely seaworthy.

Those who reached Skagway and Dyea with their ambitions intact were dumped unceremoniously ashore. Their supplies and provisions, which often weighed more than a ton, were tossed overboard onto tidal flats where the goods were frequently soaked through or wrecked.

The next challenge was to escape Skagway, a town where many of the permanent residents were con artists eager to fleece the new arrivals or talk them into "travelling arrangements" that within days would see them penniless if not dead in the wilds. "Shots were exchanged on the streets in broad daylight, and at night shouts of *Murder!* and cries for help mingled with the cracked voices of the singers in the variety halls," wrote Steele, who in early 1898 was sent to the Yukon to head the NWMP's gold rush operation. The notorious gangster Soapy Smith controlled an assortment of about 150 ruffians who, in the lawless town, did pretty much as they pleased in the saloons and brothels, where many a sucker was separated from his money. Indeed, Soapy's first achievement when he arrived in Skagway in 1897 was to put the US Marshal on his payroll – at twice the salary he was receiving from the municipal authorities. Soapy next built a fake telegraph office where the wires

Left: The *A.J. Goddard* was the first steamboat on Lake Bennett, in 1896. The sternwheeler, built perhaps in Vancouver, is seen here transporting men and supplies as they prepare for their perilous journey north to the Klondike goldfields. Note the firewood on board – necessary for firing the boilers that drove the wheel.

Below: Stampeders, who had come north by steamer seeking Klondike gold, generally landed on the waterfront at Dyea, Alaska, where they were invariably greeted with mass and muddy confusion, as well as huxters and gangs determined to defraud them of their money and goods.

Below: The thugs of the Soapy Smith Gang, who came to Skagway, Alaska, from all over the US, were once described as being bound by three things: an utter lack of conscience, a proclivity for violence and chicanery, and a talent for predation. They were also united by an all but blind allegiance to their nefarious leader seen here in the middle of the group.

Right: In the spring of 1898, the citizens of Skagway (or "Skaguay," as it is called on the accompanying document) formed a "Vigilance Committee" with the intent of ridding the town of the Soapy Smith Gang – which they were ultimately able to do in dramatic and violent fashion. The warning at right was the committee's first salvo in its war against the gang.

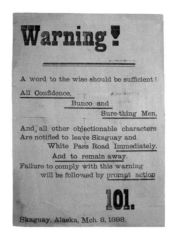

Warning !

A word to the wise should be sufficient !

All Confidence,
                Bunco and
                            Sure-thing Men,

And, all other objectionable characters
Are notified to leave Skaguay and
                White Pass Road Immediately.
                And to remain away.
Failure to comply with this warning
            will be followed by prompt action

101.

Skaguay, Alaska, Mch. 8, 1898.

Fighted by Case and Draper

went only as far as the wall (a legitimate telegraph service did not reach Skagway until 1901) and cash-laden victims were charged exorbitant fees for "sending" messages. Oftentimes new arrivals would be befriended by Soapy's men and coaxed into poker games that ended with catastrophic losses. Soapy also owned a tavern known as the town's "real city hall," as well as a variety of crooked businesses to which his thugs, disguised as newspapermen or clergymen, would send new arrivals who were either conned or robbed outright by "bandits" who would appear out of nowhere and hold up everyone on the premises. A desperate newcomer deprived of his money would often be asked to join the gang. If he refused, Soapy himself would often show up, sometimes in the guise of a preacher, and after calling for a moment of prayer, would provide the sucker with just enough money to get out of Alaska and back to civilization.

The town of Dyea, twenty miles from Skagway, was every bit as dangerous – as was Sheep Camp a little farther along, at the foot of the Chilkoot Pass. "There,"

wrote Steele, "the crimes tended to be more brutal, in that the wilderness offered fewer possibilities for discreet con games or legitimate-seeming swindles." Nevertheless, many thousands of men and women were temporarily lodged at Sheep Camp, most of them engaged in packing their supplies over the summit of the coastal mountains, all anxious to get to the headwaters of the Yukon River to build their boats for the passage down to Dawson.

Unfortunately for those still solvent and optimistic, the only routes over the coastal mountains from Sheep Camp were a pair of thousand-foot ascents, the White and Chilkoot passes, where the blizzards could be deadly in winter, and where an avalanche could, in a minute of chaos, sweep travellers off the mountain and bury them fifty feet deep in snow. At the best of times, the footing was so precarious that many prospectors, burdened by the great weight of their supplies, failed in their ascent or left their supplies by the side of the trail, where they were eventually buried in snow. By mid-1898 some three thousand pack animals, mostly horses,

A group of men is seen here digging out the bodies of the fifty-three prospectors who lost their lives in the fatal avalanche near the summit of the Chilkoot Pass on April 24, 1898.

Snow had all but buried the Canadian customs house atop the Chilkoot Pass on February 26, 1998. Nevertheless, Inspector Belcher, in charge of the station and resistant to disputes over the exact location of the border, raised the Union Jack and began collecting duties on the foreign-bought supplies of incoming prospectors and visitors.

Opposite: In order to keep the line of stampeders moving up the mountain and through the Chilkoot Pass, the climbers were required to march in step – a rhythm sometimes referred to as "the Chilkoot lock step."

had broken their legs on the route up or had grown exhausted and been shot or simply skulled with an axe. They were left to lie dead and frozen alongside the trail.

On April 28, 1898, Superintendent Steele, who, after clearing the pass had stationed himself at Bennett Lake on the far side of the mountains, received the following report from Inspector Robert Belcher, who was in charge of the NWMP customs post atop the Chilkoot:

> During the afternoon of the 24th, a storm which had been raging for a week reached its height and entirely buried my cabin and the Klondikers' caches of supplies on the summit. Six feet of snow fell that day, adding to the sixty feet already on the mountain. At seven o'clock next morning there was a lull, and large numbers of men began packing their supplies and outfits up from the Alaska side, which they had been prevented from doing for many days owing to the tempestuous state of the weather. While a number of them were

on the summit the storm increased in violence and, knowing how difficult it would be for them to descend the mountain and return to Sheep Camp, and that they could not remain on the summit and survive, they began to descend to a place called The Scales. They managed to reach a point below the mountain, but were caught there by a tremendous avalanche, which buried sixty-three of them, only ten of whom survived.

THE REWARD for those who reached the summit was entry into Canadian-controlled territory, where the Mounties stationed along the border could protect them from the likes of Soapy Smith and his boys. As many as eight Mounties occupied each of the customs posts high in the passes, offering advice, assistance and oftentimes shelter to anyone who needed it.

However, gold seekers reaching the summit of either the Chilkoot or White were by no means given an automatic welcome into the Yukon or handed a ticket to the goldfields. For one thing, the

Left: Men and women en route to the goldfields often made several trips over the treacherous Chilkoot Pass in order to transport all their food and gear. Accumulated freight often sat for several days atop the pass and on occasion got lost under the snow.

Below: Mounties relax with stampeders amid accumulated freight in front of NWMP tents in the Chilkoot Pass. The Mounties were strict in their insistence that men and women take enough food and supplies into the Klondike. Note the firewood in the background, every stick of which had to be brought up the steep and dangerous mountain.

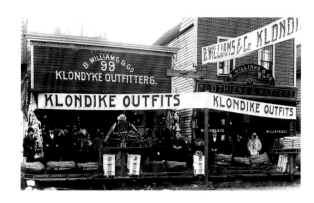

Mounties, with the backing of the territorial administration, had decreed that each visitor entering the Klondike had to bring 1,150 pounds of food. During the early months of the gold rush, food had been in drastically short supply at Bennett Lake and downriver at Dawson, creating the threat of mass starvation. "Too many people, too few groceries," wrote Sam Steele. What food was available in Dawson was so exorbitantly priced that only a successful gold miner, dance hall girl or prostitute could afford it. Eggs, imported with great difficulty by dog team, sold for $18 a dozen (compared to 5 cents a dozen on the outside). Sardines and oysters sold for $25 a tin, while bottled milk went for $30 a quart (nearly three times the price of the best French cognac in Dawson). Because of the difficulty of importing flour, even a loaf of bread or a dozen tea biscuits often sold for as much as $10.

In addition, the hopeful were required to bring their own tents, carpentry tools, mining tools and cooking utensils. Packing such weight up the mountain often required seven or eight trips – journeys that in some cases began with the help of horses but ended on foot.

As if the challenge were not great enough, prospectors were required to pay customs duty on every item of gear that they brought into the Yukon from the United States. It was often said that if prospectors from the US had waited and bought their supplies and equipment at Vancouver or Victoria, they would have saved hundreds of dollars at the Yukon border. During the winter of 1897–98, more than $150,000 was collected in duties atop the Chilkoot and White passes.

Having reached Bennett Lake at the foot of the mountains, those who had survived thus far laid out their gear in the snow, pitched their tents in temperatures that often dropped to −60°F, and began the onerous preparations for their passage downriver at spring breakup. For all of them, the construction of boats was the first order of business. This they undertook along the shores and on the ice of the eleven-mile-long body of water, or on nearby Lindeman Lake.

Klondike outfitters such as the B. Williams Co. sprang up in Seattle, Portland and San Francisco to supply clothing and gear to men and women adventurous or foolhardy enough to try their luck (and pluck) pursuing Yukon gold.

The theatre and dance-hall were an important aspect of Klondike culture during the gold rush, and dancers and actors could get nearly as rich as miners if they sold their talents and favours to the right people at the right price. While the female performers in the photo above appear to be somewhat "mature" for the rough and tumble of the Dawson City stage and gambling halls, they were nonetheless willing to take a chance, and are seen here fording the Dyea River on their way to the Yukon.

"The situation was certainly unique," wrote Steele on his arrival at Bennett Lake in February 1898.

> About seven thousand men were encamped in the immediate vicinity, and the sound of axes, hammers and whipsaws was incessant, making the place seem like one of the largest shipyards in the days of wooden hulls. East and west of us, from the Chilkoot and White passes to Tagish, nearly 60 miles east, every available nook or flat was crowded with tents."

Steele noted that on a still day the smoke rising from the cook fires of the sprawling tent city would hang like a ten-mile-wide thundercloud above the lakes.

From the time Steele arrived at the lake to the time he left for Dawson some six months later, he and his contingent of twenty policemen worked around the clock to help miners of all nationalities and walks of life to survive the ferocious winter and prepare for a safe journey into the Klondike. His office was in one end

of a hastily constructed log building that also served as the Mounties' barracks and cookhouse. There, day and night, he was visited by doctors, lawyers, clergymen, soldiers, engineers – and by "women in tights," he wrote – all of them intent on making their fortune downriver.

Even though the job of regulating the gold seekers fell to the Canadian police, only about a fifth of those on the gold trail were Canadian. The majority, by far, came from the US, with smaller numbers from England, France, Germany, the Netherlands and Scandinavia. Among them, of course, were many who had no intention of mining or prospecting but were there merely to serve those who did: dancers, prostitutes, nurses, tailors, restaurateurs. Steele wrote of one old woman in male attire who had come over the pass with a team of four goats, pulling a sleigh loaded with the makings of the laundry business she hoped to start in Dawson.

The Mounties' duties during the weeks leading up to breakup included ensuring that the boats were seaworthy and assigning a number to every vessel about to

Below: For three years beginning in 1896, thousands of prospectors gathered annually on the shores and ice of Bennett Lake, just west of the Chilkoot and White passes, to build the boats that would carry them down the Yukon River to the Klondike when the ice broke in the spring.

Fires, for both light and heat, burned round the clock in the long winter darkness, and saws hummed day and night, cutting jack pine and spruce for hull planking.

Right: Would-be prospectors from the US stand aboard their clinker-built boats on Bennett Lake, awaiting departure for the goldfields to the north. The boats were propelled by sail, pole and oar, although much of the push north came simply from the rushing current of the Yukon River.

Prospectors and Native packers made their way laboriously over the Chilkoot Trail on their way to Bennett Lake, from where they carried on by boat down the Yukon River to the Klondike. Never an easy passage, the trail was considerably less arduous in summer than winter, when the snow on it could be up to sixty feet deep.

make the trip. In addition, Steele and his men recorded the names and addresses of everyone on his way to the Klondike, anticipating the likelihood of accidents or deaths that would necessitate notifying relatives. Otherwise, the detachment was kept busy around the clock settling disputes, inspecting food, caring for the sick and burying those who died of disease or accident.

The Mounties also provided security for those who had arrived carrying large sums of money. In one instance, the managers of the banks of Commerce and British North America, who were on their way to Dawson City to do business, entrusted Superintendent Steele with $2 million, which he stowed for safekeeping under the straw-stuffed mattress of his hand-hewn wooden bed.

Finally, on May 29, the ice broke up on Bennett Lake, and the exodus north through the perilous Miles Canyon began. "I went up on the hill behind my office to see the start," wrote Steele, "and at one time counted over eight hundred boats under sail." The following day, hundreds

more began the trip. "Strange and motley were the craft," wrote Steele, "large scows with oxen, cows, horses and dogs on board; well-built skiffs; clumsy, oblong tubs, little better than ordinary boxes; light and serviceable Peterboro canoes."

The exodus marked the height of the most extraordinary treasure hunt in history. Flotillas of fervent gold hunters would be followed by thousands more, and then thousands more, as the summer of 1898 progressed. Inspector Philip Primrose, one of the first Mounties to have arrived in the Yukon, recorded in his diary that summer: "A large number had the idea that gold was to be picked up quite easily, probably on the hills or in the streets – and some, I believe, would not have known gold if they had seen it."

ON HIS OWN WAY NORTH in early June, Steele selected twenty sites along the Yukon River where NWMP posts would be established during the months to come. By this time, Steele had been appointed to the Council of the Yukon Territory and given command of the entire force of

Durable scows such as this one were used to move supplies and passengers up and down the Yukon River between Dawson City and Bennett Lake. While they were big enough to support steam engines, they were built in the Yukon where no engines were available, so were propelled by either sail or oar, with the help of the current on downriver runs.

Mounties in British Columbia and the Yukon.

Steele's arrival in Dawson was, like everyone else's, a descent into knee-deep mud along the waterfront (the result of a recent flood) and even deeper social chaos. More than a year had passed since a small detachment of Mounties had been established in Dawson City, but the town had grown so fast since its founding in 1896 that law and order was little more than a figment of the territorial government's imagination. For one thing, there were still too few officers to keep the lid on the drunkenness and violence. For another, there were far too few jail cells at NWMP Fort Herchmer to house trouble-makers intent on exploiting the chaos. The result was that all but the very worst criminals strutted the muddy streets with impunity and raised hell in the dance halls and saloons. "Even if I had cells in which to put them," Inspector Charles Constantine had written in an early 1897 report to Ottawa, "I have no men to spare to supervise them and no food to feed them." The standing rule at Fort Herchmer for several

months during the winter of 1897 was that only criminals with enough food to feed themselves for the duration of their sentences should be charged or imprisoned.

For several months the previous winter, the daily rations for a Mountie at Fort Herchmer had been two bags of tea, four ounces of bacon and twelve ounces of flour. In the town, residents had been reduced to nourishing themselves on bread, tea and whatever fish or meat they could obtain on their own or buy from local Natives. "Gold is a wonderful luxury," quipped Constantine in a report to his superiors, "but you can't eat it."

Mounties with a little ingenuity could occasionally cadge a few pounds of caribou or moose meat or a fresh-caught salmon from a local hunter. But the Mounties, most of whom were earning just $1.25 a day, had precious little purchasing power compared with the miners, many of whom paid for what flour and tea was available with gold nuggets. Even the local construction workers were earning $15 a day in the vastly inflated local economy. In some cases, dance hall girls and prostitutes

THE KLONDIKE NEWS

SAN FRANCISCO, CAL. AND

VOL. I.   DAWSON, N.W.T. APRIL 1ST, 1898.   NO. 1

OFFICE OF PUBLICATION
NO. 23 MAIN ST., SAN FRANCISCO, CAL.

COPYRIGHTED 1898 BY VIRGIL MOORE.

SUBSCRIPTION $2.00 PER ANNUM.

OUTPUT FOR 1898 $40,000,000.

FROM Nº 8 EL DORADO.
PROPERTY OF CHAS. LAMB,
VALUE $315.00

SCHMIDT L. & LITH. CO. S.F.

DISCOVERER,
GEO. W. CARMACK.

THE LARGEST GOLD NUGGET.
FOUND IN EL DORADO CREEK Nº 36 BY M. KNUSTOR
WEIGHT 36 OUNCES VALUE $530.00

Typical of the media of the day (perhaps of any day), the *Klondike News* tended to idealize its subject matter. This edition, dated April 1, 1898, depicted its cover subject, George Carmack, as a rather dapper and fanciful squire, a dilettante outdoorsman. In fact, Carmack, the San Francisco prospector who, with his common-law wife Kate and partner Jim Mason, discovered gold in the Yukon, was a hardbitten ruddy-faced adventurer, an ex-US marine, who would as soon have appeared in his underwear as in the foppish outfit shown here.

Gold was the universal currency in the Klondike during the late 1890s. Here, in front of the Lousetown Bakery, a couple of miners or tradesmen are seen paying for a loaf of bread with a carefully measured portion of gold dust.

were making as much as $1,000 a week. Bartenders, who worked around the clock, frequently ended their shifts with an ounce of gold dust in their pockets.

If the Mounties had trouble acquiring meat from area Natives, it was in part because of the general unpopularity of the force among the local tribes. In the summer of 1896, Inspector Constantine had summarily routed the local Natives from the site where the town was to rise at the forks of the Yukon and Klondike rivers. He had uprooted more of them again when he moved NWMP headquarters downriver from Forty Mile to Dawson in 1897. While the local English bishop, William Bompas, defended the Native people's right to the land they had occupied for generations, Constantine told his superiors, "When I want the land, Bompas and his Indians will go...I don't propose to be bluffed by an arrogant bishop who thinks the only people worth considering are a few dirty Indians too lazy to work."

Steele's immediate intention to build a bigger jail upon his arrival in Dawson

was initially hampered by a shortage of building materials, particularly windows, nails and hardware. What's more, when he arrived, there were few horses in town to haul timber in from the forests. Hundreds of horses had been shot the previous winter to feed the townspeople and the indispensable sled dogs that moved men and mail back and forth into the surrounding territory.

But most shortages had begun to wane with the arrival in Dawson of the seven thousand people who had survived the winter at Bennett Lake. They had brought with them their animals, provisions and manpower, as well as their tools, woodstoves and cookware. Moreover, in the summer of 1898, steamboats had begun to ply the river, bringing supplies upriver from present-day Emmonak, Alaska, on the Bering Sea. By late August of that year, fifty-six of them had arrived, disgorging not just food, basic clothing and hardware but women and whisky, as well as carpets, silk textiles and European furniture. By the autumn of 1898, Dawson's hotel dining rooms were serving champagne, truffles

AS THE GOLD RUSH peaked in 1897, hundreds of lonely men were afoot in the streets of Dawson City at night, looking for entertainment and ways to indulge their fantasies. In the saloons and gambling parlours, where the aim was to keep the men happy (and thereby extract the money from their pockets), the cancan quickly became the show dance of choice. It was sexy; it was decadent; it epitomized the energy not only of the Gay Nineties but of an explosive frontier town in which good sense and discipline were often overshadowed by the relentless dissipation that was made possible by easy and exorbitant wealth.

For the show girls, the dance was a way of displaying not only their physical allure but the thousand-dollar flounced gowns that had been imported for them from Paris, where the cancan had originated and been popularized during the mid-1800s. Dawson was, after all, the Paris of the North.

However, unlike the Parisian version of the dance, which was often performed by one dancer, the Dawson version was performed in chorus lines, with as many as a dozen athletic girls hooting and laughing as they executed the *battements* or high kicks, the *grands écarts* or flying splits, and the *port d'armes* spins performed on one leg while the ankle of the other leg was held almost vertically above the head.

The surroundings in which the dance was performed were as decadent as the cancan itself – dance halls and bars lit by French chandeliers and furnished with expensive French divans on which hucksters and investors lounged with the local dancers and prostitutes. So popular was the cancan in Dawson, and so closely associated with the early spirit of the town, that it has remained a symbol of the Klondike's golden era and excesses, and it is still danced in Dawson at Diamond Tooth Gertie's Casino.

The dancing girls of Dawson City were an irresistible lure to the men who came north during the gold rush. Note the Champagne bottles in the hands of the women furthest to the right and left in this Dawson ballroom, where the women (at least those in the photo) are outnumbered thirty-five to five by the men.

Below: By 1899, much of the mountainside behind Dawson City had been stripped of spruce and jack pine used either for lumber or in stoves to heat the buildings.

Right: Two of the more expensive items in Dawson City during the gold rush were groceries and liquor, both of which were brought thousands of miles by boat and were sold at prices that were occasionally four hundred times as high as what they fetched under normal circumstances to the south.

and caviar, which as often as not were paid for with pure gold.

Mere wealth did not, of course, cure the town's ills, many of which were the result of extreme overcrowding. In little over a year, Dawson City's population had exploded from a few hundred people to more than twenty thousand, making it the largest Canadian city west of Winnipeg. In the proliferating tent city along the waterfront where newcomers made their homes, sanitation was unknown, water often contaminated and food impossible to refrigerate. The vast and filthy encampment was an all-too-ready crucible for diseases such as typhoid, which in 1898 claimed nearly ninety lives in the town. In the graveyard partway up the mountain behind the town, the ground frost was so heavy by mid-October that as many as a hundred graves were pre-dug in September, while the soil was still workable, in anticipation of the winter's toll.

And yet the town thrived with an almost unexpected persistence and vigour. By the summer of 1899, wooden sidewalks had been installed on every street, and a pair of banks and numerous retail businesses boomed along Front and First streets: milliners, dressmakers, tailors, hardware shops, photo studios, grocery stores, restaurants. Dance halls, saloons and casinos roiled into the night, and the famed Palace Grand Theatre, constructed by "Arizona" Charlie Meadows, presented operas and vaudeville acts from around the world. When the entertainment grew dull, Meadows himself took the stage and performed wild west stunts, such as shooting cigarettes out of the mouths of willing participants. In the back streets and alleys, prostitution flourished in any of twenty or more street-side shanties and private homes. On Sunday mornings, the town's six churches were crowded.

Meanwhile, activity along the outlying creeks expanded in a fury of staking, digging and panning. And the world was kept well apprised. Foreign and Canadian journalists, including the famed Flora Shaw of the London *Times* and Faith Fenton of the Toronto *Globe*, filed regular gold-rush stories to Toronto, London and New York. The town's own newspaper, the *Klondike Nugget*, bleated its dramatic daily news to those in Dawson.

AMIDST THIS PROFUSION of productivity, dissipation and squalor, Sam Steele went to work establishing order. First, he brought dozens of additional policemen to Dawson. He sent many of them to the crude NWMP posts that had been established along the rivers and creeks, and greatly expanded the force in town. He built a jail that could house fifty or more prisoners, promptly filled it, and instituted a requirement that all guns in the Yukon be registered. The confiscated pistols and rifles (with their firing pins removed) sold for small fortunes at auction, mainly to those who cherished them as souvenirs of their time in the Klondike.

Under Steele's regime, hotels and lodging houses, whether in town or out on the trails, were obliged to keep their patrons safe and provide them with boiled drinking and wash water to counter the threat of typhoid. Saloons were strictly licensed, and the sale of liquor to anyone under the age of sixteen was prohibited.

Dawson, the city of gold, was, during its short spring and summer, also the city of mud. In this 1899 photo a team has been hitched to help pull a struggling horse and a wagonload of lumber out of the axle-deep muck along Front Street.

"The gambling houses," said Steele, "were left as we found them, wide open but closely watched, lest there should be any cheating."

Steele's prisoners were put to work in the surrounding forests, cutting and splitting firewood, which was used by the detachment and in government offices at a preposterous rate during the depths of winter. "Fires had to be kept up all night, except in my quarters," wrote Steele in his reminiscences of the era, "and the absence of it there was for self-preservation only. For had my stove caught fire, I should not have been able to escape, as it was between me and the door. I preferred to have the water bucket frozen solid every night, and to have my stove relit at six in the morning before I got out of bed."

The police and government consumed nearly one thousand cords of jack pine and spruce during Steele's first winter in Dawson – the equivalent of a pile a mile and a half long, four feet high and four feet wide. "If possible," he said, "the prisoners hated the wood pile even more than they hated me or their escorts. It was the talk of the town and kept fifty or more of the toughs of Dawson busy every day."

The story is often told of a gambler who Steele fined $50 for cheating in a Dawson casino. "Is that all?" exclaimed the gambler. "Why, I have it right here in my vest pocket!"

"And sixty days on the wood pile," added Steele. "Have you got that in your vest pocket?"

Given the poor stoves and frame buildings, fire was a constant threat, and members of the force routinely roamed the streets on winter nights looking for tell-tale puffs of smoke, ever ready to sound the alarm. During the winter of 1898, a blaze broke out, reducing two blocks of Dawson to ash before it was brought under control. "Had it not been for the Mounted Police and troops," wrote Steele, "the entire town would have been destroyed and hundreds of lives lost."

Advice from the police about nutrition, as well as daily food inspections in the tent city and restaurants, helped to reduce scurvy and limit the spread of typhoid and other communicable diseases. But with

All a miner really needed to put away a little gold once he got to the Klondike was a stream, a claim and a pan. Whether or not he became a millionaire was a function not so much of skill as of luck and persistence.

MUCH OF the gold discovered in the creeks and rivers during the Klondike gold rush had been laid down in the form of alluvial or placer deposits – in other words, gold particles or nuggets washed free of their original rock matrix and deposited in riverbed sand or gravel.

Panning was the Yukon prospector's first and easiest method of detecting and claiming that gold. Using a wide shallow pan as a receptacle, the hopeful prospector collected sand and gravel that he believed might contain gold. If water was not present in the sample, he added it and began agitating the pan. Because gold is much denser than rock, it would quickly settle to the bottom of the pan and with careful decanting could be isolated and removed.

Once the presence of gold was established, the miner invariably extracted larger quantities of sand and gravel and used a sluice box to separate out the gold. The box was essentially a man-made wooden channel, with riffles set in the bottom, over which sand and gravel were carried at an incline by a steady flow of water. The riffles were designed to create dead zones in the current to allow gold to drop out of suspension, while the lighter sand and gravel flowed out of the box as tailings.

Sometimes the gold deposits were buried deep in the banks of the rivers or streams, and their recovery required extensive, often dangerous excavation. Because most Yukon terrain was frozen solid, often to a depth of ten feet or more, miners dug down gradually by setting fires on the frozen ground. They then scraped away the gravel, lit another fire and burrowed deeper, a layer at a time, until the desired depth was achieved. Often working alone at this demanding method of excavation, miners were subject not only to cave-ins but to asphyxiation, as the hot ashes and charcoal left by the fires gave off toxic gases that could overwhelm the men if they went into the excavation too soon after the fires were extinguished.

Some ten years after the peak of the gold rush, enormous industrial gold dredges were moved into the area in an effort to claim what gold could no longer be recovered by independent surface operators. The dredges scooped massive amounts of sand, gravel and boulders out of the creeks and riverbeds, reworking the landscape, altering the locations of rivers and creeks, and leaving great heaps of tailings in their wake. The last of these, Dredge No. 4, shut down in 1966 and is now an historic landmark.

But it was the small operators – the "men who moil[ed] for gold," as Robert Service put it – who brought gold mining to the Klondike in 1897 and became the face and character of the gold rush.

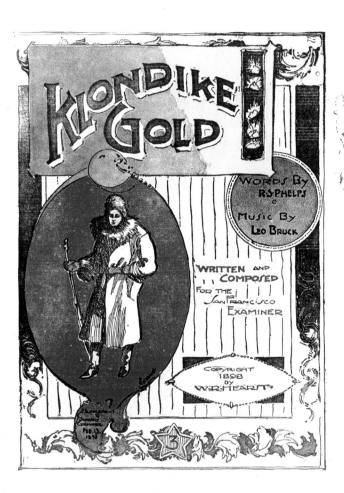

The fantasy of an exotic wilderness where one was likely to find unlimited wealth and adventure appealed equally to the public imagination and to the popular song-writers of the day. The widespread romance of it all is evidenced by sheet music published in cities as far from the Klondike, and from one another, as San Francisco, Cleveland and Chicago.

A curious and undoubtedly gleeful crowd watches as the unfortunate man in this photo was whipped publicly for stealing food in Dawson City at the height of the gold rush. A sign saying "thief" was then hung around his neck, and he was dispatched from the Klondike by dog team under NWMP guard.

sewage sitting in the streets and winter temperatures dipping to the freezing point in the town's poorly heated buildings, sickness was a formidable foe. Most of the time, the town's two government hospitals and five private ones were crowded to capacity. The town's half dozen doctors and a handful of nurses worked seven days a week, day and night. One English doctor, who had come to the Klondike looking for gold, ended up working fourteen hours a day to keep the sick alive.

Like the hospitals, the infirmary at Fort Herchmer was full of typhoid sufferers. Fortunately for the sick Mounties, Sam Steele put their interests ahead of all others in his detachment or in the town at large. "Caring for the sick was our greatest expense," he noted in his memoirs. Those in need of the most efficacious tonics were "medicated" with champagne, purchased at prices that ran anywhere from $20 to $45 a bottle. And all were fed eggs and milk, purchased with the fines imposed on those who broke the law. The Mounties occasionally commandeered a steer

or pig, paying the going rate, so that their sick comrades would be well nourished.

When funds ran out for the administration of the hospitals in late 1898, Steele, who among his other duties was chairman of the local board of health, increased the severity of fines and significantly raised the licensing fees for saloons and dance halls. That winter, more than $90,000 was collected from both sources and was poured directly into the local typhoid and scurvy wards.

While most of the offences that the Mounties had to deal with were trivial – cutting wood without a permit, selling liquor without a licence, selling bad food, refusing to pay a prostitute – the constables and officers were constantly on guard against more serious infractions. They patrolled the streets, guarded the banks and were assiduous in keeping watch over every honest miner who had staked a claim and was busily at work out on the creeks. The detachment took pride in ferreting out the histories and criminal records of every suspicious person who arrived in Dawson – and making their findings known to the officials and busi-

ness owners of the town. Steele wrote that "The true criminal class were much the same as one saw in Skagway and Dyea. Many had committed murders in other lands, had held up trains, committed burglary and safe-blowing, or were out-and-out gold thieves, but they could not display themselves openly in territory patrolled by the Mounted Police."

Not all gold-rush crimes were the work of practised criminals. In May 1898, four otherwise peaceable Native men shot at and murdered a prospector, William Meehan, who was passing their camp in a small boat, and severely injured Meehan's partner, Charles Fox. Within a couple of weeks, the Mounties had arrested the murderers, who were brought to trial in Dawson, where three of them were sentenced to death, the fourth being too young to send to the gallows. However, eight hours before they were scheduled to hang, on November 1, 1898, the executions were deferred because it was All Saints' Day, and it was considered unchristian, if not uncharitable, to hang anyone on a Christian holiday.

Innovation was the key to survival in the Klondike during the gold rush. Here, a team of goats has been hitched up to haul cargo at Bennett Lake, where, like the prospectors, the animals awaited the trip north down the Yukon River to the goldfields. While it was exceedingly difficult to bring, say, horses or cows over the mountain passes from Skagway or Dyea, the smaller goats were better suited to the trip, and perhaps more sure-footed on the steep trail.

The deferment came as a considerable shock to Toronto *Globe* reporter, Faith Fenton, who had already written an exuberant "eye-witness" account of the hanging and had sent it off to Toronto by dog team with the mail the previous day. When she heard about the stay (which, as it turned out, was in effect for six months), she went immediately and tearfully to Sam Steele, begging him to help. The chivalrous commander immediately dispatched a police dog team, which ran down the mail sled and saved the woman's job by retrieving the article.

THE HANDLING of Yukon mail was one of the Mounties' most onerous and important responsibilities. During the warmer months, mail moved easily in and out of the Klondike by steamer. But during winter, it fell to the Mounties and their dog teams to move the mail every two weeks along the frozen river between Dawson and Bennett Lake, and then over the mountains to Skagway, where it was picked up by oceangoing vessels on their way to Vancouver and San Francisco.

Among thousands of letters, often weighing as much as seven hundred pounds, the mail included bank drafts and reports, government documents and money. The run covered six hundred miles each way and was often completed, round-trip, in as little as fifteen days, by men and dogs travelling in thirty-mile relays between NWMP posts, where the exchanges were made in twenty minutes or less.

One constable from the Indian River post was able to do his thirty-mile leg in just over four hours, running behind the sled all the way. "The dogs," wrote Sam Steele, "were the well-known Labrador breed, very fierce, and they had the remarkable reputation of having at one time killed and devoured their driver."

Besides carrying the mail, the NWMP "mailmen" carried out any necessary police work en route and checked isolated cabins to make sure the inhabitants were alive and well. Those who needed care were transported atop the sleigh to the nearest police post where they were nursed back to health in exchange for a few hours of chopping wood once they were on the mend.

Below: The arrival in Dawson City of the bi-weekly winter mail via NWMP dog team invariably drew an enthusiastic crowd of those expecting letters or newspapers from home. Through the long winter darkness, when the rivers were frozen solid, mail hauled hundreds of miles by dogs from Dyea and Skagway was the Klondike's only contact with the outside world. Note the massive heap of mail aboard the sleighs.

Right: A Dawson City crowd waits for mail that, in summer, came up the Yukon River by steamboat.

The trek into the Yukon
was as tough for the
officers and constables
of the NWMP as it was
for the prospectors. But
while the prospectors
had their sights set on
fortunes in gold, the
Mounties had little
more to look forward
to than long hours,
short pay, occasionally
devilish food and heavy
loads on the trail. Their
boss Sam Steele said
eventually that build-
ing an effective NWMP
presence in the Yukon
was the most arduous
challenge of the many
he had faced, including
his participation in the
Wolseley Expedition and
the great march west.

A crowd of aspiring prospectors in fedoras and overcoats waits outside the customs house on Wharf Street in Victoria in 1896 to secure mining licences for the Klondike.

More dramatic than the run itself was the arrival of the mail in Dawson. Under Steele's regime, this celebrated event took place every two weeks and drew hundreds of the town's residents and visitors to the makeshift post office in the abandoned Palace Saloon. One legendary Christmas run brought several thousand people out onto the river to welcome the mail sleigh. Inside the post office, the mail was sorted at lightning speed by half a dozen constables and stuffed into pigeon holes, one for each letter of the alphabet. The problem for the sorters was that some of the holes ended up crammed with more than a thousand pieces of mail. Men would line up by the hundreds at the front door, where they were allowed in thirty at a time. Some were so desperate for news from girlfriends or wives that they lined up three days in advance. Victorian propriety meant that the women were given their own entrance at a side door and did not have to wait to get in. The local prostitutes quickly realized they could make money by picking up mail for prospectors who were unable to get into town or were

simply too lazy to wait in line.

In all, the mail sleighs travelled 64,000 miles during the winter of 1898, and William Ogilvie, who had taken over from Yukon Commissioner Walsh a few months earlier, estimated that the Dawson post office did business equivalent to that of the post office in a city of 150,000 people.

The only comparably busy agency in town was the claims office, where in 1898 nearly seventeen thousand claims were registered, many of which were transferred up to forty times. Men lined up for as long as three days to get into the premises, although women, as at the post office, could enter by a side door and go directly to a claims agent. Again, prostitutes were often hired by prospectors to register their claims, or were given tiny shares in those claims in exchange for their services.

By late 1898, the claims office had consumed every scrap of writing paper in Dawson, and clerks were writing out staking documents on pieces of pine board, which were kept in stacks, like building

TODAY there are roads and airports and snowmobile trails in the Yukon. But at the end of the nineteenth century, during the gold rush, the only way of travelling any distance during the long frigid winters was by dog team and sleigh.

Dogs were used by trappers, prospectors, miners and hunters – and by the northern Natives on their travels through the mountains and bush. The Mounties used dog teams to patrol the rivers, forests and gold mines, and to carry mail over hundreds of miles of frozen terrain.

Generally, the musher rode on the back of the sleigh – indeed, had to in order to keep up to dogs that could run 20 miles an hour over long stretches. Occasionally, to keep warm, or to lighten the load for the dogs, a musher would step off and run behind the sleigh, which, particularly on mail runs, often carried loads of up to seven hundred pounds.

On some runs, food was available en route for the musher and his dogs – at, say, the small NWMP outposts along the Yukon River, or at miners' cabins along the creeks. Where it was not, drivers carried simple food for themselves and frozen fish or moose meat for the dogs.

Some dog teams consisted of just three or four dogs, but many had ten or eleven, generally hitched side by side. The lead dog, hitched singly, needed intelligence, stamina, a strong instinct for keeping to the trail, and the capability to respond

quickly and accurately to the voice commands of the musher. It also had to command the respect of the other dogs.

Many types of dogs have been used in sled teams over the years, among them Alaskan malamutes, Samoyeds and Siberian huskies.

There have also been teams of less likely breeds such as foxhounds and staghounds, and more recently of crossbreeds, used for their hardiness and resistance to disease.

For the NWMP, however, the preferred dog was the durable and highly intelligent Labrador husky, a breed famous for loyalty and yet fierce when challenged or mistreated.

Native to coastal Labrador, the breed was most likely brought to Labrador by the Thule Inuit around 1300 AD. To maintain the desired

qualities of strength, stamina and intelligence, the descendants of the Thule allowed the Labrador to breed with the native wolf populations.

Undoubtedly for this reason, they resemble wolves in appearance and can weigh up to a hundred pounds. However, they are genetically distinct from wolves, as well as from any other husky.

For the NWMP of the gold rush era, the choice of Labrador huskies was obvious. The dogs' double coats protected them on the long mail runs in bitterly cold weather, their strength and aerodynamic bodies gave them speed, and their intelligence made them both trainable and responsive to commands.

There are no recorded cases of these remarkable dogs ever letting the Mounties down.

Superintendent Charles Constantine is seen here, sitting fourth from right, with the men of Fort Constantine and at least two of the four-legged members of their reliable team of Labrador huskies.

The arrival of boatloads of prospectors and other adventurers in spring was cause for excitement in Dawson City after long winters during the gold rush. Here a crowd has gathered on the muddy waterfront to welcome the first boats down the Yukon River from Bennett Lake after break-up. Larger supply and passenger boats coming the opposite direction from west coast ports, via the Pacific Ocean and Bering Sea, were met with equal enthusiasm.

Opposite: These tough Klondike gold miners, photographed in 1898, used steam, piped from above ground, to melt frozen earth and rock, so that they could burrow deeper into the candle-lit depths beneath their claim at Gold Hill in the Yukon.

blocks, in the corners of the office and in a local warehouse.

Life wasn't nearly as chaotic along the outlying creeks and riverbanks. The Mounties paid regular visits to the miners and prospectors, ever willing to help sort out a difficulty or health problem, deliver or pick up a letter, or simply assure a miner that the Mounties were present and vigilant. In the early days of the stampede for gold, there had been endless claiming and staking disputes to settle. One prospector shot one of his own investors over a discrepancy in the division of their spoils. And ownership arguments had been as common as river gravel in the claims office in town. But by 1898, the miners had settled, to extracting gold – sometimes working sixteen hours a day to do so. They panned in the creek beds and dug laboriously into the gravel and rock. Often in winter, a Mountie enjoyed a meal and a drink or two with a lonely miner, and perhaps a game of cards, before bedding down in the miner's log cabin for the night. Upon departure in the morning, the officer was occasionally given a small gold nugget as a token of appreciation for his friendship and for his efforts in keeping the Klondike safe.

Steele himself greatly respected the commitment of those whose work was the foundation of prosperity in the Yukon. "During the winter of 1899, I took several trips to the creeks," he recalled in his memoirs:

The sight was a remarkable one, the ground in some places being frozen to a depth of two hundred feet, the frost of the ice age, not of the present. The miners had to thaw out the ground with large fires of fir or pine wood until they had, after many scrapings and burnings, reached bed rock, and then had to drift along its surface to enable them to scrape up the gold… All the way up the valleys the air was full of dense choking smoke, a spectacle not likely to be seen again on this earth.

Excavating gold in this way could be dangerous in the extreme. Clay and gravel could collapse on an isolated miner in a

While many members of the NWMP wore a soft version of the iconic Mountie Stetson as early as the mid-1870s, the hat was not in common use in the force until 1894, when Sam Steele ordered dozens of the hats from the US in order to bring a measure of uniformity to his men's headgear at Fort Macleod. More were ordered in 1897 to outfit the NWMP delegation to Queen Victoria's Diamond Jubilee celebration in London, England. However, the hat, complete with leather band and four-cornered "bashing," did not become the official NWMP crown until 1904, when hundreds were ordered from the Stetson factory, then located in Philadelphia. The Stetson seen here is believed to have belonged to bugler Fred Bagley during his service with the 15th Light Horse band in Calgary.

Employees of the Dawson City branch of the Canadian Bank of Commerce, seen here in the company of miners and other account holders, prepare to ship $750,000 worth of gold dust from Dawson City in 1899. Under the security of local NWMP officers, no gold shipment was ever lost or stolen in transit to Canadian or US banks far to the south.

trice, and the buildup of fumes from the hot charcoal in the holes and drifts frequently reached toxic levels. More than a few inexperienced miners went into the drifts too soon after the fires were out and were carried out unconscious or dead.

If the miners were happy to offer hospitality to a visiting NWMP officer in exchange for his protective care, they were less sanguine about the 10 percent tax that the Yukon government imposed on their annual take of gold in late 1898 – a tax that was to be administered by the Mounties. They were even less inclined to the tax given that Commissioner James Walsh had announced, on his departure from the Yukon, that because of the new levy he would be returning to Ottawa with "more gold and material to make wealth than Caesar brought to Rome on his return from Gaul."

The problem for Steele and his men was how to measure the amount of unrefined gold extracted by each miner. The amounts brought into the banks often varied significantly from how much had been taken out of the ground or creek bed.

In the spring of 1899, rather than accepting the miners' voluntary estimates, Steele made a bold move and, as the miners prepared to start hauling out their winter's wealth, posted Mounties at the mouths of every creek where mining was going on: Bonanza, Eldorado, Dominion, Hunker, Gold Run and others. Using rough mathematical calculations, the officers assessed the productivity of each mine and recorded this to compare with the quantities of gold that the miners eventually took to the bank. While the final tax was taken on the weight that went to the bank, the field measurement helped the Mounties determine if gold was being withheld by the miner, or was being sold or traded privately before any banking was done.

"The gold output from the Klondike was very great that spring," wrote Steele. One young prospector had sifted out 1,950 pounds of gold dust, valued at $400,000 (nearly $2 million at today's values).

Almost all the gold mined in the Klondike was escorted from the creeks to the bank by a member of the NWMP. After the gold was received, weighed and paid for at the

Below: This wagonload of gold bars, leaving Dawson City under NWMP escort during the summer of 1899, has drawn an audience of duly fascinated onlookers. But the four solemn soldiers from the Yukon Field Force and the lone Mountie are clearly taking no chances that the booty will be stolen. Indeed, during the entire gold rush, no gold under Mountie guard ever disappeared.

Right: The rather grim faces and rough clothing of the Mounties and civilians of the Fort Constantine detachment tell a tale of long hours, poor pay, occasionally bad food and bitter weather during the gold rush.

"This mining business is all a gamble. Lucky if you win. The one who works the hardest is not the one who gets the rich mines; the one that knows the most about mining does not always win. The gold is not found here like in other countries, there are no indications. The green-horn as well as the expert wins. He that is lucky."

LEPHA MAE EDGREN in a letter to her sister Dottie sent from Dawson City, August 25, 1898

banks in Dawson, it was transformed into ingots, and the Mounties escorted it wherever the manager wished. For the most part, it was shipped to Seattle. As Steele reported:

The NWMP escorts had more gold in their charge, and under more difficult circumstances, than any men who have performed such duty in any country in the world. Four officers took at least five tons of ingots down the Yukon each trip – 2,000 miles of the stream through a wilderness by steamer to the ocean, then transferred it to a sea-going vessel, and finally delivered it at the bank in Seattle, another 2,000 miles distant. And this was always done without a hitch in the arrangements.

It was somewhat ironic that the Canadian Mounties, who earned $1.25 a day (50 cents of which was a special "Yukon allowance"), were risking their lives to safeguard a process that made millionaires of the men (many of them American) who owned or had mined the gold. Said Steele:

The banks usually made the officers a small present when the journey was done, but had they employed special security agents it is highly improbable that the work would have been done so well, and it would have cost at least $500 per man employed. Even then it is doubtful that the gold would in every case have gone through safely to its destination.

Another irony of the situation was that, amidst this unprecedented accumulation of wealth, few constables got to enjoy even the pittance they earned. Many lived on their 50-cent Yukon allowance and sent their regular pay of 75 cents a day home to wives and dependants. Or did not send it, as the case might be. In July of 1898, one Dawson constable's wife wrote from Picton, Ontario, addressing the post commander with the words, "My husband said I would get 15 dollars a month. Please send it at once as I am so much in need of it. I am nearly helpless and my poor children are in want of wearing material…How I wish my husband could come home, but I suppose I'll have to bear it. Please grant me this favour at once."

By comparison, bank clerks in Dawson were by this time earning $800 a year, plus board and clothing allowance, while sawyers and carpenters continued to earn more in a day than NWMP constables earned in a week. The Mounties' poverty was so well known in Dawson that the theatres regularly sent them complimentary tickets to their shows (benefiting of course by having law officers on their sometimes vulnerable premises).

It is a significant credit to the members of the force that during the Klondike rush not a single constable or officer was ever cited for, or even suspected of, dishonesty or graft. The Yukon Commissioner William Ogilvie, who took over from Walsh, said of the men of the NWMP:

The police force has a large field to fill, numerous duties to perform and vast interests to protect. And when I say that the field is filled, the duties performed and these interests protected in the highest possible manner and with the greatest efficiency, I am simply stating what everyone in this territory knows.

The relaxed attitude of the officers and constables of the NWMP's Pleasant Camp detachment (1898) would suggest that their camp was fittingly, if fancifully, named.

Note the Union Jack at right and the size of the spruce logs in the cabin – some as wide as the men's shoulders.

IN SEPTEMBER 1899, Sam Steele was recalled to the North-West Territories and replaced by Superintendent Bowen Perry. Many of Dawson's leading citizens attempted to persuade Steele to stay, but he had worked extraordinarily hard for a year and a half and was ready to go. "My time in the Klondike was the most trying that has ever fallen to the lot of a member of the NWMP," he wrote in his memoirs.

When Steele boarded a steamer at Dawson on September 26, 1899, the man chosen to bid him farewell was the wealthy ex-miner Alex McDonald, the so-called King of the Klondike, famous more for his money than his eloquence. As he thrust a bag of gold into Steele's hands, he said, "Here Sam – here y'are. Poke for you. Goodbye." Along the banks of the Yukon, thousands of people gathered from the creeks and town to cheer and wave their hats and handkerchiefs as the steamer disappeared from view.

In the brief time he had been at Dawson, Steele had brought almost miraculous changes to the town. Substantial buildings had been raised, pavement laid, streets graded and installed with drains. Drinkable water had been piped in and electric lighting introduced. A telephone system had been put in place. The town's health officer, Dr. J.W. Good, who a year earlier had described Dawson as "one vast swamp, with cesspools and filth of all kinds," now called its cleanliness and sanitation "as favourable as those to be found in any part of Canada." Moreover, Steele had treated his men with respect and dignity, had improved their living conditions and seen to it that they were well clothed and fed.

THE INCONGRUITY of it all was that no sooner had the Mounties brought order to the Klondike and settled comfortably into their role than there was no longer any need for them. By the end of 1899, the gold that had brought the hordes north – that had driven men crazy and brought a version of civilization to Dawson – had for the most part disappeared from the creeks. The miners drifted away, and with them the dance hall girls, the bankers and the gamblers. With the discovery of new gold in Nome, Alaska, in the latter part of 1899, Dawson City was all but finished as the gold capital of the world. By the end of 1900, fewer than a thousand people remained. A year after that, Dawson was a veritable ghost town.

Nevertheless, the century ended for the NWMP with a spectacular murder case when three men – a Norwegian and two Americans – were shot to death on Christmas Day as they made their way to the home of Corporal Paddy Ryan, who was in charge of a tiny NWMP detachment south of Dawson.

A few days later, a man named George O'Brien was detained at a police check-point near Tagish in connection with the crime. Proof of his guilt was eventually secured, but not before Constable Alex Pennycuick – "the Sherlock Holmes of the NWMP" – had, in his search for clues, examined every square foot of a section of spruce forest sixteen miles long and two and a half miles wide. In a subsequent and more refined search, he removed three feet of snow from a half acre of forest and screened every flake, locating in the process bullet casings, as well as bits of bone, a

Below: When the gold rush ended at the end of the nineteenth century, many of the businesses of Dawson City, even the most successful of them, were quickly gone with it. The presence of a team of sled dogs in front of the store is somewhat anomalous given that there is no snow in evidence.

Right: Thousands of Klondikers left Dawson City as quickly as they had arrived when the dream of gold faded. This group is seen at Fort Chipewyan, Alberta, as they made their way south toward home.

After a long career in
the NWMP, Sam Steele
accepted an offer to
become Commanding
Officer of the privately
raised cavalry unit, Lord
Strathcona's Horse. He
led this Canadian unit
under British command
in South Africa during
the Boer War but is said
to have detested British
orders to burn towns
and imprison Afrikaners
in concentration camps.

tooth and drops of frozen blood. He did all of this over a period of many weeks in temperatures as low as −60°F, and for his efforts was eventually cited by Sam Steele for having carried off "one of the great pieces of crime detection in history."

The bodies of the three victims, full of bullet holes, did not surface in the Yukon River until spring when the ice went out. By that time Pennycuick had collected enough evidence to have O'Brien committed to trial – in fact to the biggest murder trial in Yukon history – where he was convicted of killing the three men, plus his partner, and was sentenced to hang on August 23, 1901.

The Mounties' work on the case garnered high praise from Ottawa and the press, as well as from the trial judge who, in his summation, referred to the Mounties as "the pride of Canada and the envy of the world." It was a fitting conclusion to the Mounties' contribution to the extraordinary events surrounding the gold rush.

BY THE TURN of the century, just a handful of Mounties were needed in the Klondike.

By that time, the Boer War had broken out in Africa, and Lawrence William Herchmer, now in his fourteenth year as commissioner, was given permission to raise a police contingent called the 2nd Canadian Mounted Rifles. When the group left Halifax in January 1900, it included Herchmer, eleven officers, and more than one hundred NWMP constables. Another thirty-three Mounties joined a corps called Lord Strathcona's Horse, under none other than Lieutenant-Colonel Sam Steele.

In all, four Mounties were killed in the Boer War, while three died of disease. Many were decorated, and one, Sergeant A.H. Richardson, won the Victoria Cross.

Late in 1900, Superintendent Bowen Perry was appointed the Mounties' new commissioner, a post he would hold for twenty-two years, making him the longest-serving commissioner in the history of the force. In 1904, by command of King Edward VII, the Mounties became the Royal North-West Mounted Police. By 1905, however, the prairie would be divided into the provinces of Saskatchewan and Alberta, each with a police force of its own.

This quartet of ex-Mounties, seen frying up their dinner at Klerksdorp, South Africa, in 1902, served in the Boer War as members of the 2nd Canadian Mounted Rifles.

In 1996, Canada Post issued a block of 45-cent stamps marking the hundredth anniversary of the beginning of the Yukon gold rush. The stamps celebrated *(from left to right)*:

• Skookum Jim, who, in August 1896, in the company of his friend George Carmack and Carmack's wife, discovered an abundance of gold in Rabbit Creek off the Klondike River
• The thousands of stampeders, who came from all over North America and parts of Europe
• The North West Mounted Police, who manned the border and protected the miners and settlements
• Dawson City, sometimes referred to as the City of Gold or the Paris of the North
• The Klondike itself, Land of the Midnight Sun.

With the fading of the frontier period of Canadian history, and the establishment of provincial police forces, there seemed little need for a frontier law-enforcement agency. In 1916, Superintendent Richard Deane recorded in his journal: "Canadians as a whole are very proud of the world-wide reputation which the Force has made, but they may as well face the unquestionable fact that the Force is now on the down-grade and should be abolished before its reputation is quite gone."

By the end of World War I, the force was down to just three hundred men – the same number that had left Fort Dufferin on the great march west in 1874. Fortunately, the force was not allowed to die. In 1920, it was renamed the Royal Canadian Mounted Police, was expanded to include twelve hundred men and was given Dominion-wide responsibilities for federal and international crime.

Today the force has resumed some of its provincial responsibilities, particularly on the Prairies, and operates with nearly 25,000 men and women. While crummy pay and poor uniforms are a thing of the past – as are the drafty barracks and muddy parade grounds – the risks remain, along with the loneliness of isolated postings.

Other reminders of the bold NWMP chronicle include the bright red coat still worn on ceremonial occasions and a sense among Canadians that, for the most part, the iconic police force still represents their hopes that the laws of the country will be upheld and the integrity of their communities will be protected.

Despite the mandate
that the earliest uni-
form of the NWMP be
as free of embellish-
ment as possible, the
elaborate scripting
on the shoulder patch
from the uniform of
1874 is so cluttered and
fancified as to be all
but indecipherable.

BOOKS ARE TYPICALLY ASSOCIATED with the name of one person, the writer. However, most books would not exist were it not for the contributions of half a dozen or more creative and devoted people. This book, in particular, is a labour of many hands and talents – in particular, and foremost, those of publishers Mark Stanton, Roberto Dosil and Don Atkins. While Don has tended to be a quiet presence behind the scenes, Roberto has, with great patience and ingenuity, brought together the hundreds of illustrations that grace these pages and has applied his brilliant design skills to placing them so strikingly in their context. Mark, for his part, has spent months shepherding the project along, reading the text, offering thoughtful and incisive advice, and coordinating the efforts of everyone concerned. To both of them, I offer my sincere gratitude and respect.

Profound thanks must also be extended to the book's editors, Barbara Tomlin and Ruth Wilson, for their committed and capable handling of the text, to our astute proofreader, Merrie-Ellen Wilcox, and indexer Audrey McClellan. Beyond these committed and talented practitioners, I wish to thank to my old pal Jake Macdonald for his support, and my friends Margie Bettiol, Doug Flegel and Frank Pollari, all of whom, in their way, were indispensable to this extensive undertaking. Thanks are also due to Trish Wilson for her help and encouragement and, as always, to my children, Matt, Georgia and Eden for their love and understanding through the weeks of effort that were my own contribution to the book. My very best wishes to you all!

CHARLES WILKINS
Thunder Bay, September 1, 2010

Ahenakew, E. with Buck, R.M. *Voices of the Plains Cree.*
Toronto: McClelland & Stewart, 1977.

Atkin, R. *Maintain the Right: The Early History of the North West Mounted Police.*
Toronto: MacMillan, 1973.

Butler, W.F. *The Great Lone Land: An Account of the Red River Expedition and Other Travels in Western Canada.*
Edmonton: Hurtig, 1968.

Dempsey, H.A. *Big Bear: The End of Freedom.*
Vancouver: Douglas & McIntyre, 1984.

Haydon, A.L. *The Riders of the Plains: Adventures and Romance with the North West Mounted Police 1874–1910.*
Toronto: Copp Clark, 1911.

Hildebrandt, W. and Hubner, B. *The Cypress Hills: The Land and its People.*
Saskatoon: Purich, 1994.

Hughes, S. *The Frog Lake Massacre: Personal Perspectives on Ethnic Conflict.*
Toronto: McClelland & Stewart, 1976.

Livesay, R. and Smith, A.G. *Discovering Canada: The Mounties.*
Markham: Fitzhenry and Whiteside, 2008.

Lower, A.J. *Western Canada: An Outline History.*
Vancouver: Douglas & McIntyre, 1983.

MacEwan, G. *Sitting Bull: The Years in Canada.*
Edmonton: Hurtig, 1973.

Rees, T. *Arc of the Medicine Line: Mapping the World's Longest Undefended Border Across the Western Plains.*
Vancouver: Douglas & McIntyre, 2007.

Steele, S.B. *Forty Years in Canada: Reminiscences of the Great North-West.*
New York: Dodd Mead, 1915.

Tanner, O. *The Old West: The Canadians.*
New York: Time-Life Books, 1977.

Turner, J.P. *The North-West Mounted Police – Volume One.*
Ottawa: King's Printer, 1950.

Turner, J.P. *The North-West Mounted Police – Volume Two.*
Ottawa: King's Printer, 1950.

Wilson, G. *The Klondike Gold Rush: Photographs from 1869–1899.*
Whitehorse: Wolf Creek Books, 1997.

Woodcock, G. *Gabriel Dumont: The Metis Chief and His Lost World*
Edmonton: Hurtig, 1975.

CREDITS & PERMISSIONS

EVERY reasonable effort has been
made to trace and contact all holders
of copyright and to credit sources
correctly. In the event of omission or
error SA&D Publishers should be
notified so that a full acknowledgment
may be made in future editions.

ABBREVIATIONS

AML   Anchorage Museum
Library & Archives
ASM   Alaska State Museum
ASL   Alaska State Library
Historical Collections
AO   Archives of Ontario
AM   Archives of Manitoba
BCA   British Columbia Archives,
Royal BC Museum
CPR   CPR Archives
DCM   Dawson City Museum
GA   Glenbow Archives
GMC   Glenbow Museum Collection
GMA   Galt Museum & Archives
LC   Library of Congress
Prints & Photographs Division
MM   McCord Museum
MHS   Montana Historical Society
NGC   National Gallery of Canada
RAM   Royal Alberta Museum
RCMP   Royal Canadian Mounted Police
Historical Collections Unit
SAB   Saskatchewan Archives Board
SLSA   State Library of South Australia
TTU   Texas Tech University
Special Collections Library
UMA   University of Manitoba
Archives & Special Collections
USL   University of Saskatchewan
Libraries Special Collections
UWL   University of Washington
Libraries Special Collections
YA   Yukon Archives

FRONT COVER
GA NA-716-19

BACK COVER
Left to right: GA NA-521; LAC PA-028147;
LAC PA-139073; LAC C-001875;
LAC C-006513.

FRONT MATTER

Frontispiece: Embroidered pouch worn with the full dress uniform of the North West Mounted Police. GMC 1202
Base map: LAC E008222482

CHAPTER OPENINGS

CHAPTER 1
Paul Kane
Assiniboine hunting buffalo, c. 1851–1856
NGC 6920 (Detail)

CHAPTER 2
Richard Barington Nevitt
First whiskey spilled, 1874
GMC 74.7.11 (Detail)

CHAPTER 3
Paul Kane
Big Sanke, Chief of the Blackfoot Indians, recounting his war exploits to five subordinate Chiefs, 1848
NGC 22 (Detail)

CHAPTER 4
After a sketch by Sargent Grundy and others
The Capture of Batoche, 1885
LAC C-002424 (Detail)

CHAPTER 5
William G.R. Hind
Prospecting for alluvial gold in British Columbia, 1864
BCA PDP02612 (Detail)

CHAPTER 1
p.2: UMA Louis Riel 1858; p.3: UMA 2194738437; p.4: AO F-1066-6; p.5: AM SIS N5401; p.6: GA NA-664-1; p.7: GA NA-576-1; p.8: LAC NMC 7065; p.9: GA NA-1847-5; p.10: GA NA-1406-71A; p.11: AM SIS N5402; p.12 *top*: LAC PA-125990; *bottom*: GA NA-674-46; p.13: LAC C-078539; p.14: GMC AR-302; p.15: GA NA-3409-1; p.16 *top*: UMA 3258747290; *bottom*: LAC C-006512; p.18: LAC E010700647; p.19 *top*: GMC C-3995A; *bottom*: LAC C-002775; p.20: MM M994X.5273101; p.21: GA G-3301-E1-1857; p.22: GA M-8188; p.23: GA NA-1176-1; p.24: GA NA-3225-4; p.25: GA ND-3-4338; p.26 *top*: GA NA-207-63; *bottom*: LAC C-007229; p.28-29: TTU 67-6-4; p.30: MM II-83124; p.31 *top*: GA NA-2311-2; *bottom*: CPR A7631; p.32: LC 13514; p.35: GA NA-2791-12; p.37: UMA MSS157; p.38 *top*: LAC C-148694; *bottom*: LAC C-000773; p.39: SLSA I-14670881; p.40: LAC C-005812; p.41: CPR NS10217; p.42: LAC NLC-009768; p.43: GA NA-2246-2.

CHAPTER 2
p.47: GA NA-5501-3; p.48: GMC 74.7.77; p.49: GA NA-2003-46; p.50 *left*: GA NA-2603-2; *right*: LAC E00831546; p.51: GA NA-1149-6; p.52: RCMP 1978.45; p.53: GMC C-32710; p.54: GA NA-1175-1; p.55 *left*: LAC E002240462; *right*: LAC E002240463; p.56 *top*: GA NA-1255-4; *bottom*: GA NA-249-11; p.57: GA NA-3251-1; p.58: GA NA-249-75; p.59: GA NA-98-16; p.60: LC VAR0283; p.61: GA NA-2050-1; p.62 *left*: GA NA-3173-9; *right*: RCMP 1977.158.2; p.63: LAC C-061346; p.64 *top*: GMC C-10979A; *bottom*: GMC C-10979B; p.65: RCMP 1958.10.7-2; p.67: LAC C-081787; p.68: GA NA-65-4; p.69: LAC E0008009; p.70: LAC C-073304; P.71: LAC C-062665; p.72: GMC M-893-4-02; p.73: GA C-2417; p.74 *top*: GA NA-935-6; *bottom*: GA NA-302-2; p.75: LAC C-005874; p.76-77: GA NA-4967-57; p.78: GA NA-2928-53; p.79: GA NA-936-36; p.80: GA M8065-1; p.81: LAC PA-118754; p.82: GMA P197660233048; p.84: GA NA-3535-147; p.85 *top*: GA NA-1906-3; *bottom*: GA NA-1104-1; p.86: LAC C-062563; p.87: GA NA-1540-7; p.88: GMC C-1221A; p.89: LAC PA-135839; p.90: GA NA-98-18; p.91: LAC E007913325.

CHAPTER 3
p.94: GA NA-13-1; p.95: GA NA-1241-98; p.96: GA NA-354-1; p.97: LAC C-062697; p.98-99: RCMP 1969.20.3; p.99 *right*: GMC C-22098; p.100 *top*: RCMP 1954.31.1; *bottom*: RCMP 1954.31.4; p.101: GA NA-2206-2; p.102: GA NA-1237-1; p.103: BCA A-09080; p.104: RCMP; p.106 *top, left to right*: GA ND-37-19, GA ND-37-11, GA ND-37-22; *bottom*: GMC C-1201; p.107: GMC C-1987; p.108: LAC PA-118768; p.109: GMC C-4088; p.110: LAC E008128845; p.111: GA NA-98-12; p.112: GA NA-34-1; p.113: GMC AF-870; p.114 *left*: GA M-4403-P01; *right*: GA M-4403-P09; p.116: GA NA-1094-4; p.117: GA NA-3314-1; p.118: RAM H88.94.184; p.119 *top*: GA NA-1376-5; *bottom*: LAC E007722124; p.120 *left*: GMC R5.405A, GMC R5.405B; *right*: GMC AF-1165A; p.121: NA-3281-1; p.122: GA G3401-E1-1877-C212; p.123: GA NA-949-18; p.124: GA NA-5091-1; p.126: RCMP 1968.28.2-2; p.127: GA NA-1161-7; p.128: MHS 955-696; p.129: GA M-776-14-1877-01; p.130: MM M14374.1-2; p.134: GA M-1832-F4; p.135: GA NA-879-5; p.136: GA NA-343-1.

CHAPTER 4
p.140 *top*: GA NA-127-1; *bottom*: GA NC-21-10; p.142: GA NA-284-6; p.143: LAC C-072064; p.144 *top*: CPR NS14886-R; *bottom*: CPR NS18445; p.145: CPR NS17756; p.146: GA NA-532-1; p.143 *top*: RCMP 1969.82.1; *bottom*: RCMP 1969.20.1; p.148: CPR NS8615; p.149 *top*: LAC C-003622; *bottom*: LAC C-121918; p.150 *top*: CPR NS12968-R; *bottom*: CPR NS13230; p.151: GA NA-294-1; p.152: GA NA-3055-20; p.153: LAC C-000753; p.154-155: GA NA-782-2; p.156: GMC MI-1356; p.157: GMC C-4096; p.158 *top*: MM II-170354; *bottom*: CPR NS1340-R; p.159: GA NA-3489-42; p.160: GA NA-1063-1; p.163: GA NA-4957-66; p.164: UMA 3837953976; p.165: GMC AP-760; p.166: GA NA-363-12; p.167: LAC NMC-15955; p.168 *top*: GA NA-3811-120; *bottom*: GA NA-3205-2; p.169: LAC C-005826; p.170: GA NA-363-26; p.171: UMA 2110382767; p.172: LAC E0008112; p.173: LAC PA-118760; p.174-175: GA NA-3205-5; p.176 *top*: USL H402 ; *bottom*: SAB LAR-B6790; p.177: SAB R-A8812; p.178: LAC C-001879; p.179: GA NA-2310-1; p.180: UMA A.98-15; p.181 *left*: LAC NLC009918; *right*: LAC NLC010008.

CHAPTER 5
p.184: GA NA-2520-48; p.185 *top*: YA 000058; *bottom*: BCA H-00072; p.188: ASM III-0-1014; p.189 *top*: ASL P34-009; *bottom*: BCA D-04399; p.190 *top*: ASM III-0-866; *bottom*: ASL P39-843; p.191: YA 66; p.192: YA 872; p.193: UWL Hegg 105; p.194 *top*: UWL 26989; *bottom*: GA NA-513-47; p.195: BCA A-00515; p.196: UWL La Roche 2014; p.197 *top*: AML B64.1.43; *bottom*: ASL P-41-175; p.198: UWL La Roche 2035; p.199: BCA D-08101; p.200: YA 1243; p.201: YA KN-1898-P1; p.202: YA 1255; p.203: BCA A-05116; ; p.204 *top*: BCA B-06746; *bottom*: BCA B-06745; p.205: GA NA-912-6; p.206: UWL Hegg 3094; p.207: BCA B-08129; p.208 *left*: ASL M-75-47; *right top*: ASL M-75-48; *right bottom*: ASL M-75-29; p.209: BCA A-06744; p.210: UWL Hegg 156; p.211 *top*: UWL Hegg 2264; *bottom*: GA NA-2453-1; p.212-213: GA NA-2703-11; p.214: BCA A-04498; p.215: GA NA-919-15; p.216: GA NA-891-7; p.217: UWL Hegg 778; p.218: GMC C-22175; p.219: GA NA-964-13; p.220 *top*: GA NA-2437-5; *bottom*: UWL Hegg 496; p.222: MM MP-20249; p.223 *top*: GA NA-949-54; *bottom*: DCM 1984.50.65; p.224: GA PA-3589-5; p.225: GA NA-3378-6; p.226: LAC E002281250; p.227: GMC C-22179.

BACK MATTER
p.234: GA NA-2328-6

On July 8, 1935, sixty-one years after Commissioner Arthur French set out from Fort Dufferin with the inaugural class of Mounties on the great march west, this foursome of NWMP veterans, all of whom marched from Fort Dufferin, was honoured in the opening-day parade of the Calgary Stampede. *Left to right:* James "Cappy" Smart, Colonel James Mitchell, Colonel James Walker, and the famed NWMP bugler and band member Fred Bagley. The young driver is unknown.

LIBRARY AND ARCHIVES CANADA CATALOGUING IN PUBLICATION

Wilkins, Charles
    The wild ride : a history of the North West Mounted Police, 1873–1904 / Charles Wilkins.

Includes bibliographical references and index.
ISBN 978-0-9809304-1-2

1. Northwest, Canadian – History – 1870–1905.
2. North West Mounted Police (Canada) – History.
3. Métis – History.
4. Indians of North America – Canada, Western – History.
5. Canada, Western – History – 19th century.
I. Title.

FC3216.2.W45 2010   971.2'02   C2010-900153-2

Stanton Atkins & Dosil Publishers
Mailing address
2632 Bronte Drive
North Vancouver, BC
Canada, V7H 1M4

www. s-a-d-publishers.ca

Edited by: Barbara Tomlin and Ruth Wilson
Proofread by: Merrie-Ellen Wilcox
Indexed by: Audrey McClellan
Designed by: Roberto Dosil
Research assistant: Sandra Massey
Map routes drawn by: Colleen Wood
Colour preparation by: Ernst Vegt
Printed in Canada by: Friesens

This book's title, chapter headings, text, sidebars, and captions are set in Warnock, a typeface family designed by Robert Slimbach and released in 2000.

FIRST EDITION / FIRST PRINTING